Journal for the Academic Study of Magic

ISSN 1479-0750
ISBN 978-1906958-01-5

Published by Mandrake of Oxford, PO Box 250, Oxford, OX1 1AP, UK. http://www.mandrake.uk.net

In association with the Society for the Academic Study of Magic, c/o Dep't of Historical Studies, University of Bristol, 13 Woodland Road, Bristol, BS8 1TB, UK
http://www.sasm.co.uk/index.html

Bibliographic conventions: please cite as: Susan Johnston Graf and Amy Hale, eds, *The Journal for the Academic Study of Magic*, 5, (Mandrake, Oxford, 2009)

Copyright of individual articles remains with the author(s), while editorial, style, layout etc of the Journal is © SASM, JSM and Mandrake of Oxford 2009.

All rights reserved. No part of this Journal may be reproduced or utilized in any form or by any means, electronic or mechanical including photocopying, recording or by any information storage and/or retrieval system, without express prior permission in writing from the Publishers.

Short extracts may be reproduced for review purposes. A copy of the review, and notification of where and when it appeared would be appreciated, sent to SASM please.

Contents

Book Review Policy; Responses; Note for Prospective Authors: 4
Contributors 5
Editorial Board 6

Flavius Josephus' Terminology of Magic: Accommodating
Jewish Magic to a Roman Audience,
Philip Jewell 7

The Role of Grimoires in the Conjure Tradition
Dan Harms 40

Hermetic/Cabalistic Ritual in Christopher Marlowe's Doctor Faustus
Dana Winters 69

Italian Cunning Craft: Some Preliminary Observations
Sabina Magliocco 102

Walking The Tightrope: A Study Of Secret Astrologers
In Mainstream Professions.
J.A. Silver Frost B.A., M.A., Solicitor. 133

Martyrs, Magic, and Christian Conversion
Patrick Maille 174

"Worshiping the Devil in the Name of God" Anti-Semitism,
Theosophy and Christianity in the Occult Doctrines of Pekka Siitoin
Kennet Granholm 203

"The Witching Hour: Sex Magic in 1950s Australia"
Marguerite Johnson 286

Reviews 288

Obituaries 313

Book Review Policy:

Following debate within the editorial panel about exactly what kind of books we should be reviewing (inspired by an unsolicited review copy of a very good practical magic book that we were sent by a publisher, and which is reviewed herein) we have reached the view that we would not be doing our job properly if we ignored what occultists are writing - this would be akin to producing a Journal about French culture yet reading nothing written in French or by a French person. This does not mean that we will be reviewing every last 'how to do spells' book, occult novel or collection of magical verse that is published, but we shall endeavour to cover some of the more significant books by practitioners in this and future issues, in a proportion of perhaps 1 practitioner titles to 4-5 academic titles. Would publishers and authors who wish to submit practical occultism books for review please contact us *first*, to discuss their potential review copies and whether we are able to review them. Thankyou.

Responses:

We welcome responses to articles, written in a reasoned, academic style and of less than 1000 words. If suitable these will be included in a future edition of the JSM, with a reply from the author of the original article. Responses of a longer nature will possibly warrant the respondent writing a full article for us.

A Technical Note for Prospective Authors:

As a multidisciplinary journal receiving articles from disparate scholars trained in multitudinous methods of citation we have decided that from JSM 3 onwards we will be moving to the somewhat more straightforward *Harvard* academic referencing system; since this seems to suit the majority of our submitting authors.

Contributors

Kennet Granholm received his PhD in Comparative Religion at Åbo Akademi University (Finland) in 2005. His research interests include contemporary esotericism and the intersection of esoteric spirituality and popular culture.

Dan Harms is the Coordinator of Instruction Librarian at the State University of New York at Cortland. He lives in upstate New York, has written two books on occultism and Lovecraft's Cthulhu Mythos, and blogs at http://danharms.wordpress.com.

Dr Phil Jewell, University of Southampton. Having studied for a PhD in magic in the works of the Jewish Roman historian Flavius Josephus, I now teach a course on ancient historians at the University. My primary interests are in the fields of biblical magic and the representation of magic in Graeco-Roman literature.

Marguerite Johnson is Lecturer in the School of Humanities and Social Science at The University of Newcastle. Although trained as a Classicist, Marguerite also teaches and researches facets of English Literatue, Gender Studies and Religious Studies (particularly Neo-paganism and Witchcraft).

Sabina Magliocco is Professor and Chair of Anthropology at California State University - Northridge. She has published on ritual, festival, Italian folklore and modern Pagan religions.

J.A. Silver Frost is a solicitor and award-winning writer and was the first ever graduate of the MA in Cultural Astronomy and Astrology at Bath Spa University.

Parick Maille is assistant Professor of History at the Oklahoma Panhandle State University.

Dana Winters is an editor/writer that graduated magna cum laude from Sage College in Troy, New York, and earned a B.A. in English with Program Honors.

Editorial Board

General Co-Editors: Dr Susan Johnston Graf (Penn State University, Mont Alto, USA); Amy Hale; Dave Evans, reviews and obituary editor

Peer Review Editorial Board:

Prof Ronald Hutton (University of Bristol, UK)

Prof Geoffrey Samuel (University of Wales, Cardiff, UK)

Prof Sabina Magliocco (California State University, Northridge, USA)

Dr Dave Evans (formerly University of Bristol, UK)

Dr Owen Davies (University of Hertfordshire, UK)

Dr Robert J Wallis (Richmond College, The American University in London, UK)

Dr Matt Lee (University of Sussex, Brighton, UK)

Dr Sarah Pike (California State University, Chico, USA)

Dr Jenny Blain (Sheffield Hallam University, UK)

Dr Justin Woodman (University of London, UK)

Dr William Redwood (University of London, UK)

Production Editor: Mogg Morgan (Mandrake of Oxford)

Flavius Josephus' Terminology of Magic: Accommodating Jewish Magic to a Roman Audience

Philip Jewell

The life of Flavius Josephus was certainly not short of incident. Born in Jerusalem in 37 CE to a priestly family which could trace their line back to the Hasmonean high priest Jonathan (161-143 BCE), the young Josephus was inducted into all the major religious schools, the Pharisees, Sadducees, and Essenes, as well as sitting at the feet of Bannus, a wilderness ascetic.[1] However, as a member of the nobility, Josephus was installed as the general in command of Galilean forces at the commencement of the war with Rome in 66 CE. As the rest of Judea was shortly to find, little could stand in the way of Rome's legions; Josephus and his men were captured in the following year in the city of Jotapata. It was here, as his fellow Jews engaged in a suicide pact, that Josephus made a momentous decision, one which was to have great ramifications for the rest of his life.[2] Having been brought before the

Roman general Vespasian, Josephus claimed that God had revealed, through several dreams, that his captor was destined to become the ruler of Rome. Whether this was revelation or shrewd regard for the Roman political scene, Vespasian was intrigued enough to keep Josephus as a part of his entourage, rather than sending him to Nero in chains. Indeed, Josephus was even employed as an envoy to his people, sent by the Romans to propose surrender. Following the end of the war Josephus was encouraged by the Flavian house to record the events in what became his *Jewish War*; this was followed by the massive *Jewish Antiquities* and the shorter pieces *Against Apion* and *Life*.[3]

His works, long treasured and preserved by Christianity, present us with a remarkable account of the fateful meeting of Rome and Judea. Primarily he provides invaluable accounts of the dark events which led to the outbreak of the Jewish war of 66-70 CE, as well as writing a firsthand account of his own involvement in the war and the final siege of Jerusalem. However, his value to history is much greater than if we were to imagine him as simply an early form of the war correspondent. His *Jewish Antiquities*, a cornucopia of a history spanning thousands of years of Jewish history, is one of the earliest forms of the biblical paraphrase, whilst his *Against Apion* is a fascinating rebuttal of ancient anti-Semitic slanders. In all of these works Josephus deals with the problem of communicating the Jewish elements of his heritage and background to an imperial Roman audience, struggling to accommodate his biblical and religious traditions with the overwhelming power of Roman might. The works of Josephus are traditionally seen by scholars as a source for details on the political and military events of first century Judea, a turbulent era which transformed both Roman and Jewish life.

However, Josephus is also much more than simply a chronicler; through his works we are offered an unparalleled level of insight into the social and religious life of First-Century Judea, as well as a greater understanding of Jewish and Roman relations.

Josephus represents a unique fusion of the two worlds; his life was a rollercoaster of events in which he experienced both Roman and Jewish cultures. These experiences are exemplified by his *Jewish Antiquities* in which a synthesis between Jewish and Roman values is affected. An under-appreciated aspect of his works, however, is the extent to which magic featured as a part of his world view and as an important consideration in his efforts to correlate Roman and Jewish values. The theme of magic is often explained as simply a minor and fairly insignificant interest for Josephus (Rajak 2002, p.xii), as a straw opponent for his miracle stories (MacRae 1965, pp.128-147), or as a decorative element for the benefit of his Roman audience (Brown 1992, p.204). Nevertheless, the sheer number of magical episodes in his works, ranging from biblical paraphrases to descriptions of events witnessed by Josephus himself, in addition to a remarkable care and precision in the employment of magical terminology, suggests that he felt that magic was not only an important theme in Jewish history, but also an important bridge between Roman and Jewish culture. In this article I will not only challenge the view that Josephus held no interest in magic, but also advance the idea that Josephus was a careful employer of magical terminology and that he was well aware of the dual positive/negative nature of magic in the Roman world.

Identifying Magic

In the first century CE, "magic" constituted a shadowy category of human action, one which was increasingly of concern to Roman and Jewish law; especially in the former, unsanctioned religious activities (among which we may count magic) were readily being associated with rebellion, revolt, and insurrection. Yet, at the same time, there was a great degree of latitude with respect to the practice of magic in both Roman and Jewish worlds. In essence, the strict definition of magic, one which we would be familiar with today as being defined in concert/conflict with the idea of miracle, was far from established. Biblical literature, which formed the basis for Josephus' paraphrase of his people's history in the *Jewish Antiquities*, whilst legislating against a wide array of magicians and magical practices, is replete with episodes of both positive and negative magic. In this respect terminology became an important element in defining acceptable magical practices. For instance, we do not see any of the outlawed terms given in Deut 18:10-14 in relation to the figure of Moses, despite the fact that he engages in a contest of magic with the Egyptian magicians at Pharaoh's court (Exodus 7), uses a magical staff to effect water from a rock (Num 20:11), and creates a copper serpent figurine which magically heals the snakebites of the Israelites (Num 21:6-9). All of these actions are acceptable because they are sanctioned by God. One might prefer to term them "miracles," but this would seem to imply a categorical difference between the actions of a magician and a miracle-worker.[4] Such is not seen in biblical literature, where we can point to numerous examples of prophets practising "magic." In this respect, Elijah and Elisha are perhaps the most pre-eminent examples. They know how to decontaminate polluted waters, and make an iron axe come back up to the water's surface seemingly by magical means (2 Kings 2.19-22, 6.1-6). They also restore to life a child (1 Kings 17.19-23, 2 Kings 4.33-37). In addition, they perform healing and fertility miracles which, though not described by 'magical' terminology, nevertheless employ various ritual actions (using the prophet's staff as a magical object, throwing salt as a *materia magica* into a tainted spring, etc.) which demonstrate that more than simply the will of God was necessary to effect the various "miracles."

The first century CE was, however, a definitive era with respect to the evolution and development of theories of magic, especially in relation to the religion/magic acceptable/unacceptable dichotomy with which we are so familiar today. For this period saw a heightened interest from Roman social elites in the legality and acceptability of various religious practices, amongst which we may count what we today would call "magic," and which in Roman society was described by a dedicated and wide ranging set of terminology. However, we must not imagine that early imperial Rome had an approach to magic, involving such dichotomies as magic/negative and religion/positive, which mirrored Frazerian intellectualist models. On the contrary, there was no clear-cut dichotomy in operation; actions which invoked or involved the supernatural could be described in a multiplicity of manners dependent on not only context, but also the designs and intentions of the author. In this manner two similar ritual actions (casting horoscopes for instance) could be at once both legal and illegal. The only difference in terms of legality was supplied by those who legislated. Thus, emperors could attend magical banquets and be initiated into the mysteries of the Magi (Nero), could cast their own horoscopes (Augustus), and could have magicians on their private staff (Vespasian), whilst at the same time issuing legislation banning magical practices from Italy and Rome and conducting purges, trials, and executions of magicians as well as burning magical texts. In these laws, related to us through a number of diverse sources, the specific terminology serves to demarcate certain types of figures; such figures were readily being associated by the end of the first century CE with unsanctioned magical practices. Thus, in their descriptions of the laws passed by Augustus dealing with "magical" practices, Suetonius and Cassius Dio refer to the γοήτες, *malefici*, and μαντεῖς as those who were specifically banned.[5] In these terms we can clearly detect the roots of the modern terminology of magic (Cheak 2004, pp.260-286).

Our sources from Rome in the first century CE document eleven individual pieces of legislation which attempted to deal with the threat of magic, many of which, as recorded by the likes of Suetonius, Tacitus, Ulpian and Cassius Dio, employed distinctive magical terminology. It is this terminology through which I will primarily identify magic in the works of Josephus rather than through more artificial and functional definitions of magic; I will, however, adopt a common sense and basic definition of magic as "the art and skill of producing apparently inexplicable phenomena."[6] We may observe that there are actions which Josephus describes through this negative collection of magical terminology such as the sign prophets who disrupt Judea prior to the first revolt (i.e. the Egyptian who wants to do Moses-like miracles) and other, similar actions which are described in positive terms and without direct application of magical terminology (i.e. Moses at Pharaoh's court). For Josephus, magic is a category which can feature both positive and negative aspects. Throughout his works he is able to carefully apply magical terminology in order to describe both sides. Through several examples I will demonstrate Josephus' careful employment of magical terminology and expand upon the idea that sanction is an important consideration in his representation of both positive and negative forms of magic. It will become evident that magic was an important category of thought for Josephus, not only with respect to effecting a biblical paraphrase in his *Jewish Antiquities*, but also in promoting positive forms of Jewish religion and echoing the imperial Roman sensibilities on the subject.

Moses and Pharaoh's Magicians – *Jewish Antiquities* 2.284-288

The figure of Moses was intimately connected to the world of magic in the era of Josephus, with the events of Exodus 7, the infamous "'serpent confrontation." generating a widespread image of Moses-as-magician in Graeco-Roman sources. Despite being thought of as a biblical exegete who had no interest in magic, Josephus gave a great deal of space and detail over to his paraphrase of this event, creating an account which not only imagines Moses as a master magician,[7] but which also protects him from the anti-semitic slanders of Graeco-Roman authors who sought to portray him as a negatively defined sorcerer (γόης).[8] In order to accomplish this, Josephus carefully manages his terminology so as to create two distinct images of magic, one positive and one negative. Although his serpent confrontation is based upon the biblical versions of Exodus 7, it is clear that Josephus allowed himself a good degree of freedom in creating his paraphrase. This latitude is clear in a number of details, from the reduced role of Aaron and the downplaying of Aaron's magical rod, to additional descriptive elements which portray Moses as a Hellenistic hero, but it is particularly evident in his description of Pharaoh's magicians, as well as his attitude towards their magical skills. In the MT version of Exodus 7 we are introduced to magicians (חַרְטֻמִּים), wise men (חֲכָמִים) and sorcerers (מְכַשְּׁפִים). Of these only the sorcerer (מְכַשֵּׁף) is outlawed by biblical law (Exodus 22:18 – and there only the female version), whilst the magician (חרטם), a term most probably derived from the Egyptian term for a lector priest (*ḥry-tp*), is frequently found in Diaspora novels (Gen 41:8, 41:24, Dan 1:20, 2:2)[9] in denotation of skilled and sanctioned foreign court magicians. In something of a contrast to this fairly positive representation of magic, which, through its distinctive terminology, evokes a fairly neutral image of the magician as a religious specialist at foreign courts, the LXX version supplies a damning swathe of negative terminology in its description. Here we have wisemen/tricksters (σοφισταί), sorcerers (φάρμακος) and charmers (ἐπαοιδοί). Both of the latter terms appear in the LXX's provisions against magicians (Deut. 18:10-14). Moreover, MT describes the skills of the magicians as an art (לְהָטֵיהֶם); for LXX this art is merely harmful sorcery (φαρμακεία).

The attitude of the LXX translators seems clear, with their added associations between the Exodus magicians and the Deuteronomic laws on magic serving to further denigrate Moses' opponents. Josephus, however, having access to both texts for his paraphrase, chooses a much bolder course; it would have been a simple matter, as the LXX demonstrates, to construct a much more negative appraisal of the court magicians and set them up in a clear contrast with Moses, but Josephus instead provides a much more positive representation. For him, Pharaoh's magicians are skilled (σοφός) in an art (ἐπιστήμη); moreover, he terms them priests (ἱερεῖς), a term of high praise given his other employments, especially striking when we consider that they are nowhere thus termed in the biblical texts. In calling them priests, Josephus is linking them to an organisation (the priesthood of Egypt, a sanctioned religious body) and to ritual observances (sanctioned magico-religious rites). Likewise, the terms which describe the profession of the magicians are particularly positive, with σοφία terminology being particularly prominent in the stories of Joseph, Solomon, and Daniel, figures who were biblically famed for their magical/esoteric skills.[10] Despite having his magicians defeated again in a contest of skill and power, Pharaoh is not impressed by Moses' actions, criticizing him for imposing on him by using magic (μαγεία) and wonder-working (τερατουργία), and pointing out that he cannot hope to pose as the only expert in such matters. For a biblical paraphrase, in which our author vows to neither add nor subtract from the Hebrew records (*Ant.*1.17 cf. *War* 1.17 and *Ant.*10.218), this is a remarkable comparison between Moses and Pharaoh's magicians. Instead of miracle defeating magic, as per traditional views on Exodus 7, Josephus clearly presents this episode as a contest of magic. It is a contest of skill in which Moses is victorious.

However, in this episode there are two images of magic, one positive and one negative. Following Pharaoh's statement criticizing Moses, in which we see an acceptable, sanctioned form of magic practised by both Moses and the Egyptian magicians, Josephus has Moses offer a contrast between his works and more negative forms of magic. Here Moses refuses to disdain the skills of the Egyptians, which we might group under the heading of μαγεία; instead he offers a defence of his own skills, stating that his magical performance (φαινόμενα) derives not from witchcraft (γοητεία) or the deception of true judgement, but from God's providence and power (*Ant.*2.286). Much like the magicians, who act under the sanction and at the command of Pharaoh, Moses uses God as the sanction for his magic. In this manner we have a contrast between sanctioned (μαγεία, τερατουργία) magic and unsanctioned magic (γοητεία). The use here of the term γοητεία is particularly informative. For Josephus, γοητεία is a negative practice and a term which he uses of the darkest of villains, especially of those demagogues in the years before the war with Rome who attempted to lead the people astray through the performance of signs and wonders. Most importantly this practice is never associated with figures of authority; Josephus' γοήτες are always those figures who exist on the fringes of society and who act contrary to law, or who attempt to corrupt the masses. I will turn to Josephus' employments of γόης terminology next, but for the moment, we may see that the case of Moses at Pharaoh's court demonstrates not only that Josephus was able, contrary to the views of scholars like MacRae (1965, pp.128-147) and Betz (1987, pp.212-235) who sharply divide religion and magic, to imagine and portray positive accounts of sanctioned magic, but also that he was able to draw a contrast with more negative, unsanctioned, forms of magic.

Negative Magic – the γόης

As well as providing accounts of positive sanctioned forms of magic, Josephus also describes the activities of certain figures who clearly contravene the law in their practices. These figures, most principally described as a γόης, but also seen to be liars (πλάνοι) and deceivers (ἀπατεῳνες), are largely seen in the period before the outbreak of the war with Rome. Such figures have been portrayed as "sign prophets"

(Gray 1993, pp.112-144) due to their promises of delivering signs and wonders akin to those performed by the prophets of the long-distant past, but the employment of the term γόης by Josephus in several of his descriptions suggests that he saw them as unsanctioned magicians. In his era, the γόης had a very negative image, clearly being associated by a long list of classical authors with the practice of, often harmful, magic. It seems most likely that the term itself derives from the verb γοαν, "to utter a cry of lamentation over the dead" (Graf 1997, p.28, Dickie 2001, p.13).[11] In classical literature, however, the γόης becomes associated with a wide range of magical practices. Aeschylus (*Persae*, 687), one of the earliest to refer to such figures, describes the γόης as a religious specialist, on the fringes of society but still under its sanction, who was responsible for summoning the dead from their graves.[12] This neutral image was, however, transformed by later authors who routinely linked the γόης to negatively defined magic. Thus, Diodorus (*Library of History*, 5.55) claims that the γόης acted "just like the mages (μάγοι) do," and were able to shapeshift and create adverse weather conditions such as hailstorms and snows through their own will. This sense of the γόης as an exponent of magical and miraculous actions also is seen in Herodotus (*Histories*, 4.104-105), where they are said to have the ability to turn themselves into wolves.[13] Plato (*Laws*, 10.932ff) refers to the γόης as claiming to control the spirits of the dead in addition to misleading men through "tricks and spells and enchantments."

Increasingly the term was used as a tool for literary elites to describe those beyond the limited boundaries of a given society who either admitted to engaging in, or were perceived as engaging in, a variety of shadowy practices in which the law-abiding citizen would not be involved. The extent to which the γόης had become a negative application for magicians who wished to do harm is shown in the works of Apuleius and Philostratus. The former (*Apology*, 25-43) employs the term, in his trial on charges of practising harmful magic, in order to draw a contrast with the more religiously minded, and hence socially and state minded, μάγος. His pleas in this manner to the judge were successful, and he manages to avoid the death penalty which applied to those who practised the art of the γόης.[14] Likewise Philostratus (*Life of Apollonius*, 8.7.2) draws the negative connotations of the γόης in his description of Apollonius of Tyana's meeting with the emperor Vespasian, in which the hero stresses that his conversation with the emperor concerning the forecast of his future glory took place publicly in a temple, a place which is inimical to γοήτες who prefer the cover of night for their nefarious activities.

By the time of the early Roman Empire, the figure of the γόης was increasingly being denigrated by law, and was repeatedly linked to the actions of social and political revolutionaries. The extent to which the γόης was associated with civil disturbance, revolution, and illegal activities is seen in an excerpt from the works of Cassius Dio (*Roman History*, 49.43.5ff) who discusses the measures which Augustus and Agrippa took to secure Rome. Acknowledging the need for sanctioned soothsayers and augurs, Agrippa advises that Rome should not be a home for the atheist or the γόης, for the latter "often incite many to revolution, either by telling the truth, or, as more often, by telling lies" (Cassius Dio, *Roman History*, 52.36.2). While this passage hails from more than a century after Josephus, it is written in retrospect concerning the measures which Augustus took to secure a post-civil war Rome, particularly the expulsion, on numerous occasions, of magicians and astrologers.[15] Furthermore, Augustus is noted for his burning of thousands of Greek and Latin magical works in 31 BCE (Suetonius, *Augustus*, 31). Likewise, Tiberius executed those who were astrologers or magicians (γόης) and not Roman citizens, exiling those who were (Cassius Dio, *Roman History*, 57.15.8-9, Tacitus, *Annals*, 2.32). The extent to which the Roman authorities feared unsanctioned religious activities can be seen with the second century BCE *Senatus Consultum de Bacchanalibus*.[16] Seeking to lay down a standard for private cults and gatherings, with those unsanctioned being seen as illegal in the eyes of the law, it stated (according to Livy, *History of Rome*, 39.8-11, at least); "No one is to aspire to perform rites either in secret, or in public, or in private, or outside the city, unless he has approached the city praetor, and he has given permission on the basis of a senatorial decree, provided that not less than a hundred senators are present when the matter is debated." Livy (*History of Rome*, 39.41 and 40.43) also reports that shortly after this decree thousands of people were put to death for having practised a form of magic; though specifically covering the rites of the Bacchanalia, this decree was also used to combat the actions of figures such as the γόης, who were often portrayed as foreign religious specialists.[17]

Although not a particularly frequent term, occurring only thirteen times in all of Josephus' works, γόης and its cognate γοητεία are highly instructive for our exploration of Josephus approach to unsanctioned forms of magic. The majority of these usages refer to those who have been termed 'false prophets' or 'sign prophets' by recent scholars (Gray 1993, pp.110-117; Horsley 1981, pp.435-63); however, it could equally be seen that Josephus had in mind the Graeco-Roman meaning of a negatively defined magician when he wrote of these figures. Josephus' recognition of the negative associations of the γόης, and their connections with the world of magic, are particularly evident in the extent that he answers such charges laid against Moses by pagan critics in his *Against Apion* (2.145 and 2.161). While there are instances of the term which seem to suggest little more than deception and trickery (as in the case of Justus of Tiberius, *Life* 35-40, and John of Gischala, *War* 4.85), there are several employments which suggest that not only did Josephus imagine the γόης as a form of magician, capable of producing supernatural phenomena, but that he portrayed his γοήτες so as to accord with Roman attitudes. The most important aspect of Josephus' multiple instances of γόης terminology is the uniform depiction of these figures as opponents of the Roman order. They are not always directly connected with magical acts (though figures such as the Egyptian are clearly linked to Moses-like miracles), but they are consistently shown to be firmly dealt with by the Roman forces in Judea. There is no sense of pity in Josephus' accounts, even when he makes it clear that the Roman forces would slaughter not only the γόης but also his followers; his aim is to demonstrate that unsanctioned magic has no place in the new Rome-dominated Judea, and that such activities are often a focus for revolts and uprisings. A few examples will serve to illuminate these points.

The Deceivers and the Egyptian - **Jewish Antiquities 20.168ff, Jewish War 2.261-263**

In describing Nero's reign (*War*, 2.250ff.) Josephus turns his attention to the troubles which beset Judea, ranging from bands of robbers (ληστηρίων) to the organised terrorism of the Sicarii and the machinations of false prophets (ψευδοπροφήται) and magicians (γόητες). In every case Josephus states that the response of the Roman authorities was the same; the robbers were rounded up and crucified, while the false prophets and those who pretended to be divinely inspired were crushed by the troops of procurator Felix. In *War* 2.258, the Sicarii are seen as a new class of bandit who committed murders in broad daylight in the heart of Jerusalem and are compared to the magicians (γόητες)and deceivers (ἀπατεωνες) who, not as impure in their methods, were nevertheless more wicked in their intentions. Perhaps in an attempt to demonstrate the beneficent rule of the Romans, Josephus accuses both groups of being villains (πονηρων) who brought only ruin and bloodshed to Jerusalem. In addition, they were responsible for deceiving and deluding the populace, acting 'under the pretence of divine inspiration' (προσχήματι θειασμου), and intending to bring about 'change' (νεωτερισμός) and 'innovation' (μεταβολή) in society (*War*, 2.259). However, he does not apply the term γόης to these people, but he does point out that the procurator regarded their actions as precluding insurrection (ἀπόστασις, *War*, 2.260). Again Josephus adopts a disdainful attitude towards these men, labelling them madmen who attempted to lure the people into the wilderness where they would demonstrate divine signals of liberty (ἐκει του θεου δείξοντος αὐτοις σημεια ἐλευθερίας, *War*, 2.259). However, in *Ant*. 20.167 the parallel account uses the term γόητες, stating that they persuaded the multitude to follow them into the wilderness where the providence of God would bring forth signs and wonders (σεμεια καὶ τέρατα, *Ant*. 20.168). For the Romans, as Josephus emphasizes, such gatherings were dangerous to civil order and Roman power; hence, Felix sent his forces to destroy them (*War*, 2.260).

Furthermore, Josephus continues his catalogue of woe which befell the people under Felix with his description of an infamous figure, known only as "the Egyptian," as a false prophet (ψευδοπροφήτης) and a magician (γόης, *War*, 2.261).[18] He states that this individual was the cause for more mischief than the aforementioned groups, and that, claiming to be a prophet, he led thirty thousand to the Mount of Olives (*War* 2.261, cf. *Ant.*, 20.169 which mentions that the Egyptian led "the masses of the common people" τό δημοτικόν πλῆθος). In *Ant.* this figure is said to have "claimed to be a prophet" (προφήτης εἶναι λέγων), while in the account of this figure in *War* it is reported that he had "gained for himself the reputation of a prophet" (προφήτου πίστιν ἐπιθεὶς ἑαυτῷ) and is labelled both a false prophet (ψευδοπροφήτης) and a γόης. There are several differences between the two accounts, such as the location of the start of his journey with his following and the extent of the death toll, but such discrepancies are minor to the overall consideration of the Egyptian as a γόης. His desire was to take Jerusalem by force, but, again, Felix was on hand to thwart his efforts, killing large numbers of the crowd but failing to capture the Egyptian magician (*War*, 2.263). Here again then we have the prophetic pretensions of a magician who claims to be able to work wonders and deceives large numbers of the populace, and whose designs are interpreted as dangerous and possibly revolutionary by the Roman authorities and, thus, end in bloodshed. While we also have employments of the term in connection with figures who might be more appropriately seen as "impostors" or "deceivers," having no overt links to the promise or performance of miracles, the examples that have been discussed suggest that Josephus realised that the term γόης was a powerful indictment of figures who challenged Rome. Although he does not explicitly mention Roman laws on magic it seems quite clear that his dedicated application of the term to figures who lead rebellions or agitate against Rome is a demonstration of his awareness that the γόης is an undesirable element of Roman culture.

Theudas as Anti-Moses, *Jewish Antiquities*, 20.97-99

In addition to his defense of Moses on charges of γοητεία in the *Against Apion*, Josephus also protects his hero through his characterization of Theudas, a γόης of the author's era who mimics the actions and role of Moses. This figure combined the role of revolutionary leader with that of prophet, inspiring a large group of followers in expectation of miraculous events. Rising during the turbulent era of the procurator Fadus, Theudas the γόης is said to have "stated that he was a prophet" (προφήτης...ἔλεγεν εἶναι, *Ant*. 20.97), persuading his followers to accompany him to the Jordan River where he intended to replicate Moses' miraculous parting of the waves.[19] Such a large group of wandering people, inspired perhaps by revolutionary ideals, was a potent threat to Roman order as Josephus makes clear; Theudas and his followers were rounded up by a Roman cavalry detachment before they could reach the river. Some were killed, some imprisoned, and their leader was executed on the spot (*Ant*. 20.98). Although Theudas' intentions are debated,[20] especially in relation to his promised parting of the river, the fact that Josephus employs the term γόης in speaking of a figure who clearly evokes images of Moses is instructive. This terminology, combined with the idea that Theudas claimed to be a prophet, suggests that Theudas intended to demonstrate miraculous powers to his followers but would be doing so without sanction. Thus, whereas Moses performs the parting of the Red Sea under sanction from God, Theudas, as a false prophet, has no such backing. Josephus is quite clear concerning the punishment for magicians of his own era who attempt to replicate prophetic signs without sanction; they are hunted down and executed by the Roman authorities.

A similar scenario may be seen in Josephus' account of the Egyptian γόης who also attempted to replicate a biblical sign to his followers and who is termed a "false prophet" (ψευδοπροφήτης) by Josephus (*War*, 2.261-263, *Ant.*, 20.169-172). Such figures belong to a wider group of magicians and false-prophets who plagued Judea in the Roman era, according to Josephus, leading the masses astray with their false promises. Through detailing their violent suppression by the Roman authorities Josephus shows that they acted without sanction, and provides a direct contrast with the actions of Moses. Moses might well be a magician, performing wonderful deeds like the parting of the Red Sea, but in no sense is he a γόης. Furthermore, the wider language which Josephus uses in his description of Theudas leaves us no doubt that this figure was not only a magician, but also a lying demagogue who led the people astray. Thus, Theudas claimed that "at his command the river would be parted and would provide them an easy passage" (καὶ προστάγματι τὸν ποταμὸν σχίσας δίοδον ἔχειν ἔφη παρέξειν αὐτοῖς ῥᾳδίαν, *Ant.*, 20.98), a clear reference to magic in as much that, combined with a pretension to prophetic status, it shows him to be acting without sanction. Josephus is also careful to note that "many were deluded by his words" (καὶ ταῦτα λέγων πολλοὺς ἠπάτησεν) and that Fadus "did not permit them to reap the fruit of their folly" (οὐ μὴν ἔιασεν αὐτοὺς τῆς ἀφροσύνης ὄνασθαι *Ant.*, 20.99). Evidently, miraculous and magical signs of Israelite freedom, as performed by Moses in the ancient past, have no place in Josephus' Roman Judea; even if they did, one such as Theudas would not be performing them. This is the message contained in the description of Theudas, a figure who constituted a possible focal point for a rebellion against Roman power. Indeed, by showing that the parting of the waves was never performed by Theudas, Josephus also shows that the achievement of Moses is unique; it could never be replicated by a γόης, someone who operates outside law, order, and sanction.

In summary then, Josephus employs the terms γόης and γοητεία in connection with either the idea of deception, as with Justus and John of Gischala, or with negatively-defined magic, as with Theudas and the Egyptian. The majority of the instances of the term occur in reference to the events of the various procuratorships which ruled Judea and Galilee in the first century CE. While Josephus has a wide range of terminology for describing the various forms of criminal which plagued the land during this time, his use of γόης and γοητεία suggests that he considered magicians to be a part of this criminal class. Given the fact that Josephus uses the term ψευδοπροφήτης in connection with the γόης, we might also suggest that Josephus recognised that the term γόης referred to unsanctioned forms of magical activity. As we see in wider Graeco-Roman usage, γόης could be used to refer either directly to the performance of negatively-defined magic or to the deception of true judgement; to an extent the two ideas are consonant.[21] Josephus realised that the term γόης was a very negative form of condemnation;

he employs it in a manner which, as befitted his Roman context, consistently saw these figures as threats to the social order. The fact, too, that each of these γόητες, or at least their followers, meets with a violent end merely enhances their negative portrayal. There can be no doubt either that Josephus understood the term as a primary reference to illicit and illegal forms of magic. This can be seen in the fact that his most frequent employments of the terminology occur during the era prior to the revolt when Judea was beset with social problems often caused, according to Josephus, by those who promised miracles, wonders, and salvation. While such figures have commonly been termed "'sign prophets," the explicit use of the terminology of the γόης suggests that Josephus viewed them as magicians, using such a negative term in order not only to condemn their actions but also to show that such actions were illegal and unacceptable to the state.

Magic as an Art and Skill: Eleazar the Exorcist and the Witch of Endor

Sanctioned magic takes several forms in the works of Josephus, from stories which recount biblical legends to accounts of his own era. Here I would like to briefly discuss two cases, namely that of Eleazar (*Ant*.8.42-49) and the witch of Endor (*Ant*. 6.327-342). The case of Eleazar the exorcist provides us with further evidence for the argument that not only did Josephus consider magic to be an important facet of his culture(s), but also that he was able to conceive and describe positive forms of magic (despite the clear injunctions against it in the Bible and in Roman law). Josephus speaks of Eleazar, a contemporary exorcist who performs his art for Vespasian, in connection to another Jewish master magician, Solomon. He begins by stating that not only is Eleazar a Jew, but that he performed his exorcism in front of Vespasian, Domitian, and Titus, as well as a large gathering of officers and soldiers. Clearly, Josephus is willing to not only associate the skills of Eleazar with Judaism, but also with Roman emperors (both past at the time of the publication of the *Jewish Antiquities*, like Vespasian and Titus, and present, like Domitian). This exorcism is performed not only through the use of the name of Solomon (which could be seen to have magical power in itself) but also of incantations (ἐπῳδή). Although this latter form of magic is outlawed in the LXX text of Deut 10-14, Josephus seemingly felt no hesitance or awkwardness in using it to describe the actions of Eleazar.[22] However, it must be noted that Josephus does not mention these laws in his biblical paraphrase. This freedom allows Josephus to make use of diverse magical terminology in speaking not only of positive forms of Jewish magic, but also unsanctioned and negative forms such as that practised by the γόης.

Although we cannot be sure why Josephus leaves out these laws from his rewritten Bible, for he is by no means a consistent author in terms of creating his paraphrase (at least with respect to modern interpretations of his goal of faithfully recounting the biblical text), their omission allows him to create positive accounts of Jewish magicians through specific magical terminology (some of which is specifically legislated against in LXX). In the case of Eleazar, the instance of the term ἐπῳδή is clearly intended as a positive comment, for not only do the incantations lead to the expulsion of the demon (evidenced by the upsetting of a cup of water placed in front of the unfortunate host), but it is also linked directly to the legendary magical skills of King Solomon. On seeing Eleazar's actions, Josephus states that the understanding (σύνεσις) and wisdom (σοφία) of Solomon was clearly established, on account of which we have been moved to speak of these things, in order that all men might have knowledge of the greatness of his nature and how he was specially favoured by God and that the superiority of the king's virtue might be forgotten by no one under the sun. (*Ant*.8.49)

In this manner the magic of Eleazar receives not only the sanction of Vespasian, before whom it is performed, but also that of Solomon and, by extension, God. Again, we see an understanding of the positive art of magic being described through wisdom (σοφία) terminology. Josephus also describes the exorcisms of Solomon as an art or technique (τέχνη *Ant*.7.341), one which is of great benefit to mankind.

Through such descriptions, we may draw parallels with not only the Egyptian priests and their magical art, but also of those Jewish heroes of the biblical Diaspora novels and the witch of Endor. Indeed, the case of the witch of Endor provides a number of similarities. Not only is her profession termed a τέχνη and an episteme (*Ant*.6.340), but she is also classified as part of a group of diviners (μάντεις) and necromancers (ἐγγαστρίμυθος). Strikingly, Josephus even includes the office of the prophet (προφήτης) in this group who all practice the same art (τέχνη *Ant*.6.327). From his further comments on the witch, it is evident that Josephus wished to portray her in a favourable light. Not only are her designations as an ἐγγαστρίμυθος and a μάντις lacking in any previous condemnation through association with biblical laws on magic (both featuring in LXX Deut 18:10-14), but Josephus, going far beyond the biblical texts, represents her as obedient, loyal, kind, and accommodating. He even provides her with a lengthy eulogy in which he commends her attitude, describes her skill of necromancy as a profession, and states that her attitude is one from which everyone can learn. Thus, despite describing her as a necromancer (ἐγγαστρίμυθος) and diviner (μάντις), terms which are clearly outlawed in LXX and one of which features in reports of Roman laws on magic (so Cassius Dio, *Roman History*, 56.25.5, reports that in 11 CE Augustus passed an aedile ordinance specifically dealing with the actions of the μάντις), Josephus feels comfortable in relating her story, and representing her as a positive example of sanctioned magic. Through the careful employment of terminology, as well as demonstrating that such events occur under the sanction of monarchs and God, Josephus is able to describe Jewish magic in a manner which is acceptable to Roman culture and law.

Conclusion

In Josephus' works, then, it would appear that there are multiple approaches to the subject of magic. In addition it appears to have been an important area of Jewish culture for his representation of his people to the Romans. Through careful application of magical terminology, he is able to create both positive and negative images, from upholding the fame and repute of Moses as a master magician to the labelling of the false sign prophets and demagogues of the pre-revolt era as negatively defined magicians. However, Josephus' interest in magic is much more than simply an especial care for the correct use of magical terminology. For Josephus seems keen to communicate to his readers the power and prestige which Jewish magicians have displayed throughout history. Thus, Moses is clearly associated with the sanctioned court magicians of

Pharaoh's court, yet is shown to be their master in his contest of magic. Joseph and Daniel appear as masters of the esoteric art and are again grouped by Josephus in the category of court magicians. Solomon and Eleazar, the modern exponent of his exorcisms, are shown to be masters of magic, with the former (according to a tradition accepted by Josephus) even writing his own books on incantations and the art of exorcism, as well as proscribing magical components for the ritual. And finally, we may point to the episode of the witch of Endor, who, while described in exemplary terms as an ideal host and loyal subject of King Saul, appears as a female exponent of an art and skill which Josephus equates with the divinatory abilities of the prophets.

These episodes suggest that Josephus was not afraid of speaking of magic in connection with Judaism, so long as the correct terminology was employed and a clear hierarchy of sanction was displayed. Through his careful descriptions, Josephus is able to represent sanctioned Jewish magic as an activity which is acceptable to Rome. Unlike the γοήτες who lead astray the masses in Judea with promises of magic, miracle, and signs like Moses, and who are ruthlessly hunted down by Rome, these sanctioned magicians are carefully described by Josephus so as to prove no threat to the Roman order. Such observations suggest that the acceptability of practices which might be described as "magical" in antiquity were very much dependent on the idea of sanction. This is a general rule which Josephus seems to have taken into account, especially when we consider his repeated appeal to divine and kingly sanction for his Jewish magicians. Thus, Moses acts under the duel sanction of Pharaoh and God (the latter having already taught the three magical arts used in Pharaoh's court to Moses in a revelatory experience);

Solomon is able to write incantations and carry out exorcisms through his God-given wisdom; Eleazar performs his magic under the sanction of Vespasian and the imperial household, as well as deriving benefit from the abilities of Solomon; and finally the witch of Endor, acting only when bound by an oath, provides the skills of her necromantic profession to her king. Such views are, of course, somewhat different from the pure magic/miracle dichotomy which other scholars have adhered to in discussing Josephus' views on magic. However, as has been noted, this division, and its intentional polarities between positive and negative, is artificial, for Josephus is able to speak of acceptable forms of magical activity as well as the more traditional negative aspects. Josephus, then, displays a creative and flexible approach to magic, as well as being a careful manipulator of magical terminology. His writings are invaluable for our understanding of not only his individual approach to magic, his creative thinking, and his relationship with Rome, elements which have not received the attention which they deserve, but also for our knowledge of ancient forms of positive and sanctioned magic.

Notes

1   Josephus claimed to 'follow the party of the Pharisees' (*Life* 12). This statement has, however, received critical comment; see Mason, S. *Flavius Josephus on the Pharisees: A Composition-Critical Study* (Leiden, E.J.Brill, 1991), 342-353.

2   Although Josephus did not relate his prophecies concerning Vespasian at this point, he claims (*War*, 3.399-408) that his survival in the aborted suicide pact was due to the fact that he had to act as God's messenger to announce to Vespasian his future elevation to imperial power.

3   When citing the ancient primary sources I have used the standard editions as found in the Loeb Classical Library editions. In the case of

the works of Josephus the following abbreviations have been employed: Jewish Antiquities (*Ant.*), and Jewish War (*War*). In the case of the Bible I have used the standard notations of MT for the Masoretic Text and LXX for the Septuagint.

4 An important point to consider when looking at ancient magic is that our sources hail from an era in which the debates over the differences between magic and religion (miracle) were in their infancy. Indeed, as Nock famously stated (Nock, A.D.'Paul and the Magus', in Z.Stewart (ed.) *Essays on Religion in the Ancient World* (Oxford, Oxford University Press, 1972), 308-330, quote 314), the societies of the ancient world did not have a 'sphere of magic in contrast to the sphere of religion', though Graf (Graf, F. *Magic in the Ancient World* ((London, Harvard University Press, 1997)), 30-35) advances the case for such an embryonic distinction in the philosophical musings of Plato. Whilst Frazer's work in *The Golden Bough* (Frazer, G. *The Golden Bough: A Study in Magic and Religion*, ((London, Macmillan, 1911)) has been instrumental in advancing the magic/religion dichotomy for generations of modern scholars, a number of more recent works have highlighted the lack of distinction made by the ancient world. Scholars such as Schäfer (Schäfer, P. 'Magic and Religion in Ancient Judaism' in P.Schäfer and H.G.Kippenberg (eds.), *Envisioning Magic: A Princeton Seminar and Symposium* ((Leiden, E.J.Brill, 1997)), 19-43), Römer (Römer, T.'Competing Magicians in Exodus 7-9: Interpreting Magic in the Priestly Theology', in T. Klutz (ed.), *Magic in the Biblical World, from the Rod of Aaron to the Ring of Solomon* ((London, T&T Clark, 2003)), 12.-22) and Segal (Segal, A. 'Hellenistic Magic: Some Questions of Definition', in R. van den Broek and M.J.Vermaseren (eds.), *Studies in Gnosticism and Hellenistic Religions* ((Leiden, E.J.Brill, 1981)), 349-375) have shown that the artificial distinctions in modern critical literature are unsupported by a whole host of ancient source materials, ranging from biblical texts, to magical papyri and Graeco-Roman histories. As a result it is perhaps better to focus upon distinctions made, if at all, by individual authors, and to study the manner in which they utilise overtly magical terminology. The term 'magic' then is used in a very broad sense in this paper, with the understanding that it is a facet of what Evans-Pritchard (Evans-Pritchard, E. *Theories of Primitive Religion* ((Oxford, Oxford University Press, 1965)), 110-114) terms the 'religio-magical phenomena', in

which the idea of 'miracle' and 'magic' as mutually exclusive categories capable of clear distinction is dismissed.

5   Suetonius, *The Lives of the Caesars*, trans. J.C.Rolfe, (Loeb Classical Library, 1959), *Augustus*, 35, and Cassius Dio, *Roman History*, trans. E.Carey and H.B.Foster, (Loeb Classical Library, 1917) 49.43.4, 56.25.5.

6   Definition of 'magic' (*noun*) taken from the online version of the *Oxford English Dictionary* located at http://dictionary.oed.com last accessed on 19/07/2008.

7   See further Gager, J.G. 'Moses the Magician: Hero of an Ancient Counter-Culture?', *Helios* 21:2 (1994): 179-188, and Bloch, R.S. 'Au-delà d'un Discors Apologétique: Flavius Josèphe et les Magiciens', in N.Belayche et al., *Les Communités Religiouses dans le Monde Gréco-Romain, Essais de Définition*, (Bibliothèque de l'École des Hautes Études, Sciences religieuses 117), Turnhout: Brepols, Paris (2003): 243-258.

8   See further Gager, 'Moses the Magician: Hero of an Ancient Counter-Culture?', 179-183, Bloch, 'Au-delà d'un Discors Apologétique: Flavius Josèphe et les Magiciens', 243-258 and Smith, M. 'The Occult in Josephus', in L.H. Feldman and G.Hata (eds.), *Josephus, Judaism and Christianity* (Detroit, Wayne State University Press, 1987) 236-256.

9   The term 'Diaspora novel' refers to distinct segments of biblical texts which narrate the lives of heroes, such as Joseph (*Genesis* 37-50) and Daniel (*Daniel* 1-6), who are forced to live in foreign lands and cultures, whilst simultaneously trying to uphold the tenets, rites and traditions of their own religion.

10 Joseph; Genesis, 37-41, Solomon; 1 Kings 4: 20-21, 24-25, 29-34, Daniel; Daniel 1-3.

11 Especially relevant to the discussion of the term γόης in respect to funerary cults and the origin of the term is Johnston, S. *Restless Dead: Encounters between the Living and the Dead in Ancient Greece* (Berkeley, University of California Press, 1999), who takes issue with the shamanic connection.

12 Further support for this derivation is cited by Ogden, D. *Greek and Roman Necromancy*, (Oxford, Princeton University Press, 2001) 48, who

notes that the Byzantine *Suda* of the late tenth century CE, in speaking of the magic extant in its own time, states that the terminology of sorcery and its practitioners (the γόης) "is applied to the raising of the dead by invocation" and is "derived from the wailing (*gooi*) and the laments that are performed at tombs."

13 Herodotus (*Histories*, 4.105) also states, in an early example of the association between the γόης and deception; "I myself do not believe what they say, but they say it nonetheless, indeed swear it".

14 Apuleius, *Apology*, 29-32. The charges brought against Apuleius, including his mysterious dissection of fish (for poisons or for research?) his possession of *instrumenta magicae*, his catatonic effect on a young boy and woman, his strange cult statue kept hidden from prying eyes, and his enactment of *noctunalia sacra*, certainly seem to give grounds to his accusers arguments. In invoking the more positive aspects of the Persian magi however he is able to show that he is not a γόης but rather a form of the natural scientist or philosopher. See further Luck, G. 'Witches and Sorcerers in Classical Literature', in B.Ankarloo and S.Clark (eds.), *Witchcraft and Magic in Europe, Vol.2 Ancient Greece and Rome*, (London, The Athlone Press, 1999) 91-158 and Graf, F.'Theories of Magic in Antiquity' in P.Mirecki and M.Meyer (eds.), *Magic and Religion in the Ancient World*, (Leiden, E.J.Brill, 2002) 92-104.

15 Repeated legislation was issued during the first century CE in order to deal with the problem of magicians in Rome and Italy, especially on the advent of a new emperor. See further, MacMullen, R. *Enemies of the Roman Order: Treason, Unrest, and Alienation in the Empire*, (Cambridge, Mass., Harvard University Press, 1966) 95-127, and Gordon, R. 'Imagining Greek and Roman Magic', in B.Ankarloo and S.Clark (eds.), *Witchcraft and Magic in Europe: Ancient Greece and Rome*, (London, The Athlone Press, 1999) 159-269.

16 Clearly, the idea of unsanctioned religious activity being troubling for the Roman mind is one not limited to imperial times. Indeed, pre-imperial Rome created some detailed legislation concerning magic, such as the *Twelve Tables* and the *Lex Cornelia de sicariis et veneficus*, though these were perhaps aimed more at crimes involving murder by magical means than with magical ritual and practice. See further, Phillips, C.R. 'Nullem Crimen sine Lege: Socioreligious Sanctions on

Magic', in C.A.Faraone and D.Obbink (ed.), *Magika Hiera, Ancient Greek Magic and Religion*, (Oxford, Oxford University Press, 1991) 260-276.

17 See further Dickie, *Magic and Magicians in the Greco-Roman World*, 155.

18 For Josephus only the truly great prophets of Jewish history were entitled to be labelled as a προφήτης. Even in speaking of his own 'prophetic' experiences he hesitates to use the term, preferring to appear as a sanctioned diviner (μάντις), despite the risk that such a term was open to misinterpretation, and association with negatively-defined magic, if not carefully handled. The Egyptian certainly does not constitute a prophet for Josephus; however, as well as being a false prophet (ψευδοπροφήτης) his is also a negatively-defined magician (γόης). See further Aune, D.E., 'The Use of ΠΡΟΦΗΤΗΣ in Josephus', *Journal of Biblical Literature* 101 (1982): 419-421, and Gray, *Prophetic Figures in Late Second Temple Jewish Palestine: The Evidence From Josephus*, 116-118.

19 The model for Theudas' miraculous actions appears to be either Moses and the Red Sea (Ex. 12:29-14:30) or Joshua at the Jordan River (Josh. 3-4). However, as the latter is clearly based upon the former it would seem that Moses served as the primary model, especially since Joshua 3:7, 4:14, 4:23, all make a connection to the actions of Moses. Indeed , Gray (*Prophetic Figures in Second Temple Jewish Palestine: The Evidence From Josephus*, 115) argues that the two events had become fused in popular memory and expectation in the first century CE.

20 Hengel, M. *The Zealots: Investigations into the Jewish Freedom Movement in the Period from Herod I Until 70 A.D.*, trans. D.Smith (Edinburgh, T&T Clark, 1989) 230n.5) has suggested a further parallel between the biblical account of the Exodus under Moses and the actions of Theudas, in that both groups were armed. Whilst it is tempting to see such a parallel it must be observed that Josephus does not explicitly state that Theudas' band was armed, and that in his own version of the Exodus the Israelites (*Ant.* 2.321-349) are only armed *after* they have made the crossing.

21 Plato, in both his *Laws* (10, 908d2-4) and *Republic* (413c4, 412e7, 413b1) equates the arts of the γόης with deception, whilst Xenophon

(*Anab.* 5.7.9) uses the term in a manner which suggests the forcing of people to believe that which is patently untrue. In a similar fashion, Apollonius (Philostratus, *Life of Apollonius*, 8.7), in his debate with the Egyptian gymnophisist Thespesion, declares that the art of the γόης is simply that of causing the ignorant to believe in the non-existent and of hiding the truth. Indeed, by the time of the early Christian church the term had an essential meaning of 'deceiver'. Thus, as Morton Smith, (*Jesus the Magician*, ((N.Y., Harper & Row 1978)) 109) shows, Origen is forced to not only refute the image portrayed by Celsus of Jesus as a magician, but also to defend him from being seen as the secondary aspect of the γόης, 'a trickster trying to discredit in advance his rival claimants and rival beggars.'

22   The episode of Eleazar at Vespasian's court has been termed an example of 'white magic' (Duling, D.'The Eleazar Miracle and Solomon's Magical Wisdom in Flavius Josephus's *Antiquitates Judaicae* 8.42-49', *Harvard Theological Review* 78:1-2 (1985): 1-25), a form which was increasingly acceptable at the higher levels of Roman society; clearly Josephus was aware of this feeling, allowing him to relate a positive image of magic, and one which emphasizes the skill and power of Jewish magic and magicians. See further MacMullen, *Enemies of the Roman Order*, 125-128.

References

Apuleius. 1909, *Apology*. trans. H.E.Butler, Loeb Classical Library, Harvard University Press, Cambridge, MA.

Aune, David E. 1982, "The Use of ΠΡΟΦΗΤΗΣ in Josephus," *Journal of Biblical Literature* 101, pp.419-421.

Betz, Otto. 1987, "Miracles in the Writings of Flavius Josephus," in *Josephus, Judaism and Christianity*, ed. Louis.H.Feldman and Gohei.Hata, Wayne State University Press, Detroit.

Bloch, Rene.S. 2003, « Au-delà d'un Discors Apologétique: Flavius Josèphe et les Magiciens, » in *Les Communités Religiouses dans le Monde Gréco-Romain, Essais de Définition*, ed. N.Belayche et al., Bibliothèque de l'École des Hautes Études, Sciences religieuses 117, Turnhout, Brepols, Paris.

Brown, Cheryl A. 1992, *No Longer Be Silent, First Century Jewish Portraits of Biblical Women*, Westminster/John Knox Press, Louisville, Kentucky.

Cassius Dio. 1914, *Roman History*, trans E.Cary, Loeb Classical Library, Harvard University Press, Cambridge, MA.

Cheak, Aaron. 2004, "Magic Through the Linguistic Lenses of Greek mavgo~, Indo-European **mag(h)-*, Sanskrit *maya* and Pharaonic Egyptian *Heka*," *Journal for the Academic Study of Magic*, no. 2, pp.260-286.

Dickie, Matthew W. 2001, *Magic and Magicians in the Greco-Roman World*, Routledge, London.

Diodorus. 1950, *Library of History*, trans. C.H.Oldfather,, Loeb Classical Library, Harvard University Press, Cambridge, MA.

Duling, Dennis. 1985, "The Eleazar Miracle and Solomon's Magical Wisdom in Flavius Josephus's *Antiquitates Judaicae* 8.42-49," *Harvard Theological Review*, vol. 78, nos.1-2, pp.1-25.

Frazer, James G. 1911, *The Golden Bough: A Study in Magic and Religion*, Macmillan, London.

Gager, John G. 1994, "Moses the Magician: Hero of an Ancient Counter-Culture?," *Helios*, vol. 21, no.2, pp.179-188.

Gordon, Richard. 1999, "Imagining Greek and Roman Magic," in *Witchcraft and Magic in Europe: Ancient Greece and Rome*, eds., Bengt Ankarloo and Stuart Clark, The Athlone Press, London.

Graf, Fritz. 1997, *Magic in the Ancient World*, Harvard University Press, Cambridge, MA.

_____. 2002, "Theories of Magic in Antiquity" in *Magic and Religion in the Ancient World*, eds. Paul Mirecki and Marvin Meyer, E.J.Brill, Leiden.

Gray, Rebecca. 1993, *Prophetic Figures in Late Second Temple Jewish Palestine: The Evidence From Josephus*, Oxford University Press, Oxford.

Hengel, Martin. 1989, *The Zealots: Investigations into the Jewish Freedom Movement in the Period from Herod I Until 70 A.D.*, trans. D.Smith, T&T Clark, Edinburgh.

Herodotus. 1920, *Histories*, trans. A.D.Godley, Loeb Classical Library, Harvard University Press, Cambridge, MA .

Horsley, Richard A. 1981, "'Like one of the Prophets of Old': Two types of Popular Prophets at the Time of Jesus," *Catholic Biblical Quarterly*, vol. 47, pp.435-63.

Johnston, Sarah I. 1999, *Restless Dead: Encounters between the Living and the Dead in Ancient Greece*, University of California Press Berkeley.

Livy. 1936, *History of Rome*, trans. E.T. Sage, Loeb Classical Library, Harvard University Press, Cambridge, MA.

Luck, Georg. 1999, "Witches and Sorcerers in Classical Literature," in vol.2, *Witchcraft and Magic in Europe, Ancient Greece and Rome*, eds. Bengt Ankarloo and Stuart Clark, The Athlone Press, London.

MacMullen, Ramsay. 1966, *Enemies of the Roman Order: Treason, Unrest, and Alienation in the Empire*, Harvard University Press, Cambridge, MA.

MacRae, George. 1965, "Miracle in the *Antiquities* of Josephus," in *Miracles*, ed. Charles F.D.Moule, A.R.Mowbray and Co. Ltd., London.

Mason, Steve. 1991, *Flavius Josephus on the Pharisees: A Composition-Critical Study*, E.J.Brill, Leiden.

Nock, A.D. 1972, "Paul and the Magus," in *Essays on Religion in the Ancient World*, ed. Z.Stewart Oxford, Oxford University Press, Oxford.

Ogden, Daniel. 2002, *Magic, Witchcraft, and Ghosts in the Greek and Roman Worlds*, Oxford University Press, Oxford.

_____. 2001, *Greek and Roman Necromancy*, Princeton University Press, Oxford.

Phillips, C.Robert. 1991, "Nullem Crimen sine Lege: Socioreligious Sanctions on Magic," in *Magika Hiera, Ancient Greek Magic and Religion*, eds. Christopher A.Faraone and Dirk Obbink, Oxford University Press, Oxford.

Philostratus. 2005, *Life of Apollonius*, trans. C.P.Jones, Loeb Classical Library, Harvard University Press, Cambridge, MA.

Plato. 1926, *Laws*, trans. R.G.Bury, Loeb Classical Library, Harvard University Press, Cambridge, MA.

Rajak, Tessa. 2002, *Josephus: The Historian and His Society*, 2nd ed., Duckworth and Co., London.

Römer, Thomas. 2003, "Competing Magicians in Exodus 7-9: Interpreting Magic in the Priestly Theology," in *Magic in the Biblical World, from the Rod of Aaron to the Ring of Solomon*, ed. Todd Klutz, T&T Clark, London.

Schäfer, Peter. 1997, "Magic and Religion in Ancient Judaism," in *Envisioning Magic: A Princeton Seminar and Symposium,* eds. Peter Schäfer and Hans G. Kippenberg, E.J.Brill, Leiden.

Segal, Alan. 1981, "Hellenistic Magic: Some Questions of Definition," in *Studies in Gnosticism and Hellenistic Religions,* eds. Roelef van den Broek and Maarten J.Vermaseren, E.J.Brill, Leiden.

Smith, Morton. 1978, *Jesus the Magician,* Harper & Row, New York..

Suetonius. 1920, *Augustus,* trans. J.C.Rolfe, Loeb Classical Library, Harvard University Press, Cambridge, MA.

Tacitus. 1931, *Annals,* trans. J. Jackson, Loeb Classical Library, Harvard University Press, Cambridge, MA.

The Role of Grimoires in the Conjure Tradition

Dan Harms

Casual seekers of information on the practice of magic who look to infamous books of dark reputation, grimoires, often find only disappointment. The annals of folklore hold innumerable tales regarding such books, emphasizing the danger to mortals who seek divine power. One who possesses such a work, the stories say, is surely a master of forbidden arts, and a casual glimpse at a page may transfix an unwary reader. The complicated instructions within must be followed precisely and judiciously, lest the magician find himself following the example set by Mickey Mouse in *Fantasia*. Although stories may provide us with valuable insights into the beliefs and values of the cultures in which they are collected, they rarely tell us anything about the actual use of such books. In most cases, the situation is even worse: the contents of the grimoires themselves rarely have anything to do with the mythology surrounding them (e.g. Henning 1911, pp. 48-53; Ozanne 1915; Dobie 1930, pp. 337-338; Kerbirou 1947, p. 162; Dorson 1964, pp. 111-113).

Outside of stories relating to grimoires, folklore has long concerned itself with the collection of charms and magical formulae. The irony is that many of these charms have themselves appeared in and been disseminated *via* written collections as Stephen Bachter has pointed out regarding many such incantations collected in Germany. Within former folklore paradigms, great importance was placed upon the orality of tradition as a marker of "authenticity." As a result, researchers sought to avoid or downplay sources obviously based upon a textual tradition (Hayes 1997, pp. vi-vii). More recent scholars, influenced by the pioneering work on office culture of Alan Dundes and Carl Pagter, have been more open to the collection of written material,. Charms are seen as a form of literature, and indeed should be included and examined as part of that corpus (Dundes and Pagter 1975; see also Versnel 2002). Nonetheless, the relation between assumptions about grimoires in folklore and popular media and the actual practice of such works in particular times and places is still largely unknown. Investigation requires the examination, not only of folklore collections, but also trial records, contemporary accounts in newspapers and magazines, local histories, archaeological discoveries, reprints of magical books (both representative examples and as whole works), and similar sources (e.g. Estopañan 1942, pp. 24-38; Emery 1989, p. 115; Devlin 1987, pp. 167-184; Briggs 1953; Jones 1973; Leventhal 1976, pp. 110-119; Jones 1995, p. 100; Merrifield 1987, pp. 152, 162; Crick 1933; Powdermaker 1966 (1939), pp. 294-295; Brown and Hohman 1904; Ebermann 1914). Recent years have seen the availability of such information grow due to the respect that the study of esotericism and magic has gained in the academy. Still, despite this increasing corpus, these questions are not easy to resolve.

Even our most basic hypotheses may prove incorrect when historical sources put them to the test. For example, we might assume that ownership of a book signifies that the author has read and used it in any practice of magic in which they engage. This is not necessarily the case. In her study of nineteenth-century French newspapers, Devlin observes that some of the documented practitioners were not able to read the books in their libraries. Instead, they merely possessed them and used magic from other sources or even extrapolated from the books' illustrations for their practice (1987, pp. 165-66). This discovery is mirrored by Davies' work on the cunning folk of England, who often used such books as props to establish a practitioner's legitimacy with their clients. His findings also caution against blind use of certain categories of what is a proper "grimoire." The most popular work among the cunning folk was Reginald Scot's *Discoverie of Witchcraft* (1584), a text dedicated to the discrediting of beliefs in magic and the supernatural (Davies 2002, p. 143).

Likewise, an Italian scholar, Federico Barbierato, has turned to the records of the Inquisition of Venice to gain insight into the books used there in magical practice from the sixteenth to the eighteenth centuries. While the bias of the source might seem problematic, Barbierato uses these archives to uncover a rich undercurrent of magical activity with many surprising aspects. Even with printing, such works being illegal in Italy, a thriving trade smuggled books via multiple routes into Venice, where they were disseminated, recopied, revised, excerpted, and recreated. This market served not only the educated professions that might have been seen as the prime market, but people of every socioeconomic rank. In a striking parallel with the practitioners described by Devlin centuries later, grimoires were purchased even by the illiterate who paid others to read them aloud. The details of their practice were also eclectic; the instructions for virgin parchment or other exotic ingredients, one of the staple instructions of the grimoires, were more often honored in the breach than the observance (Barbierato 2002). These examples illustrate how what seem to be logical assumptions regarding practice can fall apart when compared with the evidence on the ground.

In the hope of illuminating these questions regarding how the books were used, this article will explore another use of magical texts within a particular tradition of practice, following the preliminary work of Patrick Polk (1999). The focus of this study is the charm-books popularized within the Pennsylvania German culture of the nineteenth and twentieth centuries. These works later received a wider distribution and were encountered frequently in the African-American magical tradition of conjure. One of the largest available archives on such material – Harry Middleton Hyatt's five-volume compilation, *Hoodoo-Conjuration-Witchcraft-Rootwork* – will be examined to discover the attitudes toward and usage of these works inside that tradition.

The Grimoires of the Pennsylvania Germans

The late seventeenth and eighteenth centuries saw the emigration of many Germans, mostly from the Palatine region, seeking farmland in Pennsylvania. Many of these, such as Johannes Kelpius and the Dunkers, sought freedom in the United States from religious persecution. This move found its parallel in the local literature, which focused on praising this new land and providing religious and instructional literature. By the first decades of the nineteenth century, most of the farmland was claimed and religious zeal had died down, leaving the Pennsylvania Germans – labeled by outsiders as the "Pennsylvania Dutch" – to the more practical business of running their isolated farms. The German publishers in the New World followed this trend by providing numerous almanacs and books of household remedies aimed at the settled, self-sufficient farmer (Robacker 1943, pp. 43-48).

Within this literature are three works that would later gain considerable influence outside of this region. Their origins are shrouded in mystery, as their authors – or, more accurately, compilers – found it advantageous to conceal their sources behind pseudonyms and false places and dates of publication. Three particular works filtered through the Pennsylvania German community, where they became the stock in trade of the "braucherei" or "hexerei," rural practitioners who attended the needs of the local farmers in matters of theft, witchcraft, and illness of humans and animals. [1]

What might be the first of these books—the fabricated origins of most of them making such determinations difficult—is *Albertus Magnus bewährte und approbirte sympathetische und natürliche egyptische Geheimnisse für Menschen und Vieh*. The first known editions bear the publication date of 1725 but likely was first issued in Brabant in 1819. This work is attributed to Albert the Great (d. 1280), the famous Dominican philosopher and theologian, around whom a tradition of false works had developed as early as the thirteenth century. This particular work derived from a number of other charm books popular in Germany at the time, most notably the *Romanusbuchlein*, a compilation of charms attributed to Saint Romanus and republished as a critical edition in 1958 by Adolf Spamer. Other sources included Staricius' *Heldenschatz* and a 1720 publication, *Der aus seiner Asche sich wieder schön verjüngenden Phönix*. The English translation, *Albertus Magnus, Approved and Verified Both Sympathetic and Natural Egyptian Secrets, for Man and Beast*, was first published in Harrisburg in 1875. The nature of the remedies varies widely – some rely entirely on substances, while others require incantations, prayers, and the sign of the cross to be efficacious. The influence of the book was broader than its circulation, with its protective prayers being sold as broadsides effective in their own rights.[2] According to the tripartite Egyptian Publishing edition from Chicago in my possession, the book was supposedly published by "Albertus Magnus" in order to alleviate the suffering of a destitute family. As promised, the remedies within cover the ailments of both animals and humans, including fever, cough, colic, and more supernatural difficulties such as witchcraft and goblins. The book also contains a number of charms for other effects, including ensuring a successful court case, emboldening a person, causing the return of stolen goods, or rendering the user immune to all types of peril.

The next work, *Der lange verborgene Freund, oder, getreuer und christlicher Unterricht für Jedermann*, was published in 1820 by a German immigrant and author, Johann Georg Hohman, a native of Elsace Township in Berks County and an author of other works of household remedies. It might be the first book on magic published in the United States, and it was certainly the most commercially successful for this period. Unlike most other authors of such books, Hohman was explicit about his identity, using testimonials by those whom he had healed as strategies to legitimize his work in lieu of the usual references to historical or mythological figures. Much of the work is derived from the *Romanusbuchlein* – in fact, the latter portion of Hohman's book is taken entirely from that work, a derivation that Hohman freely admits in his introduction by referring to a "Gypsy-book." A translated edition, retitled *The Long-Lost Friend*, was first published in Westminster, Maryland in 1855, and the book appeared in many different German and English editions afterward.[3] The contents of Hohman's work, while favoring incantations over natural remedies and highlighting an entire section dedicated to escaping the effects of weapons, are greatly similar in topic to those that appear in *Egyptian Secrets*. It is surprising, then, that little overlap exists between the two books in terms of actual spells, indicating that both were part of a larger genre of charms aimed at the same ends. This did not stop Hohman – or more likely, a later imitator – from publishing an undated version of *The Long-Lost Friend* under the title *Albertus Magnus, oder der lange verborgene Schatz und Haus-Freund* in an attempt to draw upon the recognition granted to both authors.

The third book is perhaps less geared toward a rural American market than the others, yet it has become perhaps the most infamous due to its appearance in folklore across the nation (Dobie 1930, pp. 337-38; Dorson 1964 pp. 111-13, 315-16; Ellis 2004, pp. 72-79). This was *Das Sechste und Siebente Buch Mosis, das ist, Mosis Magische Geisterkunst*, known in English as the *Sixth and Seventh Books of Moses*. Although folklore in the colonies mentions the book in connection with at least one mid-eighteenth century figure (Henning 1911, p. 49), the first printed reference to the book appears in the *Allgemeinen literarischen Anzeiger* for 1797 (Kilcher 2004). The earliest known printed edition of the *Books of Moses* appeared from the Stuttgart publisher Johann Scheible in 1851, following a supposed edition in 1849. Scheible's work contains what appear to be numerous treatises under this title, some differing from each other only superficially, along with material from such classic Faustian grimoires as *Black Raven* and *Tabellae Rabellinae Geister-Commando*.

To these, Scheible added a pirated chapter from Joseph Ennemoser's *Geschichte der Magie* on the magical practices of the Hebrews, as well as a section on "The Magical Uses of the Psalms." The latter work had a long history among Jews, and turns up repeatedly in the records of the Inquisition in New Castile (Estopañan 1942, pp. 27, 32). Godfrey Selig (not to be confused with the German Pietist and member of Kelpius' "Woman of the Wissahickon" colony, Johannes Gottfried Seelig) edited the book on the psalms and published it in 1788. Polk states that the combination of these texts would do much to enhance the work's popularity (Polk 1999). It was the 1851 edition of the *Books of Moses* that came to America and made its impact in the Pennsylvania German community. The Arthur Westbrook Company of Cleveland, Ohio, issued the first English edition in 1870, with several more following over the decades. The most popular of these was that published by William Lauron DeLaurence of Chicago in 1914. Attesting to its continued popularity, a "new revised" edition of this work, with the Secrets of the Psalms given cover billing, was published in 1985 (González-Whippler and Scheible 1991).

Despite numerous efforts to extirpate the practice of these books' remedies, they remain staples of regional belief and practice. Only a century and a half after the appearance of *The Long-Lost Friend*, many local practitioners were not aware that their extensive collection of charms had their origin in that work (Byington 1964). David Kriebel's recent fieldwork among powwowers in Pennsylvania German country confirms that all three books are still in use, though the usage of the *Books of Moses* has dropped off considerably due to its notorious reputation (2002). Nonetheless, these books would find even greater popularity due to the attention of publishers who reprinted and distributed such works throughout the United States, and even to foreign markets.

Conjure

Conjure, also known as hoodoo, rootwork, or goopher, is a set of magical techniques intended to bring about particular ends, such as healing, prosperity, and good luck. During the importation of African slaves to the New World, many ties to indigenous systems of belief and spiritual authorities were severed. As a result, those practitioners of indigenous beliefs who survived the Middle Passage became specialists who provided their new communities with spiritual services covering everything from medicine to finding a romantic partner to exacting revenge upon enemies. As many of the traditional medicinal substances were not available in this new climate, these specialists adapted materials from indigenous flora and fauna, as well as techniques from Native Americans and European Americans, to create a syncretic and unique belief system. Conjure became a means by which African-Americans, barred from practice in other fields, could become prosperous, and it attracted a considerable number of female practitioners whose career options were even more limited. Conjure's influence extended beyond the African-American community, and many doctors found a new and prosperous trade among their white neighbors. Jim Jordan, a conjure doctor from Murfreesboro, North Carolina, became the de facto leader of his small town and the owner of several business enterprises.[4]

Emancipation and the migration of African-American populations to the urban North did not disrupt the practice of conjure, but instead allowed it to reach new markets. "Doctors" – the title many conjure practitioners adopted without a formal medical degree – took up residence in these cities, selling goods that increasingly were not collected in nature but instead purchased from such "spiritual supply" companies as L. W. DeLaurence, Keystone Laboratories, and Valmor King Novelty. These companies sold not only the ingredients necessary for these remedies, but also a wide range of books – including the Pennsylvania German grimoires mentioned above (Long 2001, pp. 189-203). DeLaurence was perhaps the most notorious of these suppliers, gaining a magical reputation of his own as far away as Jamaica (Elkins 1986). In only a few short decades, these books became highly popular among conjure doctors and casual readers alike. By 1957, one folklorist reported that all three of these books were popular sellers in both Brooklyn and Harlem (Foster 1957). Even today, the Lucky Mojo site lists *The Long-Lost Friend* as one of its two best-selling books (Yronwode 2006).

The influence of Pennsylvania German grimoires on conjure practice is a direct result of the American grimoire tradition featuring more reliance upon printed sources than that found in other traditions. Although manuscript sources are not altogether lacking in the form of handwritten books or scraps on which particular charms were transmitted, the reorganization and creation of new texts that occurred in Continental contexts did not occur in this country. Most publishers were content to reprint older books instead of reassembling new ones, and most practitioners were equally unwilling to create their own, newer editions of such works. Although it is possible that some conjure doctors found their own versions of charms from a particular grimoire in other sources, I have yet to find any mention of them in the compilations of African-

American conjure beliefs published in the nineteenth century. The explicit statements by many practitioners strongly suggest that these grimoires from the spiritual supply companies were the origin of these particular charms.[5] Conjure became less popular as the twentieth century wore on due to a variety of factors. These included the increased availability of professionals such as doctors and lawyers, governmental prosecution of conjure doctors for mail fraud, and progressive African-American movements that saw conjure as a vestige of a superstitious past best left forgotten. A recent revival of conjure has occurred due to an increased interest in alternative spiritualities among African-Americans, but its impact and duration remains to be seen.[6]

The most prolific chronicler of conjure beliefs was Harry Middleton Hyatt. Born February 21, 1896 in Quincy, Illinois, Hyatt attended a wide variety of colleges after high school, eventually obtaining a bachelor's degree from Kenyon College, a bachelor's and masters degrees from Oxford University, and a doctorate in divinity from Culver-Stockton College. Having obtained his ministerial credentials, he sought to travel to Africa as a missionary, but, finding that no positions were open, he took up various positions in churches in both Ohio and New York. In 1924, he married Alma Egan Altenberg, a well-off manufacturer whose money was later channeled into the Alma Egan Hyatt Foundation (1932). This organization allowed Hyatt to pursue a career as an independent researcher into folklore.[7]

Hyatt's career began with the collection of the beliefs in his native Illinois. Working with his sister in a small geographical area, he compiled his monumental *Folklore of Adams County, Illinois* (1935, with a revised and updated edition published in 1965). While conducting this work,

Hyatt became intrigued with the various pieces of magical lore and witchcraft beliefs that he had encountered during his Adams County work. Expanding his scope to the practice of conjure in the United States, Hyatt canvassed the cities across the rural South to find practitioners of hoodoo. Hyatt spent countless hours sitting in cheap hotel rooms in African-American neighborhoods, working with local informants to locate doctors. He recorded their phrases *via* a microphone hidden under his hat on the table while negotiating with criminals and suspicious police officers alike. This fieldwork led to his five-volume compilation *Hoodoo-Conjuration-Witchcraft-Rootwork*, a tremendous collection of interviews with practitioners. Both *Folklore of Adams County, Illinois* and *Hoodoo* were privately printed, leading to the inclusion of much material that a commercial publisher would likely have excluded.

Some researchers who read *Hoodoo* were put off by Hyatt's insistence on transcribing extensive portions of his conversations with the conjure doctors (e.g. La Barre 1971). It is this thoroughness, however, which provides us with a wealth of material that in most other cases would be consigned to the dusty recesses of university archives or a fieldworker's personal notes. As such, it presents a wealth of data on the practice of conjure in the 1930s, revealing a great deal about how it was practised in the words of its practitioners. Thus, Hyatt's work provides an unparalleled window into the usage of the Pennsylvania German grimoires in that system.

The use of Hyatt's books for the assessment of the grimoires' impact is not without its issues, however. First are his unsystematic organization of the material and the lack of an index for thousands of pages. Hyatt never completed what, according to a fragmentary note mentioning similar travails in *Folklore of Adams County* (1970-78, vol. 1, p. xlii), must have been an excessively detailed and comprehensive index. Hyatt does make up for this to some extent with a detailed table of contents, though much of the material in his transcriptions is not indicated. Another problematic aspect of using Hyatt's work is that, initial appearances to the contrary, he in fact did employ various devices to ensure selection of particular materials. In at least one case, Hyatt omitted material that did not interest him simply by turning off the recording device. This might also be the case with material that Hyatt recognized as originating in written sources. In one interview (Number 1727), Hyatt turns off the tape recorder when he realizes that a recipe from *The Sixth and Seventh Books of Moses* is to follow (vol. 2, p. 1727.). This raises the question of how many other recipes Hyatt recognized as grimoire-based were removed through a process of selective recording. Nonetheless, enough such rituals from the books remain that a rough picture of their usage emerges despite this.

Hyatt also presented many of his informants' speeches in what might be described as stereotypical African-American dialects, though he does seem to have made efforts to actually reproduce speech patterns that he witnessed instead of forcing a single dialect on all his informants. Mortensen suggests that a number of possible solutions may exist for this problem, depending upon the ethnographer's preferred uses of mimesis or an imitation of the fieldwork situation that does not necessarily capture all details but nonetheless depicts what the ethnographer sees as its essential truth (Mortensen 2005, p. 118.). As I will be using data collected at quite some distance, both geographically and chronologically, however, I fear that any attempt at mimesis from a distance would likely be misleading at best. As such, I will maintain the spelling as close to Hyatt's own as possible, so others might take the opportunity to pursue their own readings.

The Perception of Grimoires in Conjure

Among practitioners of conjure, the attitudes toward written sources of charms differed considerably. The "Hoodoo Book Man," who Hyatt interviewed in New Orleans, had "read de Seven Book of Moses seven or eight year a'ready," and went on to attribute the origins of hoodoo itself to Moses and his book:

> Hoodooism started way back in de time dat Moses days, back in ole ancient times, nine thousand years ago. Now you see, Moses, he was a prophet jis' like Peter, Paul an' James. An' den he quit bein' a prophet an' started de hoodooism – what we call de *Seven Book of Moses*. (Hyatt 1970-78, vol. 2, p. 1758)

Such bold claims were particular to this individual. Nonetheless, others regarded these grimoires with some respect and were not averse to attributing their learning and success to them. The "Unkus Man" from New Orleans spoke highly of the books of "Doctor DeLong" (vol. 2, p. 1307) – most likely De Laurence, which would have included the *Sixth and Seventh Books of Moses* and the *Egyptian Secrets*. Ida from New Orleans claimed to have "learned under" the famous "Voudon Queen Marie Laveau," and only later did Hyatt realize she had learned from a book supposedly written by the legendary figure (vol. 2, p. 1666). A relative of the conjure doctor Julius P. Caesar mentioned that he "had the book at home on seals once... but I..." (vol. 2, p. 1645) – Hyatt cut him off, so we never learn what exactly happened to it. When conversation came around to the *Books of Moses*, a woman from Memphis remarked, "If ah had knowed whut chew want, ah'd brought it wit me" (Ibid., p. 1724). One wonders how pervasive such misunderstandings among Hyatt and his informants were, and if more grimoire-related material might have been collected if practitioners had been able to rely upon the non-mnemonic sources they used in practice instead of basing their descriptions strictly on recall.

Nonetheless, other doctors were more skeptical about the books and their utility in practice. An old man from Fayetteville, North Carolina, mentioned getting many occult works from the supply houses but decided that he "didn't have any part of de books" because they were sold without guarantees (vol. 2, p. 1053). According to a "Doctor" Caffrey from New Orleans, the power to work hoodoo came from birth, and "you can't get the power" from reading books (vol. 2, p. 1469). Most conjurers, as Anderson has discovered, were apprenticed to another conjurer when starting the trade while others claimed that a birthright, or the blessing of a spirit or God, brought about their power. Books could be a gateway into the practice of hoodoo, but they were usually not considered sufficient to set oneself up as a doctor. Occasionally someone attempted to do so, and other practitioners often looked with disapproval upon those who learned exclusively from written works.[8]

In keeping with this, many conjurers saw the lore in books as only a part of, or a supplement to, the spiritual blessings or training to be mastered. An informant from Savannah, Georgia, told Hyatt that she "had taken some work in certain branches of psychology an' astronomy, and then some work in black art" (vol 2., p. 1268). Hyatt interpreted this to mean mail order courses in salesmanship, knowledge of astrology, and the use of hoodoo books. When asked if she used books, Madam Collins of Memphis, Tennessee answered, "Ah can't remembah everything that ah have," suggesting the utility of the book as adjuncts to memorized lore (vol. 2, p. 1006). The "Unkus Man" from New Orleans pointed out that, even though he and others could go to "Doctor DeLong" and buy books from him, astrological differences in personality ensured that "a thousand people will come in to you and you won't find four agree on one thing" (vol. 2, p. 1307). This certainly seems to have been true on the practical use of grimoires in hoodoo.

The Use of Grimoires in Conjure

With regard to the Pennsylvania German grimoires, it was the *Sixth and Seventh Books of Moses* – or rather, the treatise "The Magical Uses of the Psalms" within – that seems to have had the greatest impact on the conjure tradition. In fact, a "doctor" from Fayetteville, North Carolina, told Hyatt outright that the *Sixth and Seventh Books* were "de onliest book dat tell yo' whut de Psalms is good fo'" (vol. 2, pp. 1522-23). Numerous practitioners throughout Hyatt describe using the Psalms as an integral part of their practice. Madame Collins recited Psalm 35, noted in the *Sixth and Seventh Books* as being used against "a lawsuit pending in which you are opposed by unrighteous, revengeful and quarrelsome people," (DeLaurence 1919, p. 155) to bring her clients success in court (vol. 2, p. 1003). A formula using Psalm 20 in conjunction with rose-water, oil, and salt to extricate oneself from a court case (DeLaurence 1919, p. 152) was a favorite of Informant 1448 from Fayetteville, North Carolina (vol. 2, pp. 1523).

Such strict adherence to the technique and goals as stated in the "Magical Uses," however, is unusual. Reading Psalm 109 over a concoction of wine and mustard for three days, the treatise says, should be used to cause an oppressor misfortune (DeLaurence 1919, p. 166). In the practice of one of Hyatt's informants, however, the rite narrows its focus to causing its target to be fired (vol. 2, p. 1141). In the "Magical Uses," Psalm 92, when said with other psalms three times over water containing the leaves of vines and myrtle, creates a magical wash that allows a man to "attain to high honors" (DeLaurence 1919, p. 164). A hoodoo practitioner in Little Rock simplified the procedure by using ordinary or holy water without the added ingredients or psalms, and using it as a potion to be drunk for good health instead of social advancement (vol. 2, p. 1322). On the other hand, other practitioners elaborated upon the rites they already had – the landlady of one of Hyatt's contacts used Psalm 48 to deal with enemies, but added that it must be read on a Monday morning before sunrise with a special prayer (vol. 2, p. 1475).

What is more surprising, given the reputation of the *Sixth and Seventh Books*, is the large number of psalm-based recipes that are not based on the book at all. Psalm 27, according to the *Books of Moses*, is used so that one will be "well and kindly received in a strange city" (De Laurence 1919, p. 154). Informant 1585 from Algiers reads the same psalm over "pecone oil" and uses this to anoint the client so they can hold the attention of a boss and obtain a job (vol. 2, p. 1072). Anointing with oil is a common procedure with other psalms, but this seems to be a new innovative technique not specified for this psalm.

Similarly, the Psalms might be blended together with local folklore and other magical traditions to create a new ritual. Nahnee, the self-described "Boss of Algiers," fused the power of Psalm 91, to which the *Sixth and Seventh Books* devoted two entire pages, with the traditional African-American story of meeting the devil at the crossroads, to create a new ritual. If one is confronted with a difficult task, they should recite the Psalm for nine days, afterward traveling to a fork in the road at midnight to meet a spirit who will render assistance (vol 2., pp. 1357-58). Other spells incorporate elements of other traditions, such as candle magic, into the psalm magic (vol. 2, pp. 1467, 1612, 1727). It is a shame Hyatt stated that he did not record more of this Psalm material (vol. 1, p. ix), possibly due to ecclesiastical bias (Smith 1994, p. 14-15).

The other materials from the *Sixth and Seventh Books* were less influential, but nonetheless occasional references show up in Hyatt's material. Notably, there are few references to the use of the seals that form the bulk of the title treatises in the *Books of Moses*, though Doctor English of Norfolk did make use of such in a protective rite (vol. 2, p. 1399), and a Memphis informant used the Sixth Table of Jupiter in conjunction with Psalm 72 to avoid a lawsuit (vol. 1, p. 288). The other treatises fared little better. A female doctor from Waycross, Georgia sought out an angel named "Peelee" before a trial, sending him to talk to the judge and the prosecutor before the trial begins (vol. 2, p. 1477). This seems to be a variant of "Pele," a name of God from the Semiphoras and Schemhamphoras portion of the book where it is noted as "he who worketh wonders" (De Laurence 1919, p. 126).

Merely because a rite is not performed in its entirety, however, does not mean it does not have influence. Ira Vands or Wands, a blind doctor from Florence, South Carolina, noted that rites to drive people insane or to get a favorable outcome at trial should be carried out "at de hour 'cordin' to de Six an' Seven Books of Moses" (vol. 2, pp. 1526-27). This is actually derived from the appendix "The Black Raven," in which a set of hours is provided for summoning spirits on various nights of the week as part of a procedure for ceremonial magic (DeLaurence 1919, p. 101). Instead of calling up demons, however, this timetable is now used as a more general ritual calendar. This same treatise provides the inspiration for the "Mojo Expert" from Memphis, who uses a vastly simplified version of the magical circle and ingredients mentioned in the text, such as "butterfly blood," in order to find buried treasure (vol. 2, pp. 1247-48). These conjurers have taken ritual instructions intended for one purpose – the calling up of evil spirits – and extrapolated from them to create new systems for other objectives.

Beyond its contents, the *Books of Moses* was seen as possessing an inherent physical virtue useful in various rites. One way to influence the judge at a trial, according to a Memphis doctor, was to either have read, or have slipped into one's shoes, the *Books of Moses* (vol. 4, p. 3688). (Given the book's size, it is likely only a few pages would be worn at a time.) Informant 1520 provides her ritual for the creation of that classic hoodoo staple, the "black cat bone," a bone that bestows invisibility, obtained by boiling a hapless feline. She claims that a thirteen-day rite of purification must be performed, during which the person must read the *Sixth and Seventh Books of Moses* without taking a drink – it can be assumed she is referring strictly to alcohol (vol. 2, p. 1730). The black cat rite is nowhere described in the *Books of Moses*, yet its inclusion here suggests that it possesses an inherent efficacy to empower a ritual.

The influence of other grimoires was also felt in the conjure community, though none possessed anywhere near the influence or reputation of the *Books of Moses*. One key example is *The Long-Lost Friend*; material from this book does turn up occasionally, but not as often as its aforementioned popularity among sellers would seem to indicate. Even Hyatt remarked upon the paucity of references to the book in his fieldwork (vol. 2, pp. 1781-82). How do we reconcile the book's popularity with the lack of its charms in Hyatt's work? It is likely the answer lies in the book's introduction, which contains the following passage:

> Whoever carries this book with him, is safe from all his enemies, visible or invisible; and whoever has this book with him cannot die without the holy corpse of Jesus Christ, nor drowned in any water, nor burn up in any fire, nor can any unjust sentence be passed upon him. So help me. (Brown and Hohman 1904, p. 141)

The book reflects a long tradition among the Pennsylvania Dutch of protective documents such as heaven's letters, fire letters, and house blessings (Yoder 2005:197-225). Combining the book's high sales with its low usage among conjure doctors, we might conclude that the vast popularity of *The Long-Lost Friend* was not so much because it was a book of charms, but because it was seen to have inherent apotropaic qualities. Nonetheless, some of the rites from Hohman's book became part of the corpus of hoodoo. An excellent example is the wagon ritual for catching a thief described in *The Long-Lost Friend* as "How to Recover Stolen Goods," also found in the *Egyptian Secrets* and the *Romanusbuchlein*. When a theft has been committed, the conjurer takes a few chips from the door through which the malefactor passed, attaches them to a wheel, and, while spinning it, speaks an incantation[9]:

> Thief, thief, thief! Turn back again with the stolen things. Thou wilt be constrained by the might of God; (three crosses) God the Father calls thee back; the Son of God turn thee about, that thou must go back; God the Holy Ghost carries thee back, till thou art at the place where thou hast stolen… (Brown and Hohman 1904, pp. 137-38)

A number of variations on this ritual are collected in Volume 4 of Hyatt's work. Once again, we see a vast disparity in techniques. Some of the practitioners seem to be working this rite straight out of a book – one New Orleans practitioner mentions that a word in "Hebrew" must be spoken for the rite, though it eludes the speaker (vol. 4, pp. 3630-31). Others are more flexible in their reading and interpretation of the rite. None presents the spoken charm in full, being content with "In de Name of de Father an' of de Son an' de Holy Ghost, bring back whut chew done took" (vol. 4, 3632) or "Thief, return de stolen goods which was taken outeh mah possession" (vol. 4, 3631), or, as a doctor from Waycross, Georgia chooses to do, leaving the exact wording unspecific (vol. 4, 3631). Doctor Glover of Charleston reflected the new urban milieu of conjure in his version of the ritual, in which an automobile wheel, after the car is placed on a jack, can substitute for the wagon wheel (vol. 4, 3631). One practitioner from Florence, South Carolina bypassed thieves entirely, putting it to use to "turn a woman roun'" (vol. 2, p. 1039) [10].

In a similar fashion, a charm from the same book "To Gain a Law Suit" also had considerable use among conjure doctors. It appears in Hohman's work as follows:

> It is said, that if one has a law-suit, and will take of the largest sage, and will write the names of the 12 Apostles on a leaf and put them in his shoe before he goes to the Court House, he will gain his case. (Brown and Hohman 1904, 122) [11]

As with the other rites, this one often accumulated elaborate procedures. A few passages from Madame Collins show how the procedure was elaborated based on the placement of the leaves, the omission of the name of Judas, and a call to another spirit:

> ...yo' git twelve sage leaves an' write the Twelve prophets' [disciples'] names on there – all but Judas. Don't write Judas' name – leave dat leaf separate. An' that leaf will go in a shoe by itself. An' then if yo' want that person tuh come free fo' murder, then yo' would use Cain as that spirit – yo' would call Cain because he slew Abel – an' have Cain to operate with that person. An' Lucifer's name wit his spirit, with those sage leaves. (vol. 2, pp. 1010-11)

A similar ritual, described by a man from Brunswick, Georgia, was performed by his grandfather, Doctor Jones. Instead of sage leaves, the twelve apostles' names are written on pieces of paper and tacked to the bottom of the courtroom chairs instead of being worn inside the shoes. Curiously enough, a copy of the *Sixth and Seventh Books of Moses* was placed above the door to the courtroom in order to complete the rite (vol. 2, pp. 1747-48). Hyatt himself had misgivings as to the accuracy of the ceremony's description, so we should examine this with caution (vol. 2, p 1747). Nonetheless, if it is accurate, it represents both how grimoire traditions might be intermingled, as well as how the supposedly inherent power of the *Books of Moses* was appropriated imaginatively for the client's benefit.

Perhaps the least influential of these three works was the *Egyptian Secrets*, but even this system had its practitioners. The "Mojo Expert" placed great stock in the book (vol. 2, p. 1249), and a love spell featuring the tongue of a turtle dove as a crucial ingredient (Albertus Magnus, n.d., p. 76) was a stock in trade for "Doctor Buzzard," who had taken on the identity of the most famous conjure doctor (vol. 2, p. 1420.).

Conclusion

If one theme has emerged from this examination of the use of the Pennsylvania German grimoires among the conjure doctors, it is the appropriation and reinterpretation of the material therein to serve the changing needs of practitioners and clients. It is striking that, despite popular depictions of the grimoire in folklore as the source of power, none of Hyatt's informants saw these books as a mainstay of their practice to be followed without question. Instead, they edited, transformed, and disseminated such material as a portion of their practice, integrating them into new social and cultural milieus and belief systems. Although the popular impression is that grimoires as powerful works with instructions that must be followed precisely, this data reinforces the impression of previous scholars that these works were utilized in creative and surprising ways as integral parts of living traditions. Whether this is true of similar works in other times and places remains to be seen.

Notes

1   An additional source of confusion with relevance to our project is that many European publishers attributed their works to New World locations, such as Philadelphia or Boston, in order to avoid the authorities' scrutiny or community censure. This makes it difficult to assess just when such books made it to the New World.

2   On *Egyptische Geheimnisse*, see Wanderer 1976: 223, Peuckert 1954, and Yoder 2005:223-24; on Albertus Magnus, see Thorndike 1923-58, vol. 2, 721-750,; on Romanusbuchlein, see Spamer 1958; on Heldenschatz and other grimoires, see Peuckert 1960 and Wanderer 1976, 223.

3   Other sources have given 1819 as the date of initial publication but this has been refuted by Heindel (2002, p. 130). See also Yoder 1976, pp. 235-36; Brown and Hohman 1904, pp. 8, 106; Heindel 2002, p. 128-142.

4   Johnson 1963. Given the modern narrative as the conjurer as hero, the role of the conjurer in maintaining the economic disparity between whites and African-Americans should not be ignored.

5   For the Continent, see Bachter 2004 and Barbierato 2002. In this sense, the situation in the United States parallels that as described by Davies with regard to Renaissance-era conjure men, who largely derived their practice from translated and reprinted Continental sources (2002:123-4).

6   Anderson (2005) and Chireau (2003) provide excellent summaries of the roots and historical development of conjure.

7   Much of this biographical information comes from Bell 1979.

8   On training, see Chireau 2003:22-23 and Anderson 2005: 99-100

9   See Spamer 1958:60, analysis 375. It should be noted that a similar rite may be found in the treatise Semiphoras and Schemhamphoris Regis, among those in the back of the *Sixth and Seventh Books of Moses*

(see De Laurence 1919, p. 133). It is possible that some of the rituals Hyatt describes might originate from that source, even though its labeling is much more prominent in Hohman's work. Nonetheless, when it is possible to distinguish between the two forms of the incantation or the particulars of the rite, every rite I have examined is more akin to that in *The Long-Lost Friend*.

10   In Germany, the same charm may have been transformed into a love spell that makes use of a sewing machine, instead of a wagon wheel, for the mechanism for the ritual. See Spamer 1958, p. 378.

11   The translation in Aurand and Hohman 1929 (p. 31) is identical in content save that there are multiple leaves to be placed in more than one shoe.

References

Anderson, Jeffrey E. 2005, *Conjure in African American Society*, Louisiana State University Press, Baton Rouge, LA .

Albertus Magnus. n.d., *The Approved, Verified, Sympathetic, and Natural Egyptian Secrets...*, Egyptian Publishing Company, Chicago.

Aurand, A. Monroe, and Johann Georg Hohman. 1929, *The „Pow-Wow" Book; a Treatise on the Art of „Healing by Prayer" and „Laying on of Hands", etc., Practiced by the Pennsylvania-Germans and Others; Testimonials; Remarkable Recoveries; Popular Superstitions; etc., Including an Account of the Famous „Witch" Murder Trial, at York, Pa.*, Aurand Press, Harrisburg, PA.

Bachter, Stephan. 2004, "Grimoires and the Transmission of Magical Knowledge," in . *Beyond the Witch Trials: Witchcraft and Magic in Enlightenment Europe*, eds. Owen Davies and Willem de Blécourt, Manchester University Press, Manchester.

Barbierato, Federico. 2002, "Magical Literature and the Venice Inquisition from the Sixteenth to the Eighteenth Centuries," in *Magia, Alchimia, Scienza dal '400 al '700: L'influso di Ermete Trismegisto*, eds. Carlos Gilly and Cis van Heerum, Centro Di, Firenze.

Bell, Michael. 1979, "Harry Middleton Hyatt's Quest for the Essence of Human Spirit," *Journal of the Folklore Insititute*, vol. 6, pp. 1-27.

Briggs, K. M. 1953, "Some Seventeenth-Century Books of magic," *Folklore*, vol. 64, no. 4, pp. 445-462.

Brown, Carleton F. and John George Hohman. 1904, "The Long-hidden Friend," *The Journal of American Folklore*, vol. 17, no. 65, pp. 89-152.

Byington, Robert H. 1964, "Powwowing in Pennsylvania," *Keystone Folklore Quarterly*, vol. 9, pp. 111-117.

Chireau, Yvonne. 2003, *Black magic: Religion and the African-American Conjuring Tradition*, University of California Press, Berkeley, CA.

Crick, Lucien. 1933, "Livres de Sorcellerie," *Le Folklore Brabançon*, 12, 71, 301-315.

Davies, Owen. 2002, *Cunning-folk: Popular Magic in English History*, Hambledon and London, London.

De Laurence, W. L. 1919, *The Sixth and Seventh Books of Moses...*, The de Laurence Company, Chicago.

Devlin, Judith. 1987, *The Superstitious Mind: French Peasants and the Supernatural in the Nineteenth Century*, Yale University Press, New Haven, CT.

Dobie, J. Frank. 1930, *Coronado's Children; Tales of Lost Mines and Buried Treasures of the Southwest*, Southwest Press, Dallas, TX.

Dorson, Richard M. 1964, *Buying the Wind: Regional Folklore in the United States*, The University of Chicago Press, Chicago, IL.

Dundes, Alan and Carl Pagter. 1975, *Urban Folklore from the Paperwork Empire*, American Folklore Society, Austin, TX.

Ebermann, Oskar. 1914, „Le Médecin des Pauvres," *Zeitschrift des Vereins für Volkskunde*, vol. 24, pp. 134-162.

Elkins, W. F. 1986, "William Lauron DeLaurence and Jamaican Folk Religion,' *Folklore* vol. 97, no. 2, pp. 215-218.

Ellis, Bill. 2004, *Lucifer Ascending: The Occult in Folklore and Popular Culture*, University of Kentucky Press, Lexington, KY.

Emery, Robert A. 1989, "Fragments of 19th-century Folk Belief in New York Court Reports," *New York Folklore*, vol.15, nos. 1-2, pp. 111-117.

Estopañan, Sebastián Cirac. 1942, *Los Procesos de Hechicerías en la Inquisición de Castilla la Nueva (Tribunales de Toledo y Cuenca)*, Instituto Jeronimo Zurita, Madrid.

Foster, James R. 1957, "Brooklyn Folklore," *New York Folklore Quarterly*, vol. 13, no. 2, pp. 83-91.

González-Whippler, Migene, and J. Scheible. 1991, *The New Revised Sixth and Seventh Books of Moses; and, the Magical Uses of the Psalms*, Original Publications, Plainview, NY.

Hayes, Kevin J. 1997, *Folklore and Book Culture*, University of Tennessee Press, Knoxville, TN.

Heindel, N. D. 2002, *The Hexenkopf: History, Healing, and Hexerei*, Williams Township Historical Society Easton, PA.

Henning, David C. 1911, *Tales of the Blue Mountains*, The Historical Society of Schuylkill County, Pottsville, PA.

Hurley, Gerard T. 1951, "Buried Treasure Tales in America," *Western Folklore*, vol. 10, no. 3, pp. 197-216.

Hyatt, Harry Middleton. 1970-78, *Hoodoo, Conjuration, Witchcraft, Rootwork : Beliefs Accepted by Many Negroes and White Persons, These Being Orally Recorded Among Blacks and Whites*, Distributed by American University Bookstore, Washington, D.C.

Johnson, F. Roy. 1963, *The Fabled Doctor Jim Jordan: A Story of conjure*, Johnson Publishing Co., Murfreesboro, NC.

Jones, W. R. 1973, "Bibliothecae Arcanae: The Private Libraries of Some European Sorcerers," *Journal of Library History, Philosophy, and Comparative Librarianship*, vol. 8, pp. 91-97.

_____1995, "'Hill-diggers' and 'Hell-raisers': Treasure Hunting and the Supernatural in Old and New England," in *Wonders of the Invisible World: 1600-1900, The Dublin Seminar for New England Folklore Annual Proceedings, 29 and 30 June 1992*, ed. P. Benes, Boston, Boston University.

Kerbirou, Louis. 1947, „Sorcellerie et Diableries en Bretagne," *Nouvelle Revue de Bretagne*, vol. 3, pp. 161-168.

Kilcher, Andreas B. 2004, "The Moses of Sinai and the Moses of Egypt: Moses as Magician in Jewish Literature and Western Esotericism," *ARIES*, vol. 4, no. 2, pp. 148-170.

Kriebel, David W. 2002, "Powwowing: A Persistent American Esoteric Tradition," *Esoterica*, vol. 4, pp. 17-29.

LaBarre, Weston. 1971, "Hoodoo – Conjuration – Witchcraft – Rootwork: Beliefs accepted by many negroes and white persons these being orally recorded among blacks and whites," *American Anthropologist*, New Series, vol. 73, no. 4, pp. 900-901.

Leventhal, Herbert. 1976, *In the Shadow of the Enlightenment : Occultism and Renaissance Science in Eighteenth-Century America*, New York University Press, New York.

Long, Carolyn Morrow. 2001, *Spiritual Merchants: Religion, Magic, and Commerce*, University of Tennessee Press, Knoxville, TN.

Merrifield, Ralph. 1987, *The Archaeology of Ritual and Magic*, B. T. Batsford Ltd., London.

Ozanne, Christine. 1915, "Notes on Guernsey Folklore," *Folklore*, vol. 26, no. 2, pp. 195-201.

Peuckert, Will-Erich. 1954, "Die Egyptischen Geheimnisse," Tidskrift Folr Nordisk Folkminnesforskning, vol.10, 40-96.

Peuckert, Will-Erich. 1960, "Johannes Staricius und sein 'Heldenschatz'", in *Folkloristica; Festskrift Till Dag Strömbäck*, ed. Dag Strömbäck, Almqvist & Wiksell, Uppsala.

Polk, Patrick A. 1999, "Other Books, Other Powers: The 6th and 7th Books of Moses in Afro-Atlantic folk belief," *Southern Folklore*, vol. 56, no. 2, pp. 115-133.

Powdermaker, Hortense. 1966, *After Freedom: A Cultural Study in the Deep South*, Russell and Russell, New York.

Robacker, E. F. 1943, *Pennsylvania German Literature: Changing Trends from 1683 to 1942*, University of Pennsylvania Press, Philadelphia, PA.

Smith, Theophus H. 1994, *Conjuring culture: Biblical Formations of Black America*, Oxford University Press, New York.

Spamer, Adolf. 1958, *Romanusbüchlein: Historisch-Philologischer Kommentar zu einem Deutschen Zauberbuch*, Akademie-Verlag, Berlin.

Thorndike, Lynn. 1923-58, *A History of Magic and Experimental Science*, Macmillan New York.

Versnel, H. S. 2002, "The Poetics of the Magical Charm: An Essay in the Power of Words," in *Magic and Ritual in the Ancient World*, eds. Paul Mirecki and Marvin Meyer, Brill, Leiden.

Wanderer, Karl-Peter. 1976, *Gedruckter Aberglaube Studien zur Volkstümlichen Beschwörungsliteratur*, unpublished doctoral dissertation.

Yoder, Don. 1976, "Hohman and Romanus: Origins and Diffusion of the Pennsylvania German Powwow Manual," in *American Folk Medicine: A Symposium*, ed. Wayland D. Hand, University of California Press, Berkeley, CA.

_____. 2005, *The Pennsylvania German Broadside: a History and Guide*, Publications of the Pennsylvania German Society 39, Pennsylvania German History and Culture Series 6, The Pennsylvania State University Press, University Park, PA.

Catherine Yronwode. 29-7-2006, "Hoodoo: African American Magic," available at http://www.luckymojo.com/hoodoohistory.html.

Hermetic/Cabalistic Ritual in Christopher Marlowe's *Doctor Faustus*

Dana Winters

The Latin verse in Christopher Marlowe's *The Tragicall History of the Life and Death of Doctor Faustus* (*Doctor Faustus*) serves multiple purposes. The Latin verse intensifies the psychological effect of the play on its audience, and it is used as a way to mock the Christian Church and Christian ritual practices during the English Reformation. When all of the fragments of verse are extracted from the play and put together in the order that the verses first appear within the text, the excerpts create a Hermetic/Cabalistic ritual, one that includes a statement of ritual intent, a conjuration, an excommunication, and a period of ritual ecstasy. Finally, further examination of the embedded ritual reveals that it is significantly influenced by the writings of Heinrich Cornelius Agrippa von Nettesheim, the renowned Renaissance occultist and magician.

Before exploring the Latin verse in *Doctor Faustus* and revealing how it forms a hidden ritual, it is necessary to examine the lives of Marlowe and Agrippa. The life of Marlowe, his upbringing, education, and later career as a spy not only bring to light the type of individual Marlowe was, but the reasons why Marlowe would embed a ritual in his play.

Meanwhile, an examination of the life of Agrippa will reveal that Marlowe had an intimate knowledge of the writings and life of the occultist. Once the connection between Marlowe and Agrippa is established, it then becomes easier to expose Agrippa's work as a major influence on Marlowe's play and the Latin verse within the text.

Marlowe was born in Saint George's in Canterbury, England, in 1564, the son of the cobbler John Marlowe and his wife Katherine (Honan 2005, p. 372). He was the second of nine children and died when he was twenty-nine years old (Honan 2005, p. 372). Marlowe's family was by no means wealthy, but as a son, he was given the best education possible. There are no official records of Marlowe's early education but it is surmised that Marlowe attended a petty school where he learned the alphabet and numbers (Honan 2005, p. 31). In *The World of Christopher Marlowe,* David Riggs (2004, p. 25) points out the primary purpose of petty school attendance for boys: petty school readied them to learn about God and to be responsible and, more importantly, obedient members of society. The curriculum was defined by whoever reigned at the time, and the tradition of defining the curriculum began with Henry VIII. The texts deemed required reading included the "*The ABC, The ABC of Catechism, the Apostles Creed, The Lord's Prayer, The Ten Commandments*, and *A Primer* or *Book of Private* Prayer," all of which had to be learned via rote memorization (Riggs, p. 26). During the years when Marlowe is thought to have attended petty school he had very few texts available to him: his father owned only a Bible (Honan 2005, p. 34). Access to texts was severely limited in Canterbury until the early 1570s, and the literature that Marlowe had access to includes several narratives, leaflets, and verses (Honan 2005, p. 34). Marlowe's exposure to religious works increased as he continued his education. He became familiar with a variety of religious rites and attended church regularly.

Marlowe attended grammar school in 1572 where he was first exposed to Latin (Honan 2005, pp. 45-46). In 1578, Marlowe entered King's School after receiving a scholarship (Honan 2005, p. 39). At King's School, Marlowe was required to recite all prayers in Latin, as well as to attend high mass every Sunday, saint's day and religious festivals, thereby giving him a familiarity with Church rituals and practices (Riggs 2004, p. 28). In *The Cambridge History of Early Modern English Literature*, David Loewenstein (2002, p. 44) states that boys in attendance at grammar school would begin an extensive study of Latin so that they could later study "select Latin authors." Edward VI and Elizabeth I insisted that William Lyly's *Latin Grammar* become the "Royal Grammar," and Marlowe would have been taught Latin from such a text (Loewenstein 2002, p. 44). Marlowe was also exposed to the poetry of Ovid and Virgil, and he would have been required to memorize specific rules for creating poetic verse. Marlowe was required "to write *controversiae*, arguing one perspective of a particular topic, then the opposite perspective" (Honan 2005, p. 55). Marlowe also learned *imitatio*, the act of utilizing other texts in order to create a new work (Honan 2005, p. 55). Ultimately, it is in King's School that the playwright learned how to rely on the works of others to create new compelling works of his own, a method common among writers during the Renaissance.

Following King's School, Marlowe would spend just over six years at the Corpus Christi College in Cambridge where he mastered Greek and Latin and had his first exposure to Aristotle with access to Leroy's

Exposition upon Aristotle's Politics (Honan 2005, p. 71). The influence of Aristotle would eventually be reflected in Marlowe's future works, including *Doctor Faustus*. While there is some evidence related to Marlowe's attendance at Corpus Christi, some of his time at the college remains ambiguous. In "Marlowe's Lives," Jeffery Meyers (2003, pp. 468-69) explains that there is a level of uncertainty about Marlowe's activities while in attendance at the college. There is evidence that Marlowe had intimate associations with secret agents, and he had an inexplicable absence from the college in 1587 (Meyers 2003, p. 468). Marlowe also suddenly had more money than could be explained; when he returned to Corpus Christi, the playwright had the funds for expensive clothing (Meyers 2003, p. 468). Further, Marlowe barely escaped several legal issues, which he could not have done without the assistance of influential patrons. He had been arrested several times for getting into violent public fights, and after being arrested for coining, he was denied his Master's, that is, until the Privy Council interceded for him (Meyers 2003, pp. 468-69). Marlowe's chief patron was Thomas Walsingham (Honan 2005, p. 5). In *Christopher Marlowe and the Renaissance of Tragedy*, Douglas Cole (1995, p. 7) explains that Thomas Walsingham was the second cousin of Sir Francis Walsingham, the head of Elizabeth's intelligence service, and it is surmised that Marlowe met Walsingham while working for the intelligence service as a spy. In light of such evidence many scholars have concluded that Marlowe had become a spy for England while he was still in attendance at Corpus Christi.

While Marlowe received a strict education, the religious instruction he received was equally strict. During the Renaissance it was by the King's order that Marlowe received certain religious teachings: "In 1536, Henry

VIII ordered that every parent must educate both children and servants in terms of specific religious instruction (Riggs 2004, p. 20). Marlowe was made to understand that disobedience was unacceptable and was considered a terrible vice (Honan 2005, p. 34). Marlowe "had an early taste of the ease with which Scripture [could] be used to quell popular dissent" (Honan 2005, p 34). Religious instruction during the Renaissance was not only for spiritual guidance and enlightenment but was also an effective means for controlling the masses.

Marlowe authored both poems and plays and was well-known for his offensive and sometimes derisive writing. According to Park Honan (2005, p. 3), "He could be outrageously insulting or perverse in his jokes or taunts . . .". In later years, many of Marlowe's contemporaries criticized his blasphemous works and behaviors. Riggs reveals the numerous accusations made against Marlowe pertaining to his blasphemous behavior by noting some of the commentary produced by contemporaries of Marlowe. Robert Greene was noted to have said: "'if the famous gracer of tragedians did not repent his blasphemies, God would soon strike him down'" (Riggs 2004, p. 1). Also, Richard Baines, another contemporary of Marlowe and a member of Queen Elizabeth's Privy Council, argued that Marlowe was an "atheist, a counterfeiter, and 'a consumer of boys and tobacco'" (Riggs 2004, p. 2). While many of Marlowe's contemporaries criticized his work, Marlowe belonged to an elite group of male writers who shared ideas with each other and acted as a support system for one another.

Many writers during the English Renaissance belonged to a coterie, a group of individuals, in this case a group of writers, which, as described in the *Oxford Concise Dictionary of Literary Terms* (2001, p. 52), is a group that shared their work with one another. Marlowe was a member of such a group; he shared a writing room with the author of *The Spanish Tragedy*, Thomas Kyd, as well as Sir Walter Ralegh [sic], and Henry Percy, also known as the "Wizard Earl of Northumberland" (Honan 2005, p. 2). In *Renaissance Magic and the Return of the Golden Age: The Occult Tradition and Marlowe, Jonson, and Shakespeare,* John S. Mebane points out the significant influence that Marlowe's coterie members had on Marlowe and his work. The coterie made Marlowe "intensely aware" of the occult tradition and made clear the debate between conventional authorities and the new wisdom people were looking to in order to understand and control the natural world (Mebane 1989, pp. 113-14). While Marlowe's coterie influenced the playwright's writing, it is also clear that Marlowe became familiar with the writings of Heinrich Cornelius Agrippa, and the occultist's work was equally influential.

Agrippa was a renowned scholar from Cologne, Germany, who studied law, medicine, and alchemy (Kastan 2005, p. 226). He produced a profound literary work entitled *De Occulta Philosophiae (De Occulta)*, a three-volume work started in 1510, that maintained and supported the existence and practice of the magical arts (Kastan 2005, p. 226). In *The Language of Demons and Angels: Cornelius Agrippa's Occult Philosophy*, Christopher Lehrich (2003, p. 2) explains the extraordinary influence that Agrippa had on Renaissance thinkers by describing him as "the touchstone, if not the key, to the mysteries of Renaissance magic." The original *De Occulta* contained three books on the philosophy of magic and, in the sixteenth century, a fourth book was erroneously attributed to him that resulted in Agrippa being recognized as a magician of the black arts (Lehrich 2003, p. 1), particularly the art of necromancy.

Necromancy can include divination, sorcery, witchcraft, enchantment and communication with the deceased (*OED* Online 1989). Interestingly, while *De Occulta* was a text about magic, some scholars question Agrippa's belief in the validity of the occult.

In *Hegel and the Hermetic Tradition*, Glenn Alexander Magee (2001, p. 33) reveals how Agrippa's work preceding *De Occulta* stirred a debate about his beliefs in the validity of the occult. In 1530, Agrippa wrote *De vanitate scientiarum* (The Vanity of the Sciences) and imparted a skeptical attitude toward all sciences, including those of the occult (Magee 2001, p. 33). Yet, in 1510 Agrippa began *De Occulta*, a work that was published twenty years later in 1533 and was based on the Cabala (Magee 2001, pp. 32-33). At first it may seem that Agrippa's works and beliefs in the magical arts were duplicitous. In *Giordano Bruno and the Hermetic Tradition*, J. B. Trapp explains why Agrippa wrote a work discrediting the occult sciences twenty years before he created a work that advocates the practice and philosophy of magic. *De vanitate scientiarum* is a device, one many occultists used when writing about magic: in the event of theological disapprobation, the author could turn to previously established work or statements made in them that contradicted the occult literature produced (Trapp 2002, p. 147). It is believed that *De vanitate scientiarum* was written as a preventive measure, a work that Agrippa could turn to if *De Occulta* led to accusations of heresy.

Agrippa studied the Cabala as well as Hermetic texts and *De Occulta* is a merging of the two schools of thought. In *The Occult Philosophy in the Elizabethan Age*, Frances Yates (1979, p. 44) asserts that *De Occulta* can be "classed as a Christian Cabala." In "Jews at the Time of the Renaissance," Arthur M. Lesley (1999, p. 845) explains that while the

Cabala was a Jewish tradition that evolved over several centuries, the Cabala was later adapted by Christians and viewed as an "ancient esoteric discipline". Agrippa relied heavily on the works of the occult writers that came before him and he was thoroughly familiar with the Cabala as well as the Hermetic tradition (Yates 1979, p. 46). Essentially, Agrippa established a text that united both Hermetic and Cabalistic beliefs.

De Occulta is a volume of work that focuses on the elements, their properties, and the use of natural, celestial, and ceremonial magic. Agrippa describes the universe as being made of three realms: the intellectual, the celestial, and the elemental, and he explains how each realm influences the realm beneath it, asserting that angels reside above the intellectual realm (Trapp 2002, p. 147). Angels influence the intellectual realm, the intellectual influences the celestial realm, and the celestial realm influences the elemental realm (Trapp 2002, p. 147). Agrippa believed that God influenced all the worlds by descending through them, and that man could ascend through and could tap into the virtues of the higher realms (Trapp 2002, p. 147). The Cabala is a form of mysticism that provides the practitioner with a method for contemplating God and knowing Him; it is also a form of "operative magic" that involves the use of the Hebrew language to invoke angels and to perform magical works (Trapp 2002, pp. 99-100). *De Occulta* is an instructional text conveying the practices of Cabalistic Mysticism: it defines a way for man to tap into the Divine and to use its power to manipulate the natural world.

While some of the magical practices Agrippa advocated are spiritually benign, not all of the magic described in *De Occulta* is positive. In some instances, Agrippa focuses on the practice of demonic magic despite the fact that much of *De Occulta* emphasizes virtuous and honorable intent (Trapp 2002, p. 149). The type of magical practices that can be derived from Agrippa's *De Occulta* rely on the virtues of the magician: if the magician has good intentions, then the outcome of any practice produced in accordance to Agrippa's text will be good; if the intentions of the magician are evil, then the result of a magician's workings will also be evil.

The evil magic that is presented in Agrippa's *De Occulta* is present in Marlowe's play. Doctor John Faustus is a doctor of divinity who has grown weary of traditional academic teachings: law, medicine, philosophy, and religion (Marlowe 1987, act 1, scene 1). He casts all of the teachings aside so that he can embrace the occult arts. Cornelius and Valdes are two characters in the play that teach Faustus the art of conjuring (Marlowe 1987, act1, scene 1). When he is alone, Faustus conjures a demon, Mephistopheles, and signs a pact. His signature consents to the exchange of his soul for twenty-four years on earth with Mephistopheles to provide him with whatever he desires (Marlowe 1987, act 1, scene 3). When the twenty-four years have ended, Faustus will be taken to Hell forever (Marlowe 1987, act 1, scene 3). Mephistopheles brings Faustus women, spells, enchantments, and gives him power (Marlowe 1987, act 2, scene 1). Continuously tempted by devils and magic, Faustus fails to repent and to ask God for forgiveness. Even after he is approached by an old man and told to repent, Faustus still does not turn to God (Marlowe 1987, act 5, scene 1). As Faustus's twenty-four years draw nearer to the time when he is to be taken to Hell, his regrets increase (Marlowe 1987, act 5, scene 1). He later confesses to the other scholars what he has done, and just before midnight on the last day of the twenty-fourth year, Faustus curses himself and Lucifer for having deprived him entry into Heaven (Marlowe 1987, act 5, scene 2). At midnight, Faustus is taken to Hell to suffer eternal torment (Marlowe 1987, act 5, scene 2). Ultimately, *Doctor Faustus* is a morality play about a man who sells his soul for knowledge and power.

Two lines in *Doctor Faustus* clearly indicate Marlowe's familiarity with Agrippa. When Faustus asks Cornelius and Valdes how to properly work magic, he aspires to be like Agrippa: "Will be as cunning as Agrippa was, / Whose shadows made all Europe honor him" (Marlowe 1987, act 1, scene 1). Faustus also has friends who are practiced in the art of conjuring, one of them named Cornelius. In *Necromantic Books: Christopher Marlowe, Doctor Faustus, and Agrippa of Nettesheim,* Gareth Roberts (1996, p. 150) explains how Marlowe first encountered Agrippa's work. Upon his death in 1576, Matthew Parker left his copy of *De Occulta* to Corpus Christi College, Cambridge, where Christopher Marlowe was a student (Roberts 1996, p. 150). Agrippa's influence on Marlowe's work is evident throughout the play, in Faustus's character, and is most evident in the Latin verse.

The characterization of Faustus matches the qualifications a magician must have in order to master the magical arts as set forth by Agrippa. As mentioned earlier, Faustus is a doctor of divinity, and the Latin verse reveals Faustus's familiarity with philosophy, medicine, and law. Agrippa asserts (1651, p. 5): "Whosoever therefore is desirous to study in this Faculty, if he be not skilled in naturall Philosophy . . . Mathematicks . . . Stars . . . [and] Theologie . . . he cannot be possibly able to understand the rationality of Magick." Since Faustus is depicted as a doctor of divinity with significant learning, the characterization suggests that Faustus has enough knowledge to fully understand the workings of magic and the consequences of its practice.

Much of the magical teachings within Agrippa's *De Occulta* appear in Marlowe's *Doctor Faustus*, which was written and rewritten, resulting in two separate and distinct texts (Kastan 2005, p. ix). The texts are currently defined as the A-text and the B-text, the A-text written circa 1590 and first published in 1604, and the B-text written twelve years after the original publication of the play, in 1616 (Kastan 2005, p. ix). The text used for the purpose of this study is the A-text, published in 1604. The differences between the texts must be duly noted; the A-text has 1,517 lines and was printed by Thomas Bushell; it is suggested that Bushell derived the text from Marlowe's original drafts (Kastan 2005, p. ix). The B-text has an additional 600 lines in its composition added after the rights to the play were obtained by John Wright (Kastan 2005, p. ix). Evidence suggests that the additional 600 lines of the play are not Marlowe's original writing: in Philip Henslowe's Diary on November 22, 1602, there is an entry about a payment made to two different playwrights, Samuel Rowley and William Byrd, to make changes to the play, specifically for the 600 additional lines (Kastan 2005, p. ix). Ultimately, the A-Text is considered a less adulterated version of Marlowe's play.

While the plays differ from one rewrite to the next, the Latin verse within each text varies little. The reader should also note that there are several verses in languages other than Latin that appear in the text that have been omitted during the process of the present analysis for clarity's sake. In the B-text, there are additional segments of Latin that do not appear in the A-text and have been subsequently omitted for this analysis.

Interestingly, there are thirty-three separate passages of Latin derived from the A-Text that remain for analysis. The fact that there are only thirty-three passages of Latin available in the A-Text suggests that Marlowe may have purposefully inserted thirty-three lines to allude to the age of Christ when he was crucified.

On the following pages, a table of the Latin in the play has been produced for easier analysis. The verse is organized into four separate sections: the Expression of Intent, the Conjuration, the Excommunication, and a Period of Ritual Ecstasy.

Table 1:

Latin Verse in the A-Text of Marlowe's *The Tragicall History of Doctor Faustus*[1]

Latin Verse followed by English translation

Expression of Intent:
"*Bene dissere est finis logices.*"
"The purpose of logic is to argue well."

"*Ubi desinit philosophus ibi incipit medicus.*"
"Where the philosopher ends, the physician begins."

"*Summum bonum medicinae sanitas.*"
"Health is the greatest good of medicine."

"*Si una eademque res legatur duobus, / Alter rem, alter valorem, rei,* etc."

"If the one and the same thing is bequeathed to two people, one shall have the thing itself, the other the value of the thing, and so forth."

"*Exhaereditare filium non potest pater, nisi,* etc."
"A father may not disinherit his son unless—"

"*Stipendium peccati mors est.* Ha! *Stipendum, etc.*"
"The wages of sin are death"

"*Si pecasse negamus fallimur, / et nulla est in nobis veritas.*"
"If we say that we have no sin, we deceive ourselves and the truth is not in us."

The Conjuration:
"*Sic probo.*"
"Thus I prove."

"*Corpus natural?*"
"Natural body?"

"*Mobile?*"
"Able to move?"

Sint mihi dei Acherontis propittii Valeat numen triplex Jehovae! Ignei, aerii, aquatici, spiritus salvete! Orientis princeps, Belzebub inferni ardentis monarcha, et Demogorgon, propitiamus vos, ut appareat, et surgat, Mephistopheles. Quid tu moraris? Per Jehovam, Gehannam, et consecratam acqam quam nunc spargo, signumque crucis quod nunc facio, et per vota nostra, ipse nunc surgat nobis dicatus Mephistopheles."

"May the gods of Acheron be generous to me! Away with the threefold power of Jehovah! Hail spirits of fire, earth, and water! The prince of the East, Beelzebub, monarch of burning hell, and Demogorgon, we beseech you that Mephistopheles may rise and appear. "Why do you delay? By Jehovah, Gehenna, and the holy water I now sprinkle, and by the sign of the cross that I now make, and by our vows, may Mephistopheles himself now rise at our command."

"Quin redis, Mephistopheles fratis imagine."
"Why don't you come back, Mephistopheles, in the shape of a friar?"

"per accidens;"
"The occasion but not the efficient cause;"

"Qui mihi discipulus."
"You who are my pupil."

"Quasi vestigiis nostris insistere."
"As if to follow in our footsteps."

"Veni, veni, Mephostophile!"
"Come, come, Mephostophile!"

"Solmen miseris, socios habuisse doloris."
"To the unhappy it is a comfort to have had the company in misfortune."

"*Consummatum est;*"
"It is finished;"

Excommunication:
"*Homo, fuge!*"
"Man, flee!"

"*Situ et tempore?*"
"In space and time?"

"*intelligentia?*"
"Intelligence?" (The Angelic influence believed to move the planets).

"*Per inaequalem motum, respectu totius.*"
"Because of unequal movement with respect to the whole."

"*Summun bonum. . .*"
"Greatest good . . ."

"*Maledicat Dominus!*"
"May the Lord curse him!"

"*Maledicat Dominus!*"
"May the Lord curse him!"

"*Maledicat Dominus!*"
"May the Lord curse him!"

"Maledicat Dominus!"
"May the Lord curse him!"

"Maledicat Dominus et omnies Sancti!"
"May the Lord curse him and all of his saints!"

Ritual Ecstasy

"Ecce signum!"
"Behold the proof!"

Nomine Domine!
"The name of God."

"Peccatum peccatorum!"
"Sin of sins!"

"Misericordia pro nobis!"
"Pity for us!

"O lente, lente, currite noctis equi."
"O run slowly, slowly, you horses of the night."

The first nine lines of Latin in the play create an expression of ritual intent where Faustus is establishing a specific state of mind. Agrippa (1651, p. 175) asserts: "We must therefore in every work, and application of things, affect vehemently, imagine, hope, and believe strongly . . .". In the first nine lines of Latin verse, Faustus is expressing his intent while simultaneously reinforcing his belief in the validity and power of magic. In "The Orthodox Christian Framework in Marlowe's Faustus," Joseph Westlund (1963, p. 192) asserts that Faustus "means to portray a psychological attitude." Faustus expresses the disheartening acknowledgement that his current studies of philosophy, medicine, law, and religion are not giving him the satisfaction he craves, and he yearns for power beyond that which is offered through his studies. Thus, Faustus reveals his discontent with logic, medicine, law, and religion and reveals his intent to use esoteric practices to realize his desire for power.

As Faustus alludes to philosophy he rejects all Aristotelian and anti-Aristotelian logic, finding that the concept of logic is not sensational enough: he refuses to believe that life's goal is to argue any issue logically (Marlowe 1987, act 1, scene 1). Faustus spurns the art of medicine when he reviews a book by Galen (Marlowe 1987, act 1, scene 1). In *Ancient Medicine*, Vivian Nutton (2004, p. 222) explains that Galen, a physician, was "indebted" to Aristotelian ideas. By viewing the works of Ramus, Aristotle, and Galen, Faustus is abandoning the teachings offered by the greatest Christian minds and preparing to embrace occult teachings.

The lines of Latin that follow the allusions to Ramus and Aristotle allude to Justinian's *Institutes*, the Roman Emperor responsible for the codification of Roman law (Kastan 2005, p. 8 n. 27). Faustus refers to the laws set forth by Justinian as "too servile and illiberal" (Marlowe 1987, act 1, scene1). His denunciation of the law is followed by the hope that The Bible will offer him knowledge and the power that he seeks (Marlowe 1987, act 1, scene 1). Yet, Faustus finds divinity too harsh in its teachings (Marlowe 1987, act 1, scene 1), and he prepares to denounce The Bible.

Two biblical verses follow the allusions to Justinian: the first is derived from Romans 6:23, and the second verse allude to 1 John 1:8 (Kastan 2005, p. 8 n. 41). Yet, the passage derived from Romans 6:23 is only a partial quotation and is therefore incomplete in terms of its intended meaning, and the verse derived from 1 John 1:8 is also incomplete in terms of its meaning because the original intent of the passage is missing without the accompanying line from 1 John 1:9. While Faustus speaks of death as the price for sin, the biblical passage in the book of Romans also explains that "God gives freely, and his gift is eternal life in union with Christ Jesus our Lord" (Rom. 6.23). Also, despite the fact that 1 John 1:8 has been quoted correctly, verse 1 John 1:9 states that "If we confess our sins, he is just and may be trusted to forgive our sins and cleanse us from every kind of wrong doing." While Faustus acknowledges the consequences for sinning, he refuses to acknowledge that he can be cleansed or forgiven. Mebane (1989, p. 114) asserts that Faustus "willfully misinterprets the Scriptures" for his own purposes: he wants to praise his intelligence," to liberate himself from the "restraints of orthodoxy" and to avoid facing his "human limitations." Since Faustus is a theologian and a scholar, it is unlikely that he would misquote biblical verse without intent. To stray from the correct quotation forces the verse to become a profane instrument, a crude inversion, and a tool to support the state of mind that Faustus has set out to establish.

Emile Durkheim (1967, p. 58) in *The Elementary Forms of the Religious* argues that in many magic rituals, what is considered sacred is made profane: "Magic takes a sort of professional pleasure in profaning holy things; in its rites, it performs the contrary of the religious ceremony." To deliberately misconstrue the meaning of the Scriptures, Faustus is blasphemous: he perverts the original meaning of the biblical verses he examines and turns the sacred word into a tool that serves his own purposes. Faustus is casting God's grace aside and using Scripture as a way to affirm his disdain for biblical teachings.

Faustus turns away from the mundane issues of logic, medicine, and law in search of consummate power (Marlowe 1987, act 1, scene 1). In *De Occulta*, Agrippa (1651, p. 127) writes of men with similar intent: "some men may elevate themselves above the powers of their body, and above their sensitive powers; and . . . receive into themselves . . . a divine vigour." Agrippa (1651, pp. 139-140) also writes about the eleven passions of the mind; the occultist's assertions suggest that the mind is moved to various states of passion including anger, boldness, desire, despair, fear, grief, hatred, hope, horror, joy, or love. Agrippa argues that all things conform to the mind of a magician "who is carried into a great excess of any passion" (Mebane 1989, p. 199). More importantly, Agrippa (1651, p. 149) explains that a "constancy of mind" is vital to every magical task: "Therefore he that works in Magick, must be of a constant belief, be credulous, and not at all doubt the obtaining the effect." Faustus is making his motivation and purpose clear, casting aside the notion of being a good doctor, and setting out to embrace the evil that accompanies excessive ambition and desire.

The conjuration follows the expression of ritual intent. After Faustus establishes a constancy of mind, the conjuration of Mephistopheles commences and is the moment when Faustus decides to prove the validity of the magical arts. The use of the phrase "Natural body" suggests that Faustus is seeking the proper astrological alignments and magical correspondences to conduct his rite. In *De Occulta* Agrippa writes (1651, p. 69): "Now if thou desirest to receive vertue from any part of the World, or from any Star, thou shalt . . . come under its peculiar influence . . . ." Faustus then calls upon the "gods of Acheron," the gods that reign over the Acheron River in Hell, as described in Dante Alighieri's *Inferno* (1999, p. 59), "the gloomy shores of / Acheron". "In Agrippa's (1651, p. A2) address "To the Reader," found at the beginning of *De Occulta*, the magician advises that "the gate of Acheron is in this book; if it speak stones, let them take heed that it beat not out their brains". Immediately following his plea to the gods of Acheron, Faustus further casts aside the grace of God and invokes the powers of fire, earth, and water to aid him in his working. In doing so, he is drawing on the power of the elements to empower his magic. One may wonder why Faustus does not call upon the element of air to aid in his rite; as noted in *De Occulta*, Agrippa writes (1651, p. 161) that the element of air was considered the glue that bound all of the other elements together. It was therefore unnecessary to invoke the element of air, as its powers would be present due to the conjuration of the first three elements.

Following the invocation of the elements, Faustus calls upon Beelzebub. In *De Occulta*, Agrippa (1651, p. 398) calls Beelzebub a false god: "Therefore the first of these are those which are called false gods . . ." In Faustus's invocation to Beelzebub he uses the words "we" and "our," despite the fact that he is working his magical rite alone. Faustus therefore relies on the "royal we." *In Talking Power: The Politics of Language in Our Lives,* Robin Tolmach Lakoff (1990, p. 183) explains that "language often metaphorically equates numbers and power," and that the "royal we, used by kings and queens to refer to themselves, suggests their largeness, their figurative majesty." Faustus's use of the "royal we" may be a play on God's representation in The Bible: "Let us make human beings in *our* image, after our likeness . . . (Gen. 1:26). The use of the "royal we" suggests that Faustus aspires to be a god, and he is already speaking like God. During the conjuration, Faustus seems to become intoxicated by his increasing power.

After the invocation of the elements, Faustus calls upon the demon Mephistopheles and questions his delay. First, it should be noted that Faustus calls on Mephistopheles specifically by name. Agrippa argues the power of names and words, both written and spoken, in *De Occulta*: "[It is in] this very voice, or word, or name framed, with its Articles, that the power of the thing as it were some kind of life, lies under the form of the signification" (1651, p. 153). Faustus seeks to control Mephistopheles, to have the demon do his bidding, and he uses the demon's proper name to call him. Secondly, Mephistopheles' appearance is delayed, and the delay is seemingly due to Faustus's momentary doubt in his magical abilities; in the Latin verse that precedes the conjuration, Faustus uses questioning phrases; the questions seem to display some doubt on the part of Faustus, and the delay of Mephistopheles' appearance is congruent with his doubt. Faustus's constancy of mind is momentarily wavering and his hesitancy may be the cause for the delay in the demon's arrival. To further affirm his state of mind, Faustus acts sacrilegiously: he sprinkles holy water and makes the sign of the cross. In doing so, Faustus is not only mocking Christ, but he is also mocking the Church's practice of blessing with holy water. Agrippa argued that "Very great also is the vertue of [water] . . . in the Religious Worship of God, in expiations, and purifications . . . Infinite are the benefits . . . being that by vertue of which all things subsist, are generated, nourished and increased" (Agrippa 1651, p. 12). Faustus sprinkles the holy water during a profane act against God, and it is a maneuver that makes his conjuration successful.

Once Mephistopheles appears, his shape is not pleasing to Faustus and he requests that the demon return in the likeness of a friar. Agrippa (1651, p. 402) argued that "angels are incorporeal, and even evil angels . . . assume bodies sometimes, which after a while they put off again . . .". It is here that Marlowe once again mocks religious officials: Robert Ornstein (1968, p. 1383) in "Marlowe and God: The tragic Theology of Dr. Faustus" argues that Marlowe views the Church as "a place of superficial rites and false authorities". Thus, the passage serves as a method for mocking the church by associating demons with clergy.

The lines that follow Faustus's demand that Mephistopheles return allude to the poem *Carmen de Moribus* (Song of Death) by William Lily (Kastan 2005, p. 18 n. 15). The English translation of the poem at *The Holy Cross College* website encourages young boys to pay respect to their teacher and to avoid lackadaisical behavior: "flee your bed in the morning, shake off soft sleep" (Ziobro 2007). Faustus beckons Mephistopheles for a third time, and the allusion to Lily's poem suggests that Faustus demands that the demon appear quickly. "As if to follow in our footsteps" also alludes to *Carmen de Moribus*, specifically to the line, "I am unwilling that you follow such crooked footsteps of habit lest, at length, you bear worthy gains from these deeds" (Ziobro 2007). The latter line suggests that one should be virtuous in all things, unless there is much to gain in the act of being immoral. Agrippa (1651, pp. 555-56) makes a similar argument in *De Occulta*: "But ye . . . sons of base ignorance . . . come not nigh our writings . . . ye may err and fall headlong into misery." Faustus is behaving immorally by conjuring a demon to gain power beyond his human limitations. The allusion to the poem could be Faustus's justification and an attempt to quiet his conscience.

Since Faustus has turned away God's grace, his sense of goodness has all but disappeared. Faustus indicates his misery. In *De Occulta*, Agrippa asserts that working with negative magic produces negative effects: "Then the celestial influences, otherwise of themselves good, are made hurtfull to us . . . Then *Saturn* darteth down anguish, tediousnes, melancholy, madnes, sadnes [sic] . . . stirrings of Divels [devils]" (Agrippa 1651, p. 470). Faustus has brought about his own misery, and the only comfort he can find is in the company of those that are as miserable as he is, in this case the company of Mephistopheles, a demon damned to Hell.

Faustus signs a pact, giving his soul freely to Satan. As pointed out by Barbara Joan Hunt (1985, p. 111) in *The Paradox of Christian Tragedy*, "It is finished" is John 19:30 and was the last words of Christ during the crucifixion. Hunt (1985, p. 111) further argues that, "Marlowe is satirizing Christianity . . . or he is underscoring Faustus' diabolical perversion of the Christian world . . .". Faustus uses the words to announce that the conjuration is complete, and that his magical working has been successful.

The excommunication follows the conjuration. Faustus's signs a pact with Mephistopheles and Lucifer, and the allusions to two biblical passages, Timothy 6:11 and Psalms 139:7-8 (Kastan 2005, p. 23 n. 73), suggest that Faustus is fully aware of the consequences of his actions. The verse, "But you, man of God, must shun all that, and pursue justice, piety, integrity, love, fortitude and gentleness," suggests that Faustus should turn away from his pursuits (Tim. 6:11). Similarly, "Where can I escape from your spirit, where flee from your presence? If I climb up to heaven, you are there; if I make my bed in Sheol, you are there" (Ps. 139:7-8), suggest that Faustus has opened his reality to Hell, that he is essentially in Hell, but that he cannot escape the will of God or his guilty conscience.

In the excommunication rite the term *"Maledicat Dominus"* appears five times. Agrippa, a firm believer in numerology and the magic of mathematics, argues that the number five represents the crucifixion of Christ as well as the "five principle wounds of Christ," and "the Seal of the Holy Ghost" (Agrippa 1651, p. 188). Further, Agrippa also notes the number five's negative aspects and argues that it is associated with the five corporeal torments in the infernal world: "deadly bitterness, horrible howling, terrible darkness, unquenchable heat, and a piercing stink" (Agrippa 1651, p. 190). Thomas B. Stroup in "Rituals in Marlowe's Plays" asserts that, "[in] a ritual in which an oath provides a contract . . . a prayer may be a malediction" (1986, p. 27). The repetitive use of *Maledicat Dominus* is an imitation of the "Papal curse by bell, book, and candle" (Stroup 1986, p. 35). Faustus's words are a clear acceptance of evil and the devil as "Lord." Finally, *"Summum bonum"* translates as "Greatest good," which is followed by the cursing, and it is as if the ritual's intent is to rid Faustus's spirit of goodness and to silence his conscience. At this point in the ritual, Faustus has reached a point of utter damnation.

Following the excommunication, the ritual moves into a period of ritual ecstasy. Faustus successfully conjures Mephistopheles and has proven his ability to work magical arts. Faustus is using the name of God in his magical practice and, once again, he is depicted as mocking Christ. While using the name of God irreverently in a magical rite can be viewed as a blasphemous act, Faustus is also attempting to achieve ritual ecstasy and to prolong the climax of the ritual. In *The Mystical Experience in Abraham Abulafia*, Moshe Idel explains that just before ritual ecstasy can be experienced the practitioner envisions the letters of the "Divine Name" and "the vision of the letters is the final stage of the ecstatic process" (1988, p. 34). Idel further asserts that: "the Name of God [is] the principal means for connection with Him; in its view, the recitation of God's Name during worship brings about the unification of the worshipper with God Himself through the very act of pronouncing" (1988, p. 42). In a mystical experience, ecstasy is achieved when the practitioner achieves a trance-like state, one in which the soul leaves the body and communes with God (Trapp 2002, p. 106). During a moment of ritual ecstasy, a practitioner would feel the celestial power of the forces he is working with; in Faustus's case, the doctor would be intoxicated by unadulterated evil.

Faustus's desire to prolong the ritual ecstasy is evident in "O run slowly, slowly, you horses of the night," a verse borrowed from Ovid's *Amores* (Kastan 2005, p. 50 n. 70). Marlowe, in an undated work, translated Ovid's poetry, and this particular line appears in Book I, Elegy XIII: *Ad Auroram ne properet*. In the poem, the narrator addresses Aurora, the goddess of the dawn and pleads with her to slow the coming of the morning so that he can have more time with his lover: "Hold in thy rosie horses that they move not" (Marlowe 1987, act 1, scene 13). In *Classical Myths in English Literature*, Dan S. Norton and Peters Rushton (1952, p. 35) explain that Helios is the god of the sun, and he drives a horse-drawn chariot that brings in the sun each morning. Aurora is a Roman goddess based on the Greek goddess Eos, the goddess responsible for opening the gates of the heavens to allow Helios to bring in the new day (Norton & Rushton 1952, p. 35). Hence, the line that appears in *Doctor Faustus* that alludes to Ovid's *Amores* indicates that the doctor seeks to prolong the night or the ritual experience.

It is clear that a ritual is embedded in *Doctor Faustus*, and the reasons why Marlowe chose to embed a ritual are numerous. Marlowe grew up during a period of societal disorder. The instability of the Church was evident in Renaissance England: from 1547 to 1558, the religious inclination changed every time a new ruler took over the throne (Riggs 2004, p. 15). Marlowe therefore "mocked religion intentionally, while at the same time paying honor to its sacred teachings" (Honan 2005, p. 31). Marlowe lived during a time period that was also extremely violent. In his adolescence, Marlowe became familiar with the price of heresy as he observed condemned men carted past his home to Oaten Hill, the Canterbury gallows (Riggs 2004, p. 14). In his adulthood, the playwright would be continuously reminded of the danger of heretical ideas and beliefs: Marlowe attended the same school as Francis Kett and had encountered him on several occasions (Honan 2005, p. 79). Kett was a Fellow at Corpus Christi and a man that would later deny the divinity of Christ, be convicted of heresy, and be sentenced by the bishop of

Norwich to be burned in a ditch (Honan 2005, p. 79). Thus, Marlowe knew full well the penalty of heresy, death being its drastic consequence. Marlowe may have been concerned about being charged with heresy and therefore fragmented the ritual within the text.

Marlowe was no stranger to English law having been arrested three times in 1592 for various acts of violence (Meyers 2003, p. 468). Interestingly, Meyers also points out Marlowe's incredible familiarity with the Privy Council; in 1593, Thomas Kyd accused Marlowe of atheism "under 'pains and undeserved tortures,' and Marlowe, in turn, was forced to report to the Privy Council on a daily basis" (2003, p. 468). What's even more striking about Marlowe's arrest record is that he was always released. Meyers contends that Marlowe had influential connections in the secret service, helping him to continually escape the full consequence of English law (2003, p. 468). Nevertheless, if Marlowe had made the inclusion of a ritual obvious within the play, he may have faced legal issues with the potential for extreme legal ramifications, despite his prestigious connections.

Concerned with being charged with heresy, Marlowe also may have feared censorship by the Privy Council. In "Marlowe's Cambridge Years and the Writing of Doctor Faustus," G. M. Pinciss clearly defines why Marlowe might have encrypted the ritual within the text instead of keeping it completely intact: "In November 1589 the Privy Council requested that the Archbishop Whitgift appoint a someone to assist the Master of the Revels in screening plays" (1993, p. 260). Since Marlowe's plays were staged, it is safe to conclude that they "did not defy the censors, however much it might have ruffled the feathers of one or another religious position" (Pinciss 1993, p. 260). The playwright was skilled when it came to writing about issues of serious debate, doing so in such a way that would allow him to reveal the issue in its entirety while still managing to avoid Privy Council censorship (Pinciss 1993, p. 260). It can be argued that if the play focused too heavily on occult subjects, the play not only risked censorship at the hands of the Privy Council, but Marlowe also risked imprisonment or death.

While Marlowe may have been concerned about censorship or being accused of heresy, he was probably equally concerned with being accused of atheism: "During Marlowe's lifetime, atheism…became the 'sin of sins'" (Riggs 2004, p. 30). During the English Renaissance, atheism was a similar but different crime from heresy, heresy being the older of the two crimes (Riggs 2004, p. 30). An act of heresy was a crime that involved the disputation of the existence of God and it also denied God's ability to intervene in one's life via the actions of the Son and the Holy Ghost (Riggs 2004, p. 30). In contrast, atheism was a crime where the individual rejected the idea that the soul was immortal, denied that heaven and Hell existed at all, and also denied the "operations of Providence" (Riggs 2004, p. 30). If *Doctor Faustus* seemed to convey the ideas of an Atheist the Privy Council might have censored the play and charged Marlowe with the crime of atheism.

Despite the fact that Marlowe faced a number of issues if he included a complete ritual in *Doctor Faustus*, he clearly included a ritual within the text, even though its form is fragmented. Mebane suggests that *Doctor Faustus* contains a dual theme. In *Art and Magic in Marlowe, Jonson, and Shakespeare: The Occult Tradition in Dr. Faustus, The Alchemist, and the Tempest*, John Mebane states (1975, p. 91): "It is a tragedy, and like many genuine tragedies it is founded upon a conflict between two irreconcilable systems of value, each of which has at least partial validity and a genuine claim to our allegiance." It is possible to consider the play as revealing the character of Faustus as one turning away from God and working against all Christian teachings, but the hidden Latin ritual may be representative of the esoteric teachings of the Renaissance period. The two opposing "irreconcilable systems" are innovatively inserted into the body of the play, the linear sequence of the play's action or plot being equivalent to the Christian understandings of the period, and the fragmented Latin verse equating to the secret understandings of Renaissance magicians.

While Marlowe may have feared legal repercussions for including a ritual in *Doctor Faustus*, it is possible that he was merely maintaining dramatic conventions. Stroup contends that it was a common practice for Renaissance writers to embed hidden material and further argues that Christian ritual can be altered and mixed with magical charms so that "the alert theatre-goer would get the fearful implication" (1986, p. 32). If the playwright was going to examine controversial issues through his work, and if he was to successfully get his plays staged, he was going to have to mask certain subjects in order to keep them from being a future source of trouble for him.

Marlowe often examined issues that were prevalent in Renaissance society and Marlowe's religious views were, in some part, based on the teachings of his father. John Marlowe may have been one of the influences for the way the playwright wrote about Christian and anti-Christian thought: Christopher's father possessed a "wary detachment" toward the community and religious practices (Riggs 2004, p. 16). As proof of John Marlowe's deficient religious practices, there is evidence that in 1569 churchwards paid a visit to Christopher's father and cited the shoemaker: "'for that he cometh not to church as he ought to do'" (Riggs 2004, p. 22). Riggs also asserts that: "Communities provide the mirror in which they learn to recognize themselves," and further suggests that Marlowe, being the son of immigrants, spent his life "on the margin of the community . . . in a place where . . . religious beliefs were constantly being discredited" (2004, p. 16). Perhaps it is Marlowe's detachment from the community and its religious structure, in conjunction with the instability of the Church that gave Marlowe his unique views of religion and God. Marlowe's writing gave him a place to explore both sides of prominent religious issues during the Renaissance.

Marlowe still may have had other reasons for fragmenting the ritual in *Doctor Faustus*. In *De Occulta*, Agrippa writes: "Therefore . . . we have folded up the truth of this science with many Enigmaes, and dispersed it in divers places, for we have not hidden it from the wise, but from the wicked and ungodly . . ." (Agrippa 1651, p. 556). According to the Renaissance magician, true occult wisdom must remain hidden from the unwise or from those that have no familiarity with magic. It is possible that Marlowe fragmented the Latin verse to keep the ritual hidden from those who might attempt to use it or from those who would not truly understand its teachings.

In conclusion, when the passages of Latin in Marlowe's *Doctor Faustus* are extracted from the play and put together in the order that they first appear, an embedded Hermetic/Cabalistic ritual containing a statement of ritual intent, a conjuration, an excommunication, and a period of ritual ecstasy become evident. In an effort to mock the Church, Marlowe cleverly embedded the text and thereby avoided the censorship of the Privy Council, as well as any legal ramifications he might have faced.

Finally, Marlowe relied heavily on Agrippa's *De Occulta* to create a play that embodies both Christian and Christian Cabalistic understandings.

Notes

1. Christopher Marlowe, *Doctor Faustus: A Two-Text Edition (A-Text, 1604; B-Text, 1616) Contexts and Sources Criticism*, ed. David Scott Kastan (New York: W.W. Norton, 2005)   1-52.

Bibliography

Agrippa, Heinrich Cornelius. 1651, *Three Books of Occult Philosophy*, trans. J. F. London, Printed by R.W. for Gregory Moule.

Alighieri, Dante. 1999, *The Divine Comedy of Dante Alighieri: The Inferno*, ed. Robert M. Durling, trans. Ronald L. Martinez and Robert M. Durling, Oxford University Press, New York.

Cole, Douglas. 1995, *Christopher Marlowe and the Renaissance of Tragedy*, Praeger, Westport.

Durkheim, Emile. 1967, *The Elementary Forms of the Religious Life*, trans. Joseph Ward Swain, Free Press, New York.

Honan, Park. 2005, *Christopher Marlowe: Poet & Spy*, Oxford University Press, Oxford.

Hunt, Barbara Joan. 1985, *The Paradox of Christian Tragedy*, Whitston Publishing, Troy, New York.

Idel, Moshe. 1988, *The Mystical Experience in Abraham Abulafia*, trans. Jonathan Chipman, State University of New York Press, Albany, NY.

Kastan, David Scott. 2005, "Introduction," in *Doctor Faustus: A Two-Text Edition (A-Text, 1604; B-Text; 1616): Contexts and Sources Criticism*, W.W. Norton, New York.

Lakoff, Robin Tolmach. 1990, *Talking Power: The Politics of Language in Our Lives*, Basic Books, New York.

Lehrich, Christopher. 2003, *The Language of Demons and Angels: Cornelius Agrippa's Occult Philosophy*, Vol. 119 of Brill's Studies in Intellectual History, Brill, Leiden.

Lesley, Arthur M. (1999), "Jews at the Time of the Renaissance," *Renaissance Quarterly* vol. 52, no.3, p. 845.

Loewenstein, David. 2002, *The Cambridge History of Early Modern English Literature*, ed. Janel Mueller, Cambridge University Press, Cambridge.

Magee, Glenn Alexander. 2001, *Hegel and the Hermetic Tradition*, Cornell University Press, Ithaca.

Marlowe, Christopher. 1987, *The Complete Works of Christopher Marlowe*, vol. 1, ed. Roma Gill, Claredon Press, Oxford.

Marlowe, Christopher. 2005, *Doctor Faustus: A Two-Text Edition (A-Text, 1604; B-Text, 1616) Contexts and Sources Criticism*, ed. David Scott Kastan, W.W. Norton, New York.

Mebane, John Spencer. 1975, *Art and Magic in Marlowe, Jonson, and Shakespeare: The Occult Tradition in Dr. Faustus, The Alchemist, and the Tempest*, DAI 35: (1975) 7316A-17A. Diss. Emory U.

Mebane, John Spencer. 1989, *Renaissance Magic and the Return of the Golden Age: The Occult Tradition and Marlowe, Jonson, and Shakespeare*, University of Nebraska Press, Lincoln, NE.

Meyers, Jeffrey. (2003) "Marlowe's Lives," *Michigan Quarterly Review*, vol. 55, no.3, pp. 468-469.

Norton, Dan S, & Peters, Rushton. 1952, *Classical Myths in English Literature*, Rinehart, New York.

Nutton, Vivian. 2004, *Ancient Medicine*, Routledge, New York.

Ornstein, Robert. (1968), "Marlowe and God: The Tragic Theology of Dr. Faustus," *PMLA*, vol. 83, no.5, pp. 1378-1385.

Oxford Concise Dictionary of Literary Terms. 2001, 'Coterie', ed. Chris Baldick, Oxford University, New York.

Pinciss, G. M. (1993), "Marlowe's Cambridge Years and the Writing of Doctor Faustus," *Studies in English Literature: 1500-1900*, vol. 33, no.2, pp. 249-264.

Riggs, David. 2004, *The World of Christopher Marlowe*, Henry Holt, New York.

Roberts, Gareth. 1996, "Christopher Marlowe and English Renaissance Culture." in *Necromantic Books: Christopher Marlowe, Doctor Faustus, and Agrippa of Nettesheim,* ed. Darryll Grantley and Peter Roberts, Scolar Press, Hants, England.

Stroup, Thomas B. 1986, "Ritual in Marlowe's Plays," in *Drama in the Renaissance: Comparative and Critical Essays,* ed. Clifford Davidson, C. J. Gianakaris, and John H. Stroupe, AMS Press, New York.

The Oxford Study Bible: Revised English Bible with the Apocrypha. 1992, ed. M Jack Suggs, Katharine Doob Sakenfeld, and James R Mueller, Oxford University Press, New York.

Trapp, J. B. 2002, *Giordano Bruno and the Hermetic Tradition,* Routledge, London.

Westlund, Joseph. (1963), "The Orthodox Christian Framework in Marlowe's Faustus," *Studies in English Literature: 1500-1900,* vol. 3, no.2, pp.191-205.

Yates, Frances. 1979, *The Occult Philosophy in the Elizabethan Age,* Routledge, London.

Ziobro. (2007), "William Lily's *Carmen de Moribus,*" Available at:http://www.holycross.edu/departments/classics/wziobro/ClassicalAmerica/Lily'sCarmenDeMoribusHP.html.

Italian Cunning Craft: Some Preliminary Observations

Sabina Magliocco

During the last decade, scholars of European history, folklore, and ethnology have increasingly turned their attention to indigenous traditions of vernacular healing. Before the widespread diffusion of medical treatments, these traditions flourished in all parts of Europe since people were dependent on them for the resolution of health problems, from the trivial to the life-threatening. They included a panoply of techniques, from the use of herbs and drugs derived from plant material, to the laying on of hands, to strictly spiritual cures, and they addressed a range of illnesses and conditions, from the ubiquitous worms and back aches to states unique to a particular cultural matrix, such as *tarantismo* and *arlìa* (De Martino 1963/2005; Staro 2005). Some healers also located lost or stolen property and performed activities now associated more with magic than with medicine: divination, love charms, counter-witchcraft and the like. The individuals who practiced these traditions were variously regarded as folk healers, wise women and men, specialists in one or more conditions, or, occasionally, witches. Indeed, one motivator behind the resurgence of interest in these traditions has been the emergence of revival Witchcraft and modern Paganism in the last half of the twentieth century. These new religions seek their roots in the folklore and folklife of Europe, and some of these roots may indeed lie in what has come to be called cunning craft.[1]

My aim in this paper is twofold: to provide English speakers and readers with an overview of Italian cunning craft, as it has been treated in the (mostly Italian language) ethnographic literature; and to suggest that the roots of Italian American Pagan Witchcraft, or Stregheria, may lie in traditions of Italian cunning craft brought to the United States (the birthplace of Stregheria) by Italian immigrants. The data is based on fieldwork, as well as on a review of existing ethnographic and archival sources: emerging from my 2005 and 2006 study of contemporary Italian cunning traditions in two regions of Italy, the Emilian Apennine and Campania, part of a joint project with Italian colleagues. Far from having disappeared as a result of the diffusion of universal health care, many of these traditions are flourishing, albeit in rural areas and under very specific social and economic conditions. A surprising feature of the study was the revelation that cunning craft was more prevalent in Emilia Romagna and along the Emilian-Tuscan border than in Campania, reversing the usual stereotypes about the Italian south being more tradition-bound than the northern regions. This inference must be treated with caution, though, as I will argue that the continued existence of cunning craft depends on a specific constellation of factors which do not respect popular stereotypes about regions. My work is thus not intended to contradict or contest that of the many fine ethnologists who have worked in the *meridione* and discovered vernacular healing traditions there; in fact, it builds upon their contributions.

I. The Context of Italian Cunning Craft: the Enchanted Worldview

Cunning traditions are part of a larger magico-religious worldview that was, and remains, deeply embedded in the everyday life of rural Italy: in the cycle of rituals and celebrations connected to the individual life cycle, the agro-pastoral year cycle and the Roman Catholic liturgical cycle (Grimaldi 1993; Staro 2005 and n.d.); in songs and musical traditions (De Martino 2005 [1961]; Del Giudice 2005; Staro 2005 and n.d.; Magrini 2003); and in the most ordinary aspects of day-to-day life (Wilson 2000) Italian rural life ways and religiosity are built upon a magical worldview that exists throughout the whole peninsula and the islands of Sicily and Sardinia. This worldview is difficult to systematize, and it differs in its particulars according to region and locality: each town may have its own unique form of it expressed through a variety of folklore genres from festivals and celebrations to legends, folktales, and beliefs. It is always framed in terms of Roman Catholicism, but includes elements that were clearly part of older, pre-Christian belief systems. Borrowing from Max Weber, I am calling it the "enchanted worldview."

In *Science as a Vocation* (1918-1919), Max Weber argued that one of the central features of modernity is its distance from the magical, the spiritual, and the religious: "The fate of our times is characterized by rationalization and intellectualization and, above all, by the 'disenchantment of the world'" (155). This disenchantment involves not only the secularization of public and private spheres, but the distancing of the subject from the spiritual on both the personal and the social levels. The disenchanted world is mostly a feature of Western elite and bourgeois urbanites. However, the sense of an interconnected universe filled with spirit and enchantment has persisted in many parts of the developed world, including rural Italy, until well into the twentieth century; in fact, it is still alive today.

A number of anthropologists have argued that all human societies recognize that multiple levels of reality exist at once – that the visible, logical world of causation exists parallel to another reality, a spiritual reality. One of the first to make this argument was Lucien Lévy-Bruhl, who argued that "primitive mentality" was characterized by a principle he called the "law of participation." In this system of thought, there was no strict boundary between the natural and the supernatural worlds; supernatural reality was not simply irrationality, but had its own form of rationality based on the association of things and ideas which would not be considered relational according to a strictly rational model. Indeed, for Lévy-Bruhl, relationality – the interconnectedness between all elements of the universe – was one of the touchstones of primitive mentality and "mystical thought" (Lévy-Bruhl, cited in Tambiah 1990, p.21). Lévy-Bruhl was criticized for making too great a distinction between "primitive" and civilized societies, repeating the errors of the unilinear evolutionary anthropologists (Evans-Pritchard 1990, p.91). Consequently, in his later work, he postulated that both "mystical thought" and rational-logical thought can coexist in any society. As Evans-Pritchard argued in his critique of Lévy-Bruhl, it is a case of multiple "levels of thought and experience" existing simultaneously within the same society (Evans-Pritchard 1990, p.91).

This is, I would argue, exactly the case that exists in contemporary Italy. It is not that the enchanted worldview is an index of primitiveness, and thus survives only in the countryside among culturally backwards people while educated and sophisticated urban dwellers cleave to a more rational standard. Rather, both worldviews exist side by side in the same society, only the enchanted worldview is more closely tied to specific social structures, economic systems, and ways of organizing labor and time. For this reason, it is easier to find in rural areas. Because it is relational, the enchanted worldview is also associated with systems in which landscape, time, labor, social relations, and religion are intimately interconnected and interdependent. When even one of these links is broken, an individual can become disconnected and removed from the enchanted worldview, as can happen when agricultural workers migrate into urban areas. This is in fact the current case of many of the circum-Vesuvian towns in Campania: they now exist as bedroom communities for the cities of Naples and Caserta. Aside from the elderly, inhabitants work and socialize outside the villages, sometimes maintaining the old family home as a summer or weekend retreat. The loss of connection with the agricultural cycle and the close social networks of village life have broken the enchantment; people remember some of the old folklore, but piecemeal and with a growing sense of nostalgia.

The enchanted worldview in rural Italy is rooted in specific pre-market economic and social systems. I hypothesize that it has persisted longest in marginal areas where small-scale agriculture and pastoralism continue to exist, often mixed with hunting and gathering as subsistence strategies. In these areas, the family remains the basic unit of social organization, but it is bolstered by the small face-to-face community – the town or village in which people know one another personally and have regular social interactions. These communities are characterized by what sociologists call "dense" networks: people's relationships to one another are characterized by multiple roles, including kinship, economic relationships, and relations of patronage. Because cunning folk do not advertise, they draw their clients from these social networks, and often have intimate, long-standing relationships with them. Italian cunning craft is typically passed down from one family member to another, and for this to happen, both relatives must continue to exist within the same social, economic, and spiritual system. This is most likely to happen in the small face-to-face community.

Because of subsistence activities associated with the land, time is organized according to seasonal cycles; these are reflected in the ritual year, even when this is dominated by the Catholic liturgical forms. These almost always are locally interpreted in ways that connect them to the economic cycle: for example, in the Campania, where wheat and hemp crops have been replaced by tobacco, which has a similar growing season, the ritual year begins near St. Martin in mid-November and extends until the end of the harvest season at St. Cosimo and Damiano in October. In pastoral areas such as Sardinia and the Apennine, May and September, the months that frame transhumance, are emphasized in local ritual practices. The exact shape of the ritual year thus differs markedly from one area to another. The symbols – the Madonnas and saints – are the same, but each township differs in the way it situates these characters within its symbolic and economic system. The enchanted worldview is not only rooted in the ritual year cycle; it is all-pervading in the individual's life cycle. It begins at birth and penetrates every phase of life and every rite of passage, from the moment of birth, when most Italian babies who are not born with a caul (*la camicia*, or "shirt," in Italian) are given a fine lawn shirt by a relative, often a godparent, to protect them against evil influences, to funerals, where a variety of beliefs about the otherworld are made manifest through practice.

The core of Italian vernacular religion is thus the correlation of its symbolic systems with *local* economic and social structures. The primary connection is never with the dominant structures of church and state. Hegemonic structures may or may not coincide with indigenous ones, but where there is no match, they are simply ignored. If a particular element does not make sense in terms of local understandings of time, space, and the nature of the world, people will treat it as though it does not exist, as if it were of no consequence. As a result, the landscape of the enchanted worldview in Italy is everywhere local.

Despite its exquisitely local character, the enchanted worldview exists throughout Italy, in both northern and southern regions, with significantly more commonalities than one might think, given the differences in language, culture and economy that characterize Italy's twenty regions. Certain concepts are ubiquitous: for example, the evil eye and its diagnosis, with very similar cures being found in all regions. Yet the enchanted worldview defies systematization. Beliefs and practices are nowhere standardized or even organized into an easily articulated set of principles; they are part of everyday life, part of praxis. German ethnologist Thomas Hauschild, who spent nearly twenty years studying Basilicata, a region in the south of Italy, writes: "There is no system, only practice" (Hauschild 2003, p.19). The practice *is* the system. Practices and beliefs of course exist within a particular cosmology, but its details seldom preoccupy its technologists.

At the same time, the enchanted worldview does not exist in isolation from dominant discourses. As Ernesto De Martino makes clear in *The Land of Remorse*, his epic study of tarantism, each successive layer of interpretation, from Christianity to Enlightenment paradigms, leaves a trace on magical traditions (De Martino 2005 [1961], p.7). The clearest illustration of this lies in the cases in which individual practitioners develop their own highly idiosyncratic systems and cosmologies based on an array of vernacular beliefs, often combined with elements from ecclesiastic or academic culture. These practitioners need to be understood as variations within the system—as part of Gramsci's "organic intellectualism," or as creative, intellectually curious individuals like the miller in Carlo Ginzburg's *The Cheese and the Worms* (1992)—illustrating the syncretic layering of interpretations, superimpositions, and rationalizations on top of very archaic material. The Pagan reclamation of these practices, and their re-elaboration by creative authors such as Raven Grimassi, is merely the latest of a series of readings to which they have been subjected for hundreds of years.

The main characteristic of the enchanted worldview is a belief in the omnipresence of spiritual beings that can influence human lives. These beings range from the dead to saints, the Virgin Mary, and Jesus (who are, after all, nothing more than particularly powerful dead). Spirits are associated with certain kinds of illnesses although the type of spirit and the type of illness are generally determined by local lore. For instance, in Basilicata, the unquiet dead are said to cause skin diseases such as erysipelas and St. Anthony's Fire (*herpes zoster*); in Campania, children who fail to thrive are said to be taken by witches on their night flights, and worn out with flying and dancing; in Emilia Romagna, Puglia, and Sardinia, spiders and/or insects are responsible for a range of illnesses from *tarantismo* to *argismo* to *arlìa*. Some scholars suggest these insects actually embodied ancestor spirits who then possess their victims through the bite or sting (De Martino 2005 [1961], pp.124; 204-6; Gallini 1988, p.25-6).

Even spirits such as saints and the Madonna, which belong to a greater Catholic pantheon, are everywhere localized: the Madonna is usually worshipped in one or more of her local manifestations, and the devout have their personal favorites based on each of the Madonna's attributes and the qualities she "stands over," or rules, and their own individual needs or interests. For example, in Monghidoro, a town in the Bolognese Apennine, there are four principal local Madonnas, each with her own sanctuary in a different geographic location, each venerated at a different time of year, and each "standing over" a particular set of characteristics, from children and fertility to grief and death. In addition, a number of local springs are ruled over by a Madonna, as are certain trees and geographical boundaries. Informal shrines are erected at these locations, and the signs of ritual activity and veneration are omnipresent there: fresh flowers, photographs, and evidence of *ex votos* are found at these locations.

Springs are associated with healing in all the regions of Italy, and the shrines there may serve to activate or commemorate specific curative rituals, often consisting of prayers and pilgrimages. In 1986, I observed a pilgrimage and curative rite at a chapel of St. John the Baptist outside the town of Thiesi on the Logudoran plateau. This chapel, located near a natural spring, had long been in the purview of a single family, the Paddeus, who yearly performed a cure for neonatal hernia on St.

John's Eve, June 24. Mothers would come with their infants from the surrounding area; some even came from other parts of the island, drawn by the reputation of Maria Paddeu, the cunning woman who performed the rite. At eventide, the pilgrims assembled outside the small chapel where Maria and her two brothers, whose participation in the rite was necessary, were making preparations. The chapel was surrounded by fig trees. For each child to be healed, Maria's brothers would cut a long vertical slit into a slender fig tree branch. The infant was stripped naked and put into Maria's arms. She then passed it three times through the split that her brothers held open, while she recited a prayer to St. John. Maria then returned the child to its mother, and again with the help of her siblings, bound the slit fig branch in burlap and tied it closed with twine. When the wood knitted together again, healing the branch, the child's hernia would be healed. This rite was followed by a mass in the chapel in which all the pilgrims participated. Afterwards, all gathered around the spring, where the water had been channeled into a large concrete trough, and bathed themselves and their children with the miraculous water. Maria explained to me that the water the spring contained became miraculously healing only at that moment, after the mass on St. John's Eve, because the saint caused it to be filled with *su balsamu* (balm). As I dipped my hands into the water, she invited me to experience its oily qualities – evidence that su balsamu had descended into it.[2] This ethnographic example captures much of the quality of traditional cunning craft in Italy: the association of ailments with saints and with key points in the year cycle (in this case, St. John, traditionally associated with children and young people, and his celebration near the summer solstice); the healing qualities linked to natural springs; the magico-religious nature of cunning craft, combining sympathetic magic with Christian prayer; the strong family-based nature of the practice; and the presence of an enchanted quality in the customs and beliefs associated with them.

For many Italians living in rural areas, the world is permeated by the spirits of the dead. "The dead are everywhere," one informant told me, "in stones, in trees, in the earth....You must learn that the dead are omnipresent" [interview w/ D.S., 6/18/06].

The dead are gone to us, their human relatives; but this does not mean they no longer exist. They manifest to us in small signs, which the living must learn to read and interpret. For example, "Diana,"[3] a forty-five year old woman in the Emilian Apennine who had lost a child, described how after his death, the area around the house and garden where he used to play was filled with butterflies. She explained how, several months later, a particular type of blue flower sprang up in the garden spontaneously, where no one had planted it. In the same way, she said, when her neighbor had lost a daughter, pink flowers of the same type had appeared in her garden. Pink and blue are linked here to the gender of the dead children, but blue was also significant to Diana because it was her son's favorite color. She interpreted the presence of butterflies and the apparently spontaneous appearance of the flowers as signs of the continuing presence of the spirits of the dead children in the natural world. The appearance of flowers as signs of the dead is idiosyncratic; but the association of the dead with butterflies and moths is traditional and recalls the ancient Greek belief reflected in the dual meaning of the word *psyche* as both soul and butterfly. In the Apennine, the appearance of a number of other creatures is traditionally associated with the dead. Besides butterflies, moths and other winged insects, these include white dogs,[4] snakes, and spiders. The last two in particular are associated in this region with an affliction known as *arlía*, in which young girls or women who have recently delivered a child lose the ability to speak (Staro 2005, pp.56-59).[5] This condition can only be cured through cunning craft, as I will explain below.

Spirits of the dead interact with the living in a variety of ways: some helpful, some not. They often feature in stories that the late Finnish folklorist Leea Virtanen called "simultaneous experience narratives," in which they appear to warn family members of the impending death of a loved one, of an imminent tragedy, or occasionally simply to offer comfort and give advice (Virtaanen 1990). They can also haunt the living, especially in places where they died, and in this form they are believed to be able to cause illness. One woman in Pianoro (Emilia) told me how her cousins had lived in a haunted mill that had once been a convent. A priest had trapped the ghosts of the nuns in a container and had put a heavy stone on top to keep them in, but when the stone was inadvertently removed, the spirits returned to haunt the place, causing her uncle to sicken [interview with T.D.E., 6/17/06]. This parallels the findings of Guggino in Sicily and Hauschild in Basilicata, where many illnesses are attributed to the restless dead (Hauschild 2003, pp.388-9; Guggino 1993, pp.41-51 ff.). Sometimes the cause is more deliberate: Hauschild's healer, Linda, described how malevolent witches raise the dead using flour and dust in order to make a *fattura*, a curse-spell (Hauschild 2003, p.261). Illnesses caused by spirits, whether accidental or deliberate, necessitate a spiritual cure, and thus a visit to a cunning woman or man.

II. The Italian Cunning Tradition

Experts who specialize in interfacing with the enchanted world are the Italian equivalents of British and European cunning folk, and much of their work consists in the diagnosis and cure of spiritual illness. Their names vary according to region; they may be known as *guaritori* (healers), *donne che aiutano* (women who help), *praticos* (knowledgeable or wise people), *fattucchiere* (fixers), *mago, maga, maghiardza* (sorcerers), and by numerous other dialectical terms. Occasionally, they may be called *streghe* (witches) behind their backs by those who either are skeptical of their powers or believe they deal in black magic. They are mostly female, as healing is an extension of women's nurturing role in society; but some male healers also exist. Hauschild (2003) found that male healers were more common in urban areas and that they were often better educated and more informed by esoteric and scientific theories than their female counterparts, reflecting the greater educational advantages that have traditionally been at the disposal of men in Italian society.

There are two principal strains of healing in Italian vernacular culture: healing through the use of herbs and spiritual healing. In some cases, both may be practiced by the same individual. Of the two, healing with herbs is considered less a matter of spiritual ability than of practical knowledge. Local plants are known as *erbe* ("herbs") if they have useful or curative properties, even when they are, in fact, trees or shrubs. Plants with no medicinal or practical use are often not even named. Depending on their nature, plants may be pounded into a poultice or dried and made into infusions or decoctions. Some healers infuse olive oil with certain herbs and use it to massage the sick.

Massimo, a healer in Monghidoro, demonstrated the traditional uses of dozens of plants: plantain, which he pounded into a poultice for bruises; horse tails, decocted into a cough syrup; blackberry leaves, made into a poultice for wounds and sprains; and St. John's wort (*ipericum*), which has a variety of applications. He also showed how a type of spider web could be used as an antiseptic bandage for a bleeding cut.

Even in the use of herbs, there are those whose use borders on the magical. Near the Apennine town of Monghidoro, Massimo and I took a long walk one afternoon during which he pointed out plants and explained their curative properties and modes of employ. Along the way, I sometimes pointed to plants and asked about their use. When I asked about mugwort, Massimo identified it (correctly) as an artemisia, and indicated that it was used, but for purposes that were not discussed – in other words, the plant was potentially harmful and associated with witchcraft. Mugwort in fact possesses hallucinogenic properties, and is toxic in large doses.

In other cases, what I presumed to be a magical function turned out to be a very social one. This was the case of the bracken fern, or *felce*. I had heard that these plants could be used in love philters, but the story turned out to be more complex. Young women used to cut bracken and dry them in the sun. These were made into an infusion that was said to be a love potion. A young woman would publicly offer this concoction to the young man who was courting her, usually at a *veglia*, festival, or work party. Before the eyes of the old women of the community, the young man could either accept the potion or refuse to drink it. Acceptance indicated he was serious about the relationship; it was tantamount to accepting an engagement. The relationship could then be treated as a trial marriage for a period of a year, with the couple cohabiting and engaging in exclusive sexual relations. When the circuit riding clerk from the town hall made it into the *borgo*, the couple would marry. Should the young man refuse to drink the potion, it indicated publicly that he was not serious in his intentions towards the young woman.

Some plants had beliefs associated with them, but no practical use. For example, hawthorn or whitethorn is associated with the Madonna in the Apennine area, and is sometimes said to have the Madonna dwelling within it. For this reason, it is said to be dangerous to cut it down.[6]

Spiritual healing, in contrast, is believed to be more connected with personal power. This is variously called *la forza* (power), *la virtù* (virtue; also attribute), or *il segno* (the sign), and is believed to be inborn. Rosa, a cunning woman from Adro (Brescia), told ethnologist Franca Romano, "My aunt told me that I had the sign in me without being aware of it. She told me that I had that gift and that I must follow her" (Romano 1987, p.191). Another healer, Margherita, explained: "I realized I had [the sign] when I was eight years old, when I would touch a broken part with my hands and right away I could tell where it was broken" (Romano 1987, p.191). But power alone is useless without the prayers, magical formulae and techniques that make up the cunning person's craft. Knowledge and power are passed on through an initiation, most commonly at midnight during Christmas Eve mass, at the elevation of the host—that magical moment of transformation in the Catholic liturgical year when the world is transformed by the birth of the Savior, and the host is transformed into his body. By association, any transformation can take place then. The knowledge takes the form of prayers that call upon a saint or the Madonna, and in some cases an accompanying technique, which varies according to the nature of the spiritual cure. These formulas and techniques are secret; they cannot be passed on to others without the healer losing her or his power, and they can only be passed on at the appointed time in the ritual cycle. Often, the communication of these formulas and techniques is the only initiation and training necessary for the transmission of simple charms. Healing knowledge and power are typically passed down within the family; in some cases, family members – typically a group of siblings (as in the case of the Paddeus of Thiesi) or cousins – must work together in order to bring about the cure. Ethnologist Augusto Ferraiuolo, working in Campania, found three aged triplet sisters who cured sprains through a ritual that involved joining three grappling hooks together, applying them to the sprained limb, and reciting a charm. The cure must be performed by three sisters; though they need not be triplets, the cure would be less efficacious if they were not (Augusto Ferraiuolo, personal communication and field notes, 2005). Occasionally knowledge may be passed to a non-family member, and in the case of more complex technologies, healers sometimes serve an apprenticeship with more experienced cunning folk. This was the case of Ada, a cunning woman in Monghidoro, who claimed that she had served seven years as apprentice to a local witch.

As scholars have documented for other parts of Europe (Davies 2003; Wilby 2005; Dömötör 1980), spirits figure prominently as the helpers of Italian cunning folk. While many ordinary Italians living in traditional communities admit to belief in spirits, and occasionally even to contact with them, cunning folk seem to possess an intensified ability to commune with them above and beyond that of ordinary people. In many areas, healing is essentially conceptualized as a battle against malevolent spirits – whether those of the unquiet dead, witches, or others. Healers need spiritual allies in these battles, and many healers claim to have them in the form of spirits who guide and help them in their craft. The nature of these spirits, once again, is highly localized as well as idiosyncratic: they may be saints, personal ancestors, or helpful dead. They may appear to the healer in dreams and visions. For example, in the 1970s, an old woman in Castellamare di Stabia (Campania) told a folklorist that St. Rita had appeared to her during a trance, touched her upon the mouth, and transmitted healing power into her (Di Nola 1993, p.40). Trance and ecstatic states are a fundamental part of communicating with the spirits; they are doorways into the spiritual world for healers and magic workers.

One Apennine healer told me that the spirit of her uncle helps her to diagnose illness and that her father's spirit appeared to her when she was pregnant to reassure her that her child was a boy and would be born healthy [interview with T.D.E., 6/17/06]. This function has also been noted by numerous Italian ethnologists, for example De Martino (1987 [1966], p.16), Selis (1978, pp.140-42), Guggino (1993, pp.62-3), and Hauschild (2003, pp.294-310 ff). "Antonia," a Sardinian healer interviewed by ethnographer Luisa Selis in the 1970s, reported being aided by three spirits in her cunning craft: a priest, who helped her to foretell the future; a physician, who helped her diagnose and cure illness; and a bandit, who helped her find stolen or lost livestock (Selis 1978, p.141). Hauschild's cunning woman "Linda" communicated with a variety of spirits of the dead in her healing work (2003, pp.294-310 ff.), and one of the cunning women I interviewed in the Apennine claimed to communicate with the spirit of the Roman physician Galen. While the spirit helpers of British cunning folk were predominantly the fairies (Davies 2003; Wilby 2005), contemporary data suggest that in Italy the spirit-helpers of cunning folk consist of the dead, the saints, and the Madonna. Although a tradition of help from fairy-like beings may have existed in the past, by the twentieth century this was no longer a custom.[7] The distinction is in some sense specious, however, as there is considerable overlap between fairies and the dead (e.g. Wilby 2005, p.69), and some scholars have suggested that fairies are in fact spirits of the dead (Purkiss 2000; Pócs 1999). The use of "familiar spirits," a term Wilby uses to cover a variety of spiritual beings, by cunning folk may be an index of the extent to which vernacular healing belongs to a very ancient substrate of European culture – one in which ancestor spirits may have played a significant role. While developing this historical link remains beyond the purview of this paper, it is a tantalizing clue that needs to be more fully explored.[8]

On the other hand, spirits of the dead can also cause illness. One informant from Pianoro (Emilia) recounted a legend of a family living in a haunted mill in which the haunting spirits were responsible for the illness and death of the father [interview with T.D.E., 6/17/06]. The healer must then intercede with the spirits causing the illness in order to persuade them to release the victim. Hauschild writes: "The *donne che aiutano* [women who help] are in constant duel with the dead" (Hauschild 2003, pp.242-3).[9]

Magical tools are part of healers' craft, but these vary greatly from one healer to another; there is no standardization. Common tools include fiber ropes or cords to bind, knives or scissors to cut away illness, mirrors, and weapons to frighten away evil spirits. Hauschild describes how Linda kept three tools on hand which she used in her craft: a *lascia*, a fiber rope made of the hair of young livestock used in *legature* (binding spells); an old pair of iron scissors, which she used to symbolically cut (and thus kill) intestinal worms; and an *arma camarata*, an old bayonet which she used to frighten the spirits of the dead (Hauschild 2003, p.253). Guggino's healers were more up-to-date in their choices, one having used a pistol instead of the more traditional knife or sword to frighten away evil spirits that caused illness in their clients.[10] Additional tools may be created as part of healing spells: charm bags, for example, to be worn upon the person as protective amulets. These may contain a mixture of ritual ingredients and religious ones: lead or iron pellets, grains of wheat, and rue, all mixed with the ashes of palms from Palm Sunday and a folded saint's image. In this artifact alone, the syncretism and admixture of layers of cunning tradition is quite evident, reflecting a combination of old beliefs about the propitiatory value of seeds, iron, and rue, overlaid with Catholic beliefs about the power of religious artifacts.

Verbal traditions, in the form of prayers and charms, are almost always a part of the cunning person's craft. Some charms take the form of a narrative, like this cure for worms from Gioia (Campania), collected by ethnologist Augusto Ferraiuolo from Giuseppe Pascale:

San Giuvanne a fianco a lu mare stava	St. John was near the sea
'a tavula 'r'oro lui faceva	Sitting at a golden table

pane sante se mangiava	Eating holy bread
acqua santa se beveva	Drinking holy water
tutte le belle fresculelle c'invitava	Inviting us to [enjoy] all the fresh [foods]
fore ch'a chille verme puzzulente	Come out, stinking worm!
ch'era schifata ra tutta la gente	Everybody was disgusted.
Tutti i giorni vene Natale,	All the days come Christmas
Giovedi l'Ascensione	Ascension Thursday
Lunneri sante	Holy Monday
Martedi sante	Holy Tuesday
Mercoledi sante	Holy Wednesday
Giovedi sante	Holy Thursday
Venerdi sante	Holy Friday
Sabate sante	Holy Saturday
La Domenica di Santa Pasqua	Holy Easter Sunday
'o verme che n'ha nate nun putrà nasce	The worm that isn't born cannot be born
e chille ch'è nate 'n terra casca	And the one that's born will fall to the ground

Oro incense e mirra	Gold, incense and myrrh
Oro incense e mirra	Gold, incense and myrrh
Oro incense e mirra	Gold, incense and myrrh

In this narrative charm, St. John is imagined as a wealthy man, eating delicious food at a golden table; not only is all his food fresh, but it is holy, for the saint feasts on the host and holy water. This food entices the worm to emerge in striking contrast to the idyllic scene painted in the beginning of the charm. The charm then mentions the holiest days of the Catholic liturgical cycle: Christmas, the Ascension, and Holy Week, culminating with Easter Sunday, by which time the worms afflicting the patient will die. The triple formula sealing the charm is "Gold, incense and myrrh," the gifts brought by the magi to the Christ Child on the day of the Epiphany.

Others are purely functional; this one, for back ache, is from Tina, a cunning woman in Pianoro (Emilia):

Per a t'abbaz'	Pear tree, I embrace you
Mell ed schina at lasz'.	Back ache, I leave you.[11]

This is to be recited early in the morning, while leaning against a pear tree and wrapping one's arms around it behind one's back.

Some charms are actually prayers. Tina gave this one to exorcise a house or building. While walking three times around the inside and outside of the building, throw salt and recite:

Sale sapienza	Salt, wisdom
Portaci pace, salute e providenza	Bring us peace, health and providence
Allontana fatture, malocchi e invidia	Keep away curses, evil eyes and envy
Lo chiedo e lo commando	I ask it and command it
In nome del Signore e della beata Vergine Maria	In the name of the Lord and the Blessed Virgin Mary
E così sia.	And so mote it be.[12]

Italian healing traditions are largely oral although some healers do possess books or notebooks of magical formulae. These are akin to medieval and early modern grimoires and the precursors of modern Neopagan books of shadows. There are also a small number of written formulae that consist of symbols such as crosses surrounded by written prayers.

The most widespread form of spiritual healing is the removal of the *malocchio*, or the evil eye.[13] Particularly in the Campania, there was scarcely anyone I spoke with, even in casual social contexts, who did not name a mother, grandmother, or aunt who performed this kind of healing. In both Campania and Emilia, the removal of the evil eye typically took the form of dripping several drops of olive oil into a dish of water that had been placed on the patient's head. By observing whether the oil diffused into the water or floated on its surface, the healer diagnosed the presence or absence of the evil eye. She then said a silent prayer that would remove the ailment. When the oil began to coalesce and float on the water in discrete bubbles, this indicated that the healing had been successful, and the evil eye had been removed. The prevalence of this form of vernacular magic, especially in Campania, is significant because this region saw a very high rate of migration to North America during the years between 1890 and 1920. It may be that the descendants of these early immigrants can now look back and interpret this tradition of healing, which is passed on in a hereditary fashion through a kind of initiation and involves practices that are certainly outside of official Catholicism, as evidence that their ancestors practiced a pagan religion.

The practice of *i segni*, "[healing by] the signs," is less widespread and requires more training. Besides prayer, the technique involves the movement of the hands over the affected part of the body in a clockwise manner. After several minutes of this, the healer moves her or his thumb vertically, then horizontally, tracing a series of signs like "X," or a sign of the cross, on the affected part. Some healers will use a sacred object, such as a small cross or religious medal, to sign. Others combine *i segni* with massage using olive oil infused with herbs or with the application of hot packs made with salt, herbs, or other materials.

More than the removal of the evil eye, signing involves close physical contact between the healer and the patient. Massimo, who heals both with traditional herbs and the signs, emphasized the importance of *disponibilità*, roughly translatable as availability or openness to others, in the personality of the sign healer. Sign healers are never paid for their work, and must accept as a patient anyone who asks them for a healing. During the period of my fieldwork, scarcely a night went by when someone did not come by Massimo's cottage to request a healing.

They must therefore be ready to make themselves open and available to their clients, never turning anyone away even when they are fatigued or might prefer some other activity, or when they are not close to the patient. Healing by the signs creates an intimacy between healer and client since it involves close physical contact. It can even serve to incorporate a newcomer into a community. When I was in Monghidoro in 2005, I suffered one of the worst attacks of sciatica I have ever experienced, probably brought on by dragging around a suitcase full of books and photographic and recording equipment. I was worked on by two different healers, Massimo and Tina, and my willingness to be worked on, to enter into the system that I was observing, may have hastened the formation of rapport with the social group I was observing. This intimacy may also explain why this particular form of cunning craft is found almost exclusively in small-scale, face-to-face communities since establishing a rapport with strangers in an urban environment is difficult and risky.

III. Witchcraft

In my own writings on Italian vernacular magic, I have consistently distinguished between local healers and magic workers, who could sometimes be accused of doing evil, and what I call the "folkloric witch," an imaginary creature of legend whose activities –killing through magic, causing terrifying nightmares, flying through the air on broom straws, and dancing around the walnut tree of Benevento, to name just a few – could only take place in the realm of folk narrative. However, this distinction is much easier to make on paper than in the minds and narratives of informants. It is clear from the stories I collected that belief in witchcraft as *maleficum* is still alive in parts of Italy. In one striking case, the tragic murder of a young man was blamed on witchcraft allegedly performed against a club of which he had been a member. The narrators claimed to have found evidence of spellwork, in the form of a witches' ladder (a piece of red string with nine knots in it) and a small pair of scissors wrapped in tinfoil hidden on the property where the club met. These items were ritually disposed of, but a local cunning woman warned of a third item on the property (none was ever found) and suggested that another club member, herself a cunning woman, might be to blame for the actions. The situation is complicated by the fact that the suspected witch calls herself one. Of all the cunning folk with whom I worked, she alone referred to herself as a *strega*. When I asked what kind of work she did, she replied, "I do what I have to do," alluding to the morally ambiguous nature of her craft. This woman asserts that she became a witch by apprenticing, as a young girl, with an older witch, who both taught her the craft and initiated her formally. Those who practice vernacular healing, cunning craft, and the removal of spells and curses become easy, natural targets when something goes wrong in the community, and they are often the first to be blamed.

Legends of witches working as part of a secret society are also alive and well in modern Italy. In Benevento, the legendary meeting place of witches, many people remembered very specific legends from their childhoods about witches who were well-known members of the community, and who, it was said, met secretly with other community members to work magic. Several described witchcraft to me as an initiatory organization that passed its secrets on only at Christmas during midnight mass, just as the ability to heal is transmitted. Again, the threads linking the cunning tradition with beliefs about witches are subtle but unmistakable. Here we are beginning to find some of the parameters that not only form a part of European witchcraft beliefs going back at least to the fourteenth century, but that are also part of the structure claimed by Italian American Streghe: witchcraft as a secret, communal activity, handed down within families and through apprenticeships, much like cunning craft.

IV. Italian Cunning Craft and Italian American Witchcraft

The Italian cunning tradition has a number of traits that suggest that some aspects of modern Stregheria, or Italian American Pagan Witchcraft, may derive from it in part and that many Italian Americans who today see themselves as carriers of Stregheria grew up in families that preserved aspects of the rural Italian enchanted worldview. Like modern Paganism and revival witchcraft, the way of life in which the enchanted worldview flourished was organized around a ritual year that followed the cycle of the seasons. The moon and sun were believed to influence rhythms of work and production. Women were recognized as life-givers and nourishers and were closely involved in the maintenance of shrines to a feminine divine figure, the Virgin Mary. The immigrant ancestors may have been carriers of a tradition of healing that involved herbal and magical practices. They may have kept notebooks of charms and prayers that were precursors of today's Wiccan books of shadows. Their tools may have included knives, swords, and other weapons designed to frighten away malevolent spirits, and their craft involved communication with spirit helpers who took the form of ancestor spirits. Since these traditions could often be conflated with witchcraft in popular narratives, it is possible that this link persisted into the second, third, and fourth generation after immigration, giving contemporary Streghe the impression that their ancestors belonged to an organized, hierarchical, but secret society of witches. It is also important to stress here how Italian cunning craft differs from modern Stregheria as described in the works of Charles Leland, Leo Martello and Raven Grimassi. It is emphatically not a pagan religion. There is no mention of a goddess and god, nor are deities ever drawn down into the bodies of practitioners. The Wiccan ritual framework also is entirely absent from it. Italian cunning craft exists within a largely Catholic worldview, albeit one permeated with ancestor spirits, magical practice, and other elements that mark it as vernacular, rather than ecclesiastical, in nature.

Research in the Folklore Archives of the University of California at Berkeley, which contain items collected from 1962 to 2005, confirms that some elements of Italian cunning craft were brought to the United States by immigrants in the late nineteenth and early twentieth centuries. By the 1960s, however, these elements existed in highly decontextualized form. The interconnectedness that characterizes the enchanted worldview in Italy could not survive in the Little Italies of the United States: the sacred landscape of springs, trees, and chapels that linked saints, spirits, and states of illness and health were beyond the scope of the New World experience. By the 1960s, ethnic neighborhoods, too, were changing as the second and third generations left them for the suburbs. For contemporary Italian Americans, who often lack the knowledge with which to contextualize the family memories of cunning craft that may have persisted into the twenty-first century, Stregheria provides a framework into which these disparate, and by now decontextualized, beliefs and practices may be united and systematized.

As each successive generation interprets esoteric material according to the reigning dominant paradigms and predominant discourses of the time, the discourse of reclamation is itself but the latest of these to be layered upon this material.

Notes

1. Although historians have found some similarities between cunning folk and practitioners of modern Witchcraft, on the whole the differences outweigh the similarities; see, for example, Hutton (1999:84-111) and Davies (2003:196-7).

2. I cannot claim that the water felt any different to me than ordinary water.

3. A pseudonym.

4. This parallels associations in Celtic literature, in which white dogs with red ears were associated with the realm of the dead.

5. Cf. the association of spiders with *tarantismo* by De Martino, 2005 [1961]; and of winged ant-like insects with the Sardinian *argismo* by Gallini, 1988. Both scholars in fact hypothesize that underneath these cures of medieval origin there may have been an earlier belief in the presence of spirits of the dead in insects and spiders.

6. Cf. folk beliefs from Great Britain, where this plant was thought to belong to the fairies – with very similar prohibitions against disturbing it.

7. See the work of Hennigsen (1993) on the *donne di fuori*, Sicilian spirits somewhere in between witches and fairies in nature, and their connection with healing; and also my own 2004 article.

8. Wilby, following the suggestion of Carlo Ginzburg (1989), links it with shamanism. I do not wish to enter into a discussion here of the merits of this link; but it seems there are significant differences between shamans and cunning folk, and the spirits with which they work. I am thinking here of late Neolithic sites along the Tiber River, where archeologists have found human burials under or near the hearths of human habitations, in what perhaps constituted a practice

linked with ancestor veneration. Since ancestor worship persisted in Etruscan and Roman times, this link is perhaps one that could be more fully explored.

9   Translation by Consuelo Griggio-Kuhn; I am grateful to her for her invaluable help with the intricacies of Hauschild's text.

10 These instruments recall the tools of modern Pagan Witches, whose altars, like those of vernacular healers, are places where the relationship to the spirit world is negotiated and maintained (Magliocco, 2001). Modern Witches may not use their sacred blades to frighten away the dead, nor their cords to bind them; but the parallels are striking. It is not clear at this point whether the weapons entered into cunning craft from Renaissance ceremonial magic, or whether ceremonial magicians borrowed them from the cunning tradition.

11 Interview with T.D.E., 24 August 2005.

12 Interview with T.D.E., 24 August 2005.

13 This practice has been exhaustively studied by scholars, and because of that I only touch on it briefly here.

References

Davies, Owen. 2003, *Cunning Folk: Popular Magic in English History*, Hambledon & London, London.

DeMartino, Ernesto. 2005, *The Land of Remorse: a Study of Southern Italian Tarantism*, Translated by Dorothy Louise Zinn, Free Association Books, London. [Originally published in 1961 as *La terra del rimorso*. Milano: Il Saggiatore.]

_____. 1987 [1966], *Sud e magia*. Feltrinelli, Milano.

Di Nola, Alfonso. 1993, *Lo specchio e l'olio: le superstizioni italiane*, Laterza, Bari.

Dömötör, Tecla. 1980, "Cunning Folk in English and Hungarian Witch Trials," in *Folklore Studies in the Twentieth Century*, ed. by Venetia Newall, Brewer Woodbridge, UK.

Evans-Pritchard, E. E. 1990 [1965], *Theories of Primitive Religion*, Clarendon, Oxford.

Gallini, Clara. 1988, *La ballerina variopinta: una festa di guarigione in Sardegna*, Liguori Editore, Napoli.

Ginzburg, Carlo. 1992, *The Cheese and the Worms: the Cosmos of a Sixteenth Century Miller*, Translated by John and Anne Tedeschi, Johns Hopkins University Press Baltimore, MD.

_____. 1989, *Storia Notturna*, Einaudi, Torino.

Grimaldi, Piercarlo. 1993, *Il calendario rituale contadino*, Franco Angeli, Torino.

Grimassi, Raven. 1999, *Hereditary Witchcraft*, Llewellyn, St. Paul, MN.

_____. 2000, *Italian Witchcraft*, Llewellyn, St. Paul, MN.

_____. 1995, *The Ways of the Strega*, Llewellyn, St. Paul, MN.

Guggino, Elsa. 1993, *Il corpo è fatto di sillabe*, Sellerio Editore, Palermo.

Hauschild, Thomas. 2003, *Magie und Macht in Italien*, Merlin Verlag, Gifkendorf.

Hobsbawm, Eric and Terence Ranger, eds. 1983, *The Invention of Tradition*, Cambridge University Press, Cambridge.

Hutton, Ronald. 1999, *Triumph of the Moon: a History of Modern Pagan Witchcraft*, Oxford University Press, Oxford.

_____. 2005, "Seasonal Festivity in Late Medieval England: Some Further Reflections," *English Historical Review*, cxx/485, pp. 66-79.

Leland, Charles Godfrey.1990 [1890], *Aradia, or the Gospel of the Witches*, Phoenix Publishing, Custer, WA.

_____. 1892, *Etruscan Roman Remains*, T. F. Unwin, London.

Lévy-Bruhl, Lucien. (1966 [1910]), *How Natives Think*, Translated by L. A. Clare, Washington Square Press, New York.

Magliocco, Sabina. 2004, "Witchcraft, Healing and Vernacular Magic in 19th and 20th Century Italy," in *Popular Magic in Modern Europe*, ed. Owen Davies, Manchester University Press, Manchester, UK.

_____. 2001, *Neo-Pagan Sacred Art and Altars: Making Things Whole*, University of Mississippi Press, Jackson, MS.

_____. 2002, "Who Was Aradia? The History and Development of a Legend," *The Pomegranate* 18 (2002), pp. 5-22.

_____. 2005, "Imagining the Strega: Folklore Reclamation and the Construction of Italian American Witchcraft," in *Performing Ecstasies: Music, Dance, and Ritual in the Mediterranean*, ed. Luisa Del Giudice and Nancy van Deusen, The Institute of Mediaeval Music, Ottawa, Canada.

Pitré, Giuseppe. 1889, *Usi, costume, credenze e pregiudizi del popolo siciliano*, Giuffé, Palermo.

Pócs, Éva. 1999, *Between the Living and the Dead*, Translated by Szilvia Rédey and Michael Webb, Central European University Press, Budapest.

Tambiah, Stanley J. 1990, *Magic, Science, Religion and the Scope of Rationality*, Cambridge University Press, Cambridge.

Romano, Franca. 1987, *Guaritrici, veggenti, esorcisti*, Gangemi Editore, Roma.

Staro, Placida. 2005, "Reconstructing the Sense of Presence: Tarantula, *Arlìa* and Dance," in *Performing Ecstasies: Music, Dance and Ritual in the Mediterranean*, ed. Luisa Del Giudice and Nancy Van Deusen, Institute of Medieval Music, Ottawa, Canada.

_____. n.d, *Il canto delle donne antiche: con garbo e sentimento*, Edizioni LIM, Lucca, Italy.

Virtanen, Leea. 1990, *That Must Have Been ESP! An examination of psychic experiences*, Indiana University Press, Bloomington, IN.

Weber, Max. 1946, "Science as a Vocation," in *Essays in Sociology*, trans. and ed. H.H. Gerth and C. Wright Mills, Oxford University Press, New York.

Wilson, Stephen. 2000, *The Magical Universe: Everyday Ritual and Magic in Pre-Modern Europe*, Hambledon and London, London and New York.

Interviews:

Interviews with Tina Degli Espositi, August 24, 2005 and June 17, 2006.

Interview with "Diana Stellari," June 18, 2006.

Walking The Tightrope: A Study Of Secret Astrologers In Mainstream Professions.

J.A. Silver Frost B.A., M.A., Solicitor.

Introduction

This qualitative collective case study of five unconnected astrologers, who all receive their principal remuneration from mainstream professions, illustrates the precarious position of those who attempt to balance *orthodox* jobs with *heterodox* interests. It reveals the incidence, degree and source of discrimination experienced by astrologers within the workplace, and society generally, and examines how the reported, substantial, increased use of astrology takes effect within a society that historically outlawed the subject and set a precedent for the persecution of its adherents.

Astrology is contemporarily being practiced in a wide sphere of social activity, but those employed in conventional occupations are convinced that secrecy about their astrological interests, and particularly the use of astrological techniques within their professions, is still essential to protect them from ridicule, social ostracism or dismissal. The higher one climbs in the academic world, the less acceptable astrology becomes, and the greater the degree of secrecy that is deemed appropriate.

The informants are all keen to express their astrological views openly and to use astrology in their work and to benefit society generally, but they feel inhibited from *coming out* by their previous experiences of discrimination and their recognition of on-going scepticism. They all desire a solution to their dilemma and wish to educate the public, especially sceptics, as to the *true nature* and potential benefits of astrology, and to publicize scientific evidence supporting it, but they claim that this is prevented by censorship, which is instigated by the media and educational institutions.[1]

Astrology Under Attack

Astrology, as a discipline, has possibly been in existence for thirty-five to forty thousand years (Marshack 1972), and Western astrology, as it is still practiced today, can be traced back to circa 2200 BCE (Campion 2000, pp509-554). Records of attacks on astrologers by theologians, academics and scientists can be traced back through various sources for at least two millennia.[2] This has periodically necessitated that its practitioners shape-shift wherever possible or become completely invisible in order to fit the prevailing *Zeitgeist*. Otherwise they could become locked in perennial battle or even become outlawed for their epistemological offences. Theologians, who were concerned to ensure that all interpretations of celestial phenomena were in keeping with their own respective monopolies on the nature of existence, established the heterodoxy of the subject. Astrology found itself outside the scope of any mainstream religion as it became defined as "heretical", "magical" or "occult." Subsequently, its heterodox status was compounded by its inability to prove itself as either "normal" or "natural" on the definition of mainstream science: in spite of astrologers' persistent efforts to fit themselves into the scientific genre, by attempting to prove the subject to be objectively "true," astrology is instead defined as "paranormal" or "supernatural" by the mainstream.

Astrology and the Academy

According to Curry (1992b, pp. 274-291), it was during the late seventeenth century post-Reformation period that it became fashionable for the intellectual middle classes to mock and ridicule astrologers and their claims. This, he asserts, came about as a result of astrologers' association with radical political ideas and initially entailed them simply being defined as "vulgar." Subsequently, this discrimination developed into harassment and exclusion from universities and academic circles, and then eventually prosecution. It reached the stage where it became intellectual suicide to even mention the "A" word within the hallowed portals of academia, unless the intention was to deride the subject and ridicule its proponents, and this set the scene for the sardonic tone that came to be adopted by academics. This is evidenced in a paper entitled "The Study of Wretched Subjects" by Neugeberger (1951, p. 111), an historian who recorded it as a lamentable academic duty to have to study and record facts about a subject such as astrology, and this is an attitude which has survived among some academics to this day. In contemporary academic circles, astrology is still viewed pejoratively: by historians as an antiquated magical practice; by psychologists, as cognitive error, the positive testing of which can be put down by scientists to statistical artefacts; and by sociologists and anthropologists as ritual practice, or a 'symptom' of post-modern crisis.

In spite of this history, which saw opponents of the subject attempting to stamp it out by prosecuting and actively encouraging persecution of its practitioners, in 1997 Bauer & Durant (pp. 55-72) were nevertheless recording a marked increase in the belief in and use of astrology in contemporary British society. Taking these factors together with the fact that adherents of similarly categorised 'occult' subjects have been reporting discrimination here and abroad from opponents who are seemingly unwilling to make room for such beliefs and practices, the totality of these considerations indicated that there might be scope for a worthwhile investigation into how exactly British astrologers experience the alleged boom in their trade, and particularly those who are fully integrated into the orthodox sectors of society, where the subject was still seemingly heterodox.

There are no previous studies about discrimination against contemporary British astrologers, however, there are many studies around this subject which can be drawn on and cited as relevant. Examples include Davies (1999) and Curry (1992), who both write about the historical persecution of British astrologers by prosecution of their practices; Berger (1999) and Orion (1995), who study contemporary American witches and Pagans, and include sections telling of persecutions for their beliefs; Fischler (Tiryakian 1974), who looked at reactions to contemporary French astrologers, and Greenwood (2000) and Luhrmann (1994), who each considered the heterodoxy of witchcraft and magic in contemporary British society and the scepticism faced by adherents. These subjects are all considered to be "occult" and therefore fall outside the social norm. Greenwood writes: "The term 'occult' is loose and all-embracing, and can refer to a variety of practices ranging from Spiritualism to alchemy or astrology. It is often used by outsiders in a derogatory way to describe that which is seen to be heretical to orthodox beliefs" (2000, p. 2). It is that heterodoxy which will be considered in this paper.

The significance of the subject was highlighted by Bauer and Durant (1997), who were researching the phenomenon of astrological belief in contemporary British society. They established that astrology has become a booming industry, with astrologers being consulted by many thousands of people, a fact not overlooked by the scientific sceptics, for example Prof Dawkins, who accused all astrologers of being charlatans who enjoy vast riches from defrauding their vulnerable clients (1995). Bauer and Durant echo Adorno's opinion (1994) that those who turn to astrology are "semi-erudite," and they posit a profile of a typical serious believer in astrology as a young, single, female, of mediocre educational achievement, who attributes scientific status to astrology, and has an intermediate level of scientific knowledge. They do, however concede that "it may be regarded anthropologically, as an alternative world-view deserving of attention and respect in its own right" (1997, p. 69).

Methodology

The sample is of five informants who all self-describe as astrologers and who all rely on income from paid employment. They were selected for the widest possible variety across the professions and include informants from the medical profession, the criminal justice system, and the world of business and finance. Some also have teaching experience and are published authors. They will all be referred to by their job titles since the paper is about employment issues across the orthodox sphere.

One astrologer is a company director who has been working as chief executive of a "medium sized company" for the last decade, having been with that company in various executive roles for two decades. Her role is "strategic and financial" and involves "high level decision making." Before joining the company, she had worked as a professional astrologer and had taught astrology.

Another informant is a recently retired member of the medical profession. He has been qualified in medicine for over three decades, worked to the top of his profession, having been "involved in political policy decisions at the highest level." He has written textbooks and trained registrars, and been behind some innovative new ventures in the NHS. Astrology is listed as one of his several "heterodox intellectual pursuits."

A further interviewee worked as a medical secretary for the last fourteen years and was specifically selected as contrast to the Doctor, with the ideas of Adorno and Bauer and Durant in mind regarding lesser qualified women believers. This lady was also a professional astrologer and author, had taught astrology for around two decades, and had been involved in organized astrological groups.

Another astrologer had worked as both a Probation Officer and a youth offending team member for over fifteen years and had reached management status within the criminal justice system. She had not succeeded financially as a professional astrologer but had taken a keen interest in the subject, especially psychological astrology, for several decades.

The fifth member of the sample was a personal coach whose work in astrology and "NLP (Neuro-Linguistic Programming), modern hypnosis, timeline therapy and psychobiology" brought insufficient income so that he had to rely on his wife's income from accountancy. Initially selected by contrast to the rest of the sample, and by way of control, to see whether self-employment as an astrologer outside of the orthodox job market differed from paid employment within it, his wife's profession became a material factor by fitting in with the patterns being expressed by the other informants.

Each of the sample astrologers was asked to describe their day job, their level of experience in astrology, and the degree of integration between the two, if any. They were asked about the response of their employers and colleagues to their astrological interests. If not volunteered, they were asked to give examples of any personal experiences of discrimination, and where supplied, they were asked for dates and whether this situation had changed over the years. They were asked whether they felt at liberty to freely and openly express their astrological interests and whether they felt protected by the law in so doing. At the end of the interview they were asked what the solution might be to the difficulties they had each expressed regarding the status of astrology within the orthodox spheres of society.

They all related intimate detailed experiences, and each interview was of significance in its own right. Each person had a telling history to relate, and in that respect, the study produces five important intrinsic case studies. However, the combination of the interviews produces a significant instrumental, collective study of an issue which is of importance generally, namely the perceptions of a contemporary community currently undergoing bias and discrimination against their worldview. Although the sample is undeniably small, it is of representative value. To use the language of Philip Runkel (1990), it was possible to "cast the nets as widely as possible" and "test a few specimens," in order to learn about the 'entire species' by examining a small sample.

Collective case studies can be designed to be representative, but in a small sample the representative value is hard to defend (Stake 1995, p. 5). For this reason, the present qualitative method was moulded, in so far as it was possible, with quantitative features, by structuring the interviews quite tightly, and asking the same questions of each interviewee. The resulting interviews were analysed, compared and contrasted, and in spite of the size of the sample, it is asserted that patterns emerged whereby the interviewees were found to be mutually corroborative in their assertions. This indicated representative value and appeared to justify further, more extensive studies, which were subsequently carried out.[3]

Juggling Jobs

All of the astrologers interviewed were living on a salary from conventional employment, even though the majority would much rather earn a living from astrological consultancy. All except the Doctor had tried to achieve this at some time, however, all except the Company Director expressed an inability to make ends meet and had been forced to resort to the 'day job' to supplement or replace the astrological income. Hence the reason for astrologers relying on paid employment and their need to balance a day job with an astrological worldview. Similarly, the Personal Coach's wife would rather be teaching yoga but was waiting for his income to stabilize so that she could give up accountancy.

Having an astrological worldview and being in command of astrological techniques became part of the person and their way of thinking and dealing with life: all of the astrologers viewed life through an astrological lens and spoke fluent *astrologicalese*, peppering their conversation with planetary vocabulary and mythical allusions. It seemed to be natural for them to think in astrological terms and unnatural to exclude astrological thinking from the daily work situation: all of them used astrology as part of their paid employment, and the Company Director even retained a specialist company astrologer at her own expense to increase profitability.

Secret Astrologers

All of the sample, except the Personal Coach, considered it necessary to be secretive about the use of astrology in their day jobs, and it was only considered safe to speak openly about it in limited circles. The Probation Officer, when asked, "Do you use astrology in your day job as a Probation Officer or Manager?" replied, "Usually secretly!" and admitted to using astrology on virtually a daily basis to discover probation clients' childhood and personality traits, the general background that triggered their criminal behavior, and what brought each offender to the attention of the criminal justice system. But, she pointed out: "I would sort of almost do it on the sly really." Her secrecy had developed with experience: "I've become even more secretive as I've got older. I'll have a chart and look at it at home, and then come to work and offer my observations, which they wouldn't know had been based on my astrological knowledge." She had used it with "a number of clients … occasionally with their consent," but says "I had to be careful 'cos I could probably have got sacked for that. So I had to be really careful how I approached it … I was probably very devious." Although she felt strongly that astrological tools could make her work organization operate more efficiently, she would not suggest it openly: "I don't feel confident enough to say to my managing group, 'Here's a chart for this organization. This is where you're going wrong. That's my perspective on the organization. That's the tool I'm using in my analysis'." When asked whether she ever told anybody that her insights came from astrology, she replied: "Only if I was doing the chart with them. Only if they'd engaged and consented in some respects. Only if they already knew that this is what I'm doing, then, yes I would … but I'm wary … I'm quite wary of being too open." She had encountered other persons professionally, who also had astrological interests, but they were few and far between, and the secrecy employed prevents recognition of like-minded people: "… it is unusual to meet someone who's got a healthy interest in the subject, but because we're secretive about it we wouldn't actually know if that person was or wasn't." To be safe, she ensured that "…the people that would know about it would always be the secretarial/admin. staff."

The Medical Secretary said that although there was rarely an opportunity to use astrology in her daily routine of work, due to lack of contact with patients, she did so whenever the opportunity arose. For example, in one temping job for a psychiatric consultant with patients who came in for short term traumatic events and critical illnesses, she would note patients' dates of birth and "just do a quick glance at their transits and notice that they'd come in to the psychiatric wing at the beginning of the transit and, low and behold, at the end of the transit they'd be discharged!" She indicated that she would use astrology more if there were more connection between her work and astrology, in fact, she said: "I wouldn't be able to stop myself!" She did keep an eye on her boss's transits and pointed out: " … if he were to ask me what was going on in his chart when he was having a bad time last year, I could have told him that he'd got the Saturn/Pluto opposition right on his Sun, … but he never asked and, therefore, I never told him." In fact, due to his "distaste for it," the subject had been carefully avoided and had "never **ever** been mentioned in the whole ten years" she'd worked there, even though the consultants knew about it when they appointed her and would freely discuss other personal matters, like her grandchild. Astrology was kept firmly in its place among the secretarial staff where it was acceptable to openly discuss it and where, she states: "it's kind of snowballed to all my working colleagues asking me at various times do you know 'what's happening in my life' and 'would you just have a look at my chart?'." Occasionally, some of "the younger doctors … not consultants," had shown curiosity and enquired about the purpose of the ephemeris, which always sits on her desk, and following her explanation, she asserts, "they'll be quite happy to accept it and not be resistant." Nevertheless, she explains that ever since she became an astrologer, there had always been a segregation of her astrological interests from her "day job," and she reports: "I've always lived and worked … like two separate lives."

The Company Director had had no hesitation in using astrology quite widely within her company, because "it pervades every area really." She said: "When I started working in the company it was the most obvious thing. I mean, the company was going through a crisis and I happened to know some of the astrological background to that, so it was a normal thing to apply astrology to what I was doing." She went on: "I integrate astrology into business more than I work as an astrologer and a business woman, and I'm becoming more and more a business woman who is using astrology within it." She had also felt that astrology was only going to be accepted among the secretarial staff: "It was OK for a PA, or the girls in the office, I mean the girls in the office talk about astrology and read Jonathan Cainer or whatever they read, ... that's fine ... but it's supposedly a 'low level girl thing,' so for the PA to be into astrology was fine, it was all part of that office culture really." She had initially used astrology herself secretly in various departments and without the knowledge of any of the other heads of department while she had been working her way through the ranks towards her current position. However, because the needs of the company had exceeded her own knowledge and astrological ability, she had appointed a business astrologer, at her own expense, who had a specialization in company matters. A chain of successful decisions followed, which aroused other people's suspicions within the company, and she was quizzed about her unusual decisions and corresponding successes: "After about two or three years of me using astrology 'on the quiet' ..., people started asking me questions." Eventually she felt forced to admit to the use of astrology. Once word got out that astrology was helping with the success of the business, to her surprise, the other departmental heads also took to using astrology, and it then became accepted practice within the company. However, the barriers of secrecy were not removed at this stage, but were merely relocated. It was thought that in all probability "shareholders aren't really bothered" about astrology being used to enhance profits, but there was apprehension about disapproval from "...the people we depend upon, like the banks ..." and other people in the business world "... who could ridicule you." For this reason, the astrologers' bills were disguised: "...we put them through as 'business consultancy' and we said to [X] not to mention anywhere on the bill that she was an astrologer." The Company Director would not and could not stop using astrology, but explains: "You have to be cautious. I'm always cautious, I'm always cautious that if I'm going to be attacked ... I'm very, very careful not to put myself in a position where I will be attacked."

The Doctor confessed to integrating astrology "to a degree" within his day job. He says that it never "became a central core" but "...it was an adjunct to understanding ... it didn't drive the case in any kind of way, but it was an adjunct to sometimes understand the paradoxes, which seemed to be coming up..." He admitted to doing "quite a lot of charts" over a period of about seven years, using astrology a couple of times a month, yet only "...occasionally discussed them with patients, because I did this in my office without anybody really knowing". He explained: "Maybe I'd share it, and maybe I wouldn't, depending really on the person. You know, if I felt that they were prepared to countenance it as part of the work, I would bring it in, but if I felt that it didn't help, or it was going to sort of create difficulties for me, because nobody really knew that I was doing this [I did not share it]. Nobody. My secretary didn't even know. I had a closed door. I locked the door." The Doctor had several other "heterodox interests" and was certainly not alone within his field. He shared his secret interests with others, as and when he happened across them: "I had some really interesting registrars who came through, and they were as quiet about their background interests as I was about mine! And that was very fascinating." He said: "I just shared in my intellectual … kind of … curiosity really … with my trainees…" and he then watched them "…go on to very interesting situations in their own jobs." Even in situations where a "mutual regard" arose and "interesting spiritual conversations" occurred, he nevertheless felt the need to tread cautiously, and said, "[I] always kept kind of careful about where my line was."

The Personal Coach reported no secret use of astrology in his daily work, and stated categorically that he felt totally at liberty to express his beliefs anywhere and in front of any people. Nevertheless, he had been upset when his wife, an accountant, did not tell her professional work colleagues that she was married to an astrologer, because "she was embarrassed," and when he had wanted to do a Ph.D. in an astrology related subject, he had found himself in a very precarious position. As a self-employed person, he did feel at liberty to self-describe on official documents as "Astrologer," but he objected to the term "alternative," and lamented the lack of an officially recognized category: "I can't find a box for it; I have to tick 'other' and I protest because I'm not an 'other'."

Discrimination

Each of the sample was asked to give their own reasons why they considered secrecy to be necessary. They all gave examples of verbal abuse, ridicule, humiliation, or reprimand, together with their individual thoughts about the likely consequences that they might suffer if they were to be discovered using astrology in their work or even entertaining thoughts that astrology may have some validity within a mainstream context.

The Probation Officer's experiences of bias went back to her teenage years, and she professed that there were "too many to mention." She remembered arguing with her boyfriend about sun-signs when she was sixteen; she recalled her father accusing her mother of witchcraft for learning astrology at college when she had been nineteen, and she was "wondering why she was faced with that kind of prejudice." Her own reticence to openly use astrology arose because it had "met with such a high level of resistance and ridicule" that she had "become a bit of a tortoise ... and you back into your shell again and shove your head back in again and think, 'hmm – shit, I'd better be careful about this'." While training as a student probation officer, she was "... told that you can't possibly say anything about astrology because it has no validity whatsoever." She had "quite innocently and naively" analysed "a young lad who had about 4 or 5 planets in Aries" as a "very self-centred young man, who needed to learn the lesson of balance, which was the opposite of what he was at the time" at which, her manager "just looked *horrified*!!! Absolutely **horrified** and told me I should never, ***ever, ever, ever*** make any reference to astrology in my work with offenders ***ever***. And that was quite disturbing and that stayed with me as well."

Other than that, colleagues "just take the piss out of you and treat you like a bloody idiot" because "they assume that if you're into astrology you're not particularly intelligent" and will say: " 'Well, you're an intelligent woman ... how can an intelligent woman like you believe in that?', " which she finds "quite annoying." She admitted to a degree of victim consciousness now and related it to the history of persecution of astrologers, but insisted "there is also a good deal of very real ridicule and discrimination still actively occurring." She says: "I don't think its safe ... I still don't think its safe ... in the past ... even 50/60 years ago, someone who had astrological beliefs might have been deemed mentally unstable or even taken to an asylum. You know, it's **that** serious. I'm not saying someone's going to cart me off to an asylum nowadays, but your credibility as a person would be undermined by your beliefs." The media were accused of contributing to the problem by portraying sun-sign astrology as "a laugh," and treating Russell Grant as "an object of total ridicule," and also because, whenever there is a serious consideration of it, "they just come out with the old ... 'well, you can't scientifically prove it, therefore it's a load of crap'." She goes on: "they always bring out a really famous psychologist, whose name I can't remember ... who is famous for slagging off astrology ... he calls them all *charlatans* ... and he's always on TV whenever astrology is raised as a subject." She sees the media as taking a firm line to "ridicule or just discredit us in general." She concludes that astrology will have to continue to be used secretly: "I think nobody likes to be ridiculed ... I don't want to look stupid." She regrets that individual astrologers are obliged to tolerate "such attacks personally ... rather than the astrological fraternity uniting as a group." She observes that "it's much harder to attack a group" but since "we're all fragmented all over the place" individual attacks are likely to persist.

The Medical Secretary confessed that she "used to get very upset when people criticised or ridiculed" her, and she told of being "accosted by Born Again Christians," and was told to stop "doing the work of the devil" by her sister who became a Baptist. A bookshop assistant had once directed her to "the mumbo jumbo" section when she had enquired about the location of astrology books, and she said that it was quite typical to fall into conversation at a party about occupation and work to find yourself in the midst of a *"full on ... almost a verbal attack."* She echoes the Probation Officer's comments, saying: "there is some sense with the very intelligent that anybody who does or is interested in astrology is a little less intelligent." The usual argument, she says, is that "people who are intelligent just wouldn't give it the time of day." She experienced this while being interviewed for her current post by "hardened" consultants, "...very 'old school' types...," who wanted to know how she reconciled "alternative" subjects with working for a conventional medical hospital. Her response was that she thought of her interests as *complementary* and she comments that it was *"them* that couldn't reconcile it, not *me."* She had set up several courses to teach astrology in the early 1980's and had encountered direct censorship from one university because "the Head of Astronomy opposed it and said *'definitely, definitely* we're not having astrology here'," even though she was taken on by every college in that county.

The situation of a medical secretary being interviewed by a panel of overtly sceptical medical consultants provides an interesting contrast to the private thoughts of an actual consultant, who was himself a secret astrologer. By virtue of some highly cautious manoeuvring and the avoidance of awkward situations, the Doctor didn't *"actually* experience criticism" directly because he "managed *somehow* or other to remain secret about it." However, he had witnessed enough to know what would be tolerated by the "we-know-better-than-anybody-else, I'm-a-little-God kind of medical view" that he had encountered, and found so "*profoundly* disturbing." He had seen a homeopath reduced to tears by other doctors on more than one occasion, and perceived "the rational sceptical medical culture" as being "quite *vicious*." He had been shocked to see the Association for Jungian Analysts "sweep Liz Greene and others off the advisory board" when they went "very *hyper-rational*" and watched them "cut out all the *irrational* stuff ... and the astrology completely *evaporated*." He decided that his own personal interests were best kept hidden in order to fulfil his greater purposes, which included high-level policy decisions and innovative new schemes. He believed that heading NHS projects would have been denied him "if they knew that I was some sort of *screaming loony* astrologer." For him, it was a considered decision: "So my own interests I kept as quiet as possible simply because it was *dangerous* for my career and also for my other interests."

He had witnessed "a lot of very, very interesting discrimination" at the top managerial levels of a government department, especially "against ideas that were outside ... 'the conventional'." He had experienced some near misses himself and recalls one particular occasion where he was directly asked about his belief in astrology during some light-heartedness at a policy panel meeting for ministerial matters where "we went around the table more or less 'do you believe in that stuff?' and I found, when it got to me - this is a real piece of denying Christ three times - I just simply giggled and said something like 'it's all very intriguing' and I didn't say anything more." He avoided saying whether or not he believed it, and joined in the laughter, but adds: "in fact, that *could* have been an opportunity for me to say 'well actually I've been interested in this for years and I've done many charts' and that would have been the end of my political credibility as a policy maker. I'm telling you, it was close as that, do you get me?" He was in no doubt as to the consequences of discovery: "The point is that I would have definitely been disempowered, I would have been politically *dismembered* by some people and I could have been attacked." He speculated about the effect on his academic career: "Then it could have gone into 'wonder what he talks to his registrars about.' Then it could have gone to the [X college] 'is he fit to teach registrars'. . . . 'do we want him to do that lecture course anymore when this man's as mad as a hatter - he might be a good doctor, but good God, he's got these crazy ideas'."

The Company Director considered herself to be in a prime position to know just how dismissive others would be of astrological belief, having once been a sceptic herself. She confessed that she'd "thought it was a load of rubbish" and had been "very sceptical" before she "actually saw the evidence" for herself. With her reformed attitude she now says: "I can see why people would ridicule it. My answer to people who ridicule it is 'go and find out about it and then ridicule it' because what they're ridiculing is not the astrology that I'm using or the astrology that I know." She attributes the frequent ridicule of astrologers to "the history of astrology" and its connection with "magic and superstition" and says that "people rejected it" believing that "it's non-scientific" but without knowing anything at all about it and without testing it for themselves.

She had found it difficult enough to prove herself in a hostile, male dominated business world, mixing with the "old school network types who've all been to the same public school" and who "will try and humiliate you and put you down and they'll gang together quite often." She thought the CBI, the Institute of Directors, accountants, financiers and bankers were hostile, especially to women, and unlikely to ever change. She says: "I'd heard things like I was described as 'wacky', 'not too bright'" and says, "the last thing I wanted was for them to have something on me that could **prove** that I was an idiot." Consequently, in spite of the enormous successes experienced by her company seemingly as a result of using astrology as a tool for forecasting trends, which resulted in "the best sale the company had had in years," the Company Director nevertheless anticipated opposition and humiliation. She confessed to some paranoia, however, and confessed that her experiences had not been as bad as anticipated: "I've now discovered that my fear was that *everybody* was going to ridicule me, but what I found out in reality was there's no way *everybody* was going to ridicule me. In any situation, *some* people might ridicule you, and *some* people wouldn't." Having "come out" and given an interview on television, she expressed surprise and relief that "nobody *ever* ridiculed it. *Nobody*. I've not had any negative feedback from that programme." However, she does believe that her position as a major shareholder in a family company affords her considerable protection so that she is actually "*unlikely* to be attacked or fired or made a scapegoat for using astrology. But I wouldn't be that confident if I worked for somebody else. If somebody else were to come in and take over the business, I would keep quiet again; I wouldn't admit to it."

The Personal Coach had experienced many adverse reactions when he told people he was an astrologer, reactions such as Christians pressing him to "accept Christ," telling him "that's not the way," and "phone calls at 1 o'clock in the morning saying 'you're evil'." He volunteered that he was a Pagan, so he understood persecution very well, and had been made to feel "wary": "I've, felt completely … almost … stunned." With no fear of losing his job, however, he felt able to engage when challenged by "people who say 'this is bollocks'." He reports no experiences of humiliation or ridicule within his own self-employed working environment, but by contrast, his wife who is an accountant with a "prestigious company" had been too embarrassed to tell her professional colleagues what her husband did for a living. This had caused some matrimonial discomfort when she strenuously defended her position to keep his work a secret.

"Coming Out"

When The Personal Coach did eventually press his wife to "come out" and she commented to the training team at her workplace that their Myers-Briggs questionnaires were based on the work of Carl Jung who was "into astrology and alchemy," he tells how she was promptly removed from the training room and "interrogated in an intimidating fashion." The issue of "coming out" was, in fact, a relevant issue to all interviewees, but there was a broad span of attempts among them with varying degrees of success. The Doctor had never attempted to "come out" during the entire course of his career, taking the view that discretion was the better part of valour, and when asked whether or not he felt protected by the law to freely express his beliefs, he replied, "not protected, because I knew that my reputation was going to live or die by what *I* said, nothing to do with what *the law* said." On his retirement, however, he gave his "valedictory presentation," feeling that he could get away with whatever he wanted at this stage. This was a controversial talk to all the professors in the department, and he could see that "a third of them thought it was *voodoo* and were very confronted and scared;" however, "the middle third were *intrigued*, and the junior part of the department, ... all the young doctors ... thought it was *fabulous*!" By contrast to the support of the newer doctors, who "thought it was *absolutely wonderful*," he got "... a *very cool* reception from the professor . . . ."

He regretted the lost years of silence, believing that his metaphysical worldview had been "gifted" to him and that he would "very much like to make available for other people" because "it's got illumination for some of the issues that confront us at the moment." He raised the issue of the loneliness of the outsider, referring to being "*totally* alone" except for his wife and a few "close friends" who "share very similar views, over all this stuff." He said: "I really would like to have more of a dialogue and debate. I don't want to be so kind of ... *isolated*. I've been very, very isolated for 20 years, saying very little in public." His resolution, following retirement, was to "come out" and risk the consequences, and he planned to give public talks "... which are really completely central to my kind of core thinking about this sort of thing ... some of them are in front of 2 or 3 hundred people, so I have 'come out' in that sense." He intended to continue as a consultant into retirement and said that he was now "not terribly bothered" about being found out: "... if it, sort of, shuts down my medical/legal work, it would just have to do so. I can't spend the rest of my life sitting under a toadstool." He explained: "These things are too important for me personally and I've been *waiting*, time wise, in my life to be able to write more fully and do the research more fully." He stated his intention to write several books now on the areas of his "special interests."

By contrast, the Probation Officer had already been "out" and gone back under cover as a result of her experiences. However much benefit she deemed her organization might have gained from the use of astrology as a diagnostic tool, she declares herself unwilling to try again in the present climate, saying, "I don't feel *confident* enough." She states that she would very much like to "come out", "if we had safety in numbers…," and "…if the subject was more acceptable within wider society." But she saw it unlikely to occur, since astrologers had never been given the chance to express the validity of their subject. She was encouraged by the fact that public figures like Madonna, Nancy Regan, and Princess Diana had admitted openly using astrology and considered that it "helped with public acceptance," but qualified it with, "Its easier for them though … 'cos they're mega rich and powerful and famous," and adds, "not a lot can touch them. And they're used to critical press anyway." She echoed the Doctor's lack of confidence in the protection of the law, saying, "I can express my views without being thrown into prison … So, on that basis … 'yes' … I don't feel that I'm going to be *sectioned* by a doctor if I say I've got the beliefs that I've got. But you might not necessarily 'come out' with it at work!"

The Company Director had been wrestling with her need to "come out" for several years. She held back because of the hostility she anticipated from the male-dominated world of finance. During the mid 1990s she decided "to hell with it" and agreed to be featured in various interviews and on a television programme as "a client of a business astrologer." She confesses: "I did various interviews but always with either a false name or not giving anything away." One television interview, in particular, had a profound effect. She had been "interviewed by Joan Bakewell on *Heart of the Matter*," and reports,

> "I'm in the dark, ... and I felt, ... I felt like a *rape* victim, you know? Because they had an actress's voice, which unfortunately sounded like me anyway ... and they had me in the *dark*, in silhouette ... and I felt almost as if I'd been raped. Yeah, I felt *terrible*. I felt 'why am I in the *dark*?' and I remember saying at the astrology conference ... I remember standing up and saying, 'I'm *coming out*! I'm coming out of the closet! I'm not prepared to *do* this anymore!'"

She did take courage, and gradually "came out" as she progressed in seniority through her own company, and the effects had not been as devastating as she had anticipated. The other managers had started to use astrology; she had become more relaxed about mentioning it; and eventually, the managing director established "a constant line to our astrologer" for himself. This gave her the confidence to appear openly on television for the *Witness* programme on Channel 4, which "seemed quite a *sympathetic* programme" so she "thought 'to *hell* with it' ... 'let's do it' ... if there was ever a time to do it ...I mean, you know, ... publicity is publicity, so, as long as they weren't sending us up, there was a very positive side to having our brand and our name on ...." She reports some positive feedback from high profile people and no negative feedback at all from that experience.

Despite these positive experiences within the safe environment of a family business, where she was unlikely to " be fired or made a scapegoat for using astrology," she nevertheless would still not refer to astrology in the world of finance: "I'd *love* to go to the bank manager and say "don't *worry* we've got some *great* Jupiter transits coming up!" (Laughter.) She explained how she was "*struggling* to get money from the bank" in spite of the almost guaranteed "run of luck" and "good sales this summer" promised by a "Jupiter Grand Trine." She sighed, "I wish there was a bank that used astrological information because nobody *believes* that!" A regular bank would say "… 'the trend is down, so you can't come and tell us that it's just suddenly going to pick up.' You know? But in fact, you *can* say, 'it's going to suddenly pick up' if you know that Jupiter, Uranus, … whatever, … because it *works*!"

The Medical Secretary had been "out" with her employers right from the beginning because it had been apparent from her CV. Nevertheless, although it appeared to be acceptable for it to be openly discussed with other secretarial staff, it seemed to her to be totally off-limits with the consultants, who appeared to be consciously avoiding the subject. She was acutely aware that astrology has its place, and that place could only be among its "friends": "You can't go into a room full of new people and, you know, just sort of start talking about … 'oh, did you see Venus in the sky tonight' … or 'what do you think about this Mars Pluto square that's coming up next week?' … You can't *do* that … and I feel quite sad about that … unless I'm actually in a group of astrologers." Having witnessed the experiences of fellow professional astrologers, it was remarked upon that astrologers who are "out" get a very raw deal from the press. She gave examples of professional astrologers, known to her, who had been censored by the press when trying to defend astrology publicly against the sceptics: "[X] was involved in a great long argument with somebody in the *New Scientist* in the early [19]90's. It was about the validity of astrology." .... "Well I think the upshot of it was that they didn't print [X's] reply." Another incident was reported regarding the then astrologer for *The Daily Mail,* and she said: "I felt so *helpless,* and I think that's how probably a lot of astrologers have felt. You feel as though you can't *do* anything because you're up against the *whole system.*"

The Solution

It became clear throughout the recording of the interviews that having an astrological interest was generally viewed as a "problem," in terms of social acceptability; so, each informant was asked what the solution might be. Common themes arose from their diverse replies, including the education of "the ignorant" about the usefulness of astrology, the need for unity within the astrological community, and, allowing time and the evolutionary course to take their path. The general feeling was that things were improving, either because the astrologer had learned to be secretive or because the others had been educated about the value of astrology and had become more tolerant, and even accepting.

The Personal Coach said, "We need to be activists to have a positive outcome." He suspects that there are many people, "all thinking the same stuff, but all too frightened to tell anyone 'cos they don't dare to be different," and he foresees a gradual "coming out" led by activists such as himself who assist with "an evolutionary consciousness, coinciding, obviously, with the changing law, so it becomes safer." He anticipates a time when "It's not scary anymore to be individuals. It's not scary anymore to be who you are. It's not scary anymore to just be yourself." He explains, "It's all part and parcel of a philosophy that's becoming more prevalent … what's happening is there's less of a need for people to attack it." His way of dealing with attack is to enter into "an educational process," interact in the sceptic's "own theological language" and argue until "they can't attack you any more because there's a big question mark" over their position so that "suddenly, they're on my side."

The Probation Officer lamented the distinct lack of unity within the astrological community, caused by "the present corporate image of the AA" (Astrological Association) which she found "a bit elitist and very white." She declared: "its *very* unusual to meet a black person," and complained that the AA leaders are "a little bit old-fashioned in some respects … they're not particularly dynamic." Since "we live in a multi-cultural, multi-ethnic society," it was not helping being so "very *white*, very *male*, very *middle-class*," and she noted that in order to "get other people onboard" and "get different communities involved in the subject" it was necessary to "spread our wings a bit." She pinpointed ignorance among the sceptics, who comprise two categories, scientific and religious, as being the core problem underlying the poor social status of astrology. She anticipated difficulty because "You can't break down ignorance so easily," and advocated educating people, following Newton who "believed in alchemy as well as astrology," despite being "presented as this pure new scientist," and who challenged sceptics to study the subject before attacking it. She says, "Sometimes it's useful to quote him because when they are ignorant they think they've studied the subject.

They think they know about the subject when they know nothing at all. And they don't want to find out. That's the problem." Sceptics are, she suggested, "brought up to think along one path," are resistant to "having to think a bit differently," and are propelled by "the fear of having their world blown apart if they find out about this subject." She says, "It's a bit *scary* changing your worldview." She concedes that astrologers have been partly to blame for wrongly presenting purely a sun-sign image of astrology, but, in spite of this, "Things are changing … certainly over the past 20-30 years they've changed. Businesses are using astrology … but they're using it secretly! But they are using it."

The Medical Secretary took a similar view, explaining how she had broken through her religious sister's ignorance by educating her as to what astrology was about: "I tried to explain to her really that astrology is just *one* of the routes, … *one* of the paths to the same end really, and when I did explain to her what it was all about … she calmed down, and she's been fine ever since." She considered that if astrologers were allowed positive input into television programs that much public ignorance could be dispelled, but this was prevented by the ITC Code. Longer term changes required educating people and astrologers properly, and this was a major problem because of the lack of a recognisable career path by comparison to other professions.

The Company Director took the view that time would bring about a gradual evolutionary change. She had noted that women and younger people were already "9 times out of 10, open to astrology" whereas "8 out of 10 men," needed scientific proof, which was "going to be exceptionally difficult in the case of astrology." She considered that in the main, the "old school people" who typically "run the CBI and the

Institute of Directors" and are accountants, financiers, bankers, and people like that" would never change because, they held such "very fixed beliefs," and because "it goes against their sense of logic." Although " ... having said that, every so often, when you talk about it, you find somebody you never expected, who's deeply into something like this ... and they could be at the top of an organization...." She did not blame the sceptics for their cynicism, saying, "I was very sceptical when I was ... before I actually saw the evidence myself." By contrast, she notes that "people who were born in the, certainly in the '60s and possibly early '70s who are now, today, being infused into this world that I work in ... have a completely different way of thinking, ... a different outlook" and indicates that "people like Anita Roddick and Richard Branson, who are a new type of business person" are "much more radical in their thinking" and are making things easier than the "old school" with their "negative reactions." The business world, she explains, was results-orientated, and this had ultimately broken through the barriers of scepticism within her own company. Astrology, quite simply, brought positive results, and once it was proven to work successfully in her own organization, she then had the opposite problem and had to apply sanctions to *stop* the staff from using it so much. Even those who had been the most sceptical had become avid users. To scoffing sceptics, she says: "Maybe they think we're all deluded, I don't know, but if the business is doing well ... what talks? Certainly in financial circles, it's evidence."

The Doctor said, "I think there will be a gradual drift towards more openness about it, and I think there are a number of ways that that will happen. A lot of it will be very intellectualized." He offers as example two books which are "very important 'must reads'," which "give people who need rational, particle based, intellectual explanations of paradoxical ideas and mysterious happenings, something to hang onto" by explaining it in "a cloud of synchrony." He explains that those sorts of books provide an "intellectual route in for some sceptical people ... to edge their way comfortably and decently and in academic departments" towards such issues. He differentiates between "some people who are more naturally able to deal with the kind of paradox and live with it comfortably, and other people have to resolve it." In the Doctor's opinion, "it needs some fundamental questions being asked ... and some people are asking those questions, but they're not in the university departments, those kind of people." He points out that the world of academia effectively censors that which may be studied, and proved, and he compares the contemporary position of astrology with what he witnessed at the Association for Jungian Analysts: "The people involved were all forced to have to satisfy national accreditation boards that couldn't acknowledge too much *voodoo*, as it were, on the course. Rather like your course at the moment: can't teach actual *astrology* because that wouldn't cut it ... the EGC wouldn't *approve* of Bath Spa University College having the course ... but you can be taught *critical application* to 'the nonsense,' ... but not 'the nonsense'."

Precariously Balanced

Most of the previous studies cited relate to witches, Pagans, and magical practices, which are categorised as "occult" and therefore deemed "heretical" to the current prevailing "orthodox beliefs" and tend to be defined, at least in part, by Christianity. Greenwood writes about "contemporary witches' own mythology of 'the Burning Times'" as "a powerful metaphor for their oppression by the dominant rationalist culture, symbolised by Christianity" (2000, p. 7). The astrologers reported that the majority of their verbal encounters were with Christians, and their own history certainly reveals two millennia of attacks from Christians at various junctures, of which the astrologers in the sample seemed at least vaguely aware. However, contemporary astrologers' equivalent metaphor would probably be the conflict their predecessors encountered with the law, and the fear of prosecution and incarceration experienced by those who went before. Few astrologers today are unaware of the arrest of William Lilly and the trials of Alan Leo, and this seems to represent the legacy of prejudice they have inherited from a past of persecution. Moreover, the law in relation to their subject changed as recently as 2008[4] and caused a flurry of panic as astrologers who are "out" debated the interpretation and possible consequences.

The major contemporary oppressor apprehended by these particular astrologers, however, appeared to be the scientific worldview, which has percolated into academia, and seems to dictate what it is fashionable to believe in intelligent circles. This is supported by a perennial scepticism and sarcasm which astrologers must endure through the press and at the hands of intellectuals who value only "the rational." These attitudes have evidently survived since the late seventeenth century (Curry 1989, 1992) and the results of it were clear: the Doctor was probably the highest qualified and the most deeply embedded in the academic/scientific fraternity, and he was the most cautious and secretive. The Medical Secretary, although from a similar environment, was probably the most open within her workplace, but only amongst the support staff. The Company Director and Probation Officer both came up against question marks against their intelligence, which had otherwise been presumed to be sound, considering their qualifications and professional status, and the self-employed Personal Coach only experienced scepticism vicariously, through his wife from her accountancy practice.

Luhrmann also noted that "despite magic's growing appeal, at some point in their practice – for some throughout their practice – magicians confront scepticism" (1994, p. 293), and she records how they rationalize and explain the continued practice of magic to the sceptics. Astrologers also rationalise their craft and can even relate a history of scientific experimentation into its claims. However, scientists who have had positive results, and some who merely mentioned an interest in doing the research, themselves report having been ostracised from the academic community and have experienced persecution themselves. Hynek, a professor of astronomy, declared that "for an astronomer to have anything whatsoever to do with anything remotely related to astrology seems enough to rule him out of the scientific fraternity" (Gauquelin 1974, pp. 13-14). Eysenck and Nias comment that "established scientists … have often found it best to say nothing, rather than incur derision: only a few have had the courage to admit that 'there might be something in it' " (1982, p. 5.) Therefore, in spite of Bauer and Durants' finding that astrology is now thriving, it seems that it will only be tolerated or relished within certain sectors of society, while remaining most unwelcome in others.

It is not surprising then that the research of Bauer and Durant revealed the vast majority of serious believers in astrology to be young, semi-literate females, since those within the "forbidden zones" would be unlikely to own up to a "serious interest in astrology." If astrology is indeed only acceptable as "a low level girl thing," then their findings may well have been distorted by the secrecy of managerial and higher qualified staff, since only secretaries and administrative support staff are going to admit to their belief in astrology. Those who are part of the scientific fraternity, or profess to any intellectual ability, would likely take our Doctor's view and distance him or herself from astrology in order to retain any degree of social dignity. No such issue appears to arise for those seeking fame and fortune, since it is clear from the popular press that footballers, pop stars, musicians, royalty and politicians' wives have all "come out" as users of astrology without backlash. Whereas money and fame may afford protection against the swing of the social tide, if a person wants acceptability and respect in circles which consider themselves to be intellectual or of academic standing, then it seems they will not willingly admit to holding astrological beliefs.

Theodore Adorno writes: "the fact that people 'choose' astrology … somehow indicates a lack of intellectual integration which may be partly due … to expanding semi-erudition" (1994, p. 69). As the sample in this study discovered, it is not uncommon for astrologers to be accused by their critics of being semi-literate; however, these particular astrologers surely cast serious doubt on the above assertion: they would be more suitably described as highly intelligent, intellectual, deeply philosophical, and certainly highly educated. All except one had higher degrees, half were teachers and authors, and one even wrote textbooks for postgraduates and had risen as high as academia would allow within the scientific world. If these are representative, and on-going studies are suggesting it to be so, then doubt must be cast on Adorno as well as Bauer and Durant, and further research is warranted. It is cautioned, however, that astrologers such as those in this study may be hard to find, since over half of them were not even members of astrological organizations.

With negative, preconceived notions circulating about the typical believer, and the experiences they all report, it is perhaps understandable that the employees in the sample felt such an imperative need for secrecy and discretion, and that they apprehended trouble were they to expose their astrological interests. The Doctor studiously avoided exposure during his employment, and only hinted at it on his retirement. The Company Director kept it quiet for years. The Personal Coach had no employer and did not feel the need to keep quiet, but his wife certainly did not want to discuss the subject at her workplace. The Probation Officer was the exception to this, but retracted very quickly having naively presumed that it would be acceptable to use what she considered to be an accurate and probative analytical tool. The Medical Secretary felt safe speaking with other secretaries, but understood it to be *taboo* with more highly qualified personnel.

Luhrmann found that magicians also preferred "to insulate their claims from sceptical criticism" to avoid "subjecting them to scoffing outsiders" (1994, p. 273). Berger went so far as comparing witches to homosexuals, saying that since both "are marginal groups within the culture; their members often keep their identity hidden" (1999, p. 68) She suggests that Phelan's four-stage model of lesbian communities applies equally to Neo-Pagans: "Witches, like homosexuals, fear – often with good cause – that their "coming out" will have negative repercussions on them, ranging from rejection by family and friends to difficulties at work"(Berger 1999, p. 68). The astrologers in this study would certainly echo that sentiment. Their need for secrecy was a self-defence mechanism that sprang from the vulnerability they felt in having to precariously balance their day jobs with their astrological interests. They expressed a deeply-felt urge to "come out," but it was only partly for personal reasons and had more to do with bringing the wonder of astrology into the open so that it might be utilized freely for the benefit and advancement of society generally. Orion describes American Pagans as having similar philanthropic motivations (1995, pp. 225-228).

In 1933 Jung asserted that scientific materialism and empiricism had become the new religion, or even creed, of the age, the *Zeitgeist*, and he warned of the dangers of transgressing it: "To think otherwise than our contemporaries think is somehow illegitimate and disturbing; it is even indecent, morbid or blasphemous, and therefore socially dangerous for the individual. He is stupidly swimming against the social current" (Jung, Ch IX, paragraph 5). The astrologers in this sample felt their illegitimacy keenly and recognized the extent to which they were swimming against the social current. This mirrors Luhrmann's finding that magicians "live in a society in which their magic is intellectually rejected and socially disavowed" (1995, p. 292). Astrologers clearly sense the danger in their situation, but they have put themselves into that position by their choice to think outside of the *Zeitgeist*, which, it seems, has changed little over many years in relation to astrology. This is primarily because it has still not satisfied the scientific criteria for acceptability within the orthodox field of academia, and so it remains firmly on the outside.[5] This creates a problem for those who believe the claims of astrology, who use it, and try to earn a living by it, but from the perspective of the sceptics, it is the very fact that people "believe in" astrology that is the problem.

Most of the astrologers believed that proving the truth of astrology, educating their attackers, and reasoning with them was the answer to their dilemma. The ability to freely publicize and teach astrology was seen as the steps necessary in order to stop the routine ridicule and unacceptability of the topic. However, direct censorship of the material through the media and indirect censorship of that which may be taught within universities are seen as major obstacles to the achievement of this goal. Meanwhile, astrologers prefer to lie low in the trenches.

Although the Company Director and Probation Officer conceded that reticence to "come out" could be based in part on a little paranoia inherited from a history of persecution of astrologers, their fears and apprehensions appeared to be very well-founded and based on cogent reasoning and valid complaints about past experiences. They rightly acknowledged that they could no longer be burned at the stake, imprisoned, or committed to an asylum for their beliefs, but they were under no illusions at all about the political dismemberment and social ostracism that they anticipated taking place instead. The Personal Coach was the only one who felt complete freedom to practice and discuss astrology, but he was the only self-employed practitioner working outside the mainstream. However, he was not financially independent and relied on his wife's income, and she in turn was obliged to adhere to the social niceties in the same way as the rest of the sample.

Popular newspaper reporting gives the impression that the scientific sceptics of astrology hold all astrologers to be charlatans and all believers to be their victims. Dawkins (1995) implies that astrologers all make vast sums of money out of vulnerable clients and stated that they ought to be prosecuted for trading. In fact, not one of the current sample was able to make a living out of astrology, and they were all obliged to take a day job or to live on a spouse's earnings from orthodox employment. Wherever astrology was practiced, it was done for free and to be of service. Astrology was practiced more for love than money, was studied in a spirit of intellectual enquiry, and was pursued out of passion. It enjoyed more the quality of a calling than a mode of employment. Nevertheless, Dawkins has his wish, since the criminal sanctions against professional astrologers have been reintroduced.

Patiently Poised

More questions were raised by this small study than were answered, and further studies were undertaken as a result. In spite of the small sample used in this initial study, there were several recurrent themes running throughout the interviews, and the stories of the interviewees were mutually corroborative. They each found themselves in the precarious position of having to balance paid employment with an astrological worldview because it was not possible to earn sufficient income from the practice of astrology. Each person interviewed displayed evidence of genuine *bona fides*, and they were all committed to an astrological worldview, which they hoped to utilise in dedication to the service of those who might be benefited by their astrological skills.

In undertaking these interviews it was striking that the interviewees' accounts of verbal abuse, harassment, and hostility, were related in such a matter-of-fact manner and as though it were an occupational hazard. There was frequently an air of sadness about the interviewees and occasionally a sense of hopelessness and even despair. Astrologers have evidently come to expect to have to endure routine ridicule, censorship, insult, and even humiliation. The response to one question, "Have you ever been ridiculed about your astrological beliefs?" in a follow up survey, was simply, "Of course," and this illustrates the resignation which is evident with many astrologers.

Astrology is clearly being used widely in contemporary society, but there are apparently double standards being used, since it appears to be being practiced under a cloud of secrecy and censorship. If this study is representative, and only the people working in jobs outside the mainstream are admitting to holding an astrological worldview, then it is likely that there are many others using it secretly within academia and orthodox professions. People could well be merely paying lip service to the *Zeitgeist* but acting secretly against it, which suggests the existence of a community of secret astrologers scattered throughout the professions, who are dangling on a thread and walking the tightrope between orthodoxy and heterodoxy.

Notes

1 Sincere gratitude is due to the covert astrologers who agreed to being interviewed despite their apprehensions of the risk to their professional status and reputation in the event of their exposure: thanks go to each and every one for their time, co-operation, and sincerity. Their trust is greatly appreciated in disclosing their secrets. This paper was written in 2003 as the first in a series of similar studies that commenced at Bath Spa University for the M.A. in Cultural Astronomy and Astrology, and are continuing at PhD level at the University of the West of England pursuant to a thesis entitled: *From*

Persecution and Prosecution to Dignity and respectability: A Study in the Law's Responses to the Epistemologically Marginal Beliefs and Practices of Astrologers. Other papers include: *Why are professional Astrologers not Jailed for Fraud?* and : *Prisoners of Conscience: A Study in Contemporary Discrimination against Astrologers:* an M.A. dissertation.

2   Examples include: Cicero, *on divination*, (trans. W.P. Falconer) Cambridge, Mass., Harvard University Press, 1929; Augustine, *City of God*, London, Penguin, 1972, pp. 354-430; Zoller, *Fate, Freewill and Astrology*, London, Ascella (undated); Curry, *Prophesy and Power*, 1989; and Curry, "Astrology in Early Modern England: the Making of a Vulgar Knowledge", in *Science, Culture and Popular Belief in Renaissance Europe*, Eds; Pumfrey, Rossi & Slawinski, Manchester University Press, 1992, pp. 274-291; Allan Chapman, "Astrology on Trial: The Case Against," *Astronomy Now*, December 1990; Kurz, "Objections to Astrology", *The Humanist*, Washington, American Humanist Association, September 1975

3   These took the form of my MA dissertation "Prisoners of Conscience" Bath Spa 2003, unpublished and my doctoral research "From Persecution and Prosecution to Dignity and Respectability" UWE ongoing.

4   Consumer Protection from Unfair Trading Regulations 2007, in force from April 2008.

5   There has been much scientific testing of astrology and much debate about the results. See for example, Bok, "Objections to Astrology", *The Humanist*, Washington, American Humanist Association, 1975; Dawkins, "The Real Romance in the Stars", *The Independent on Sunday*, 31 Dec 1995; and summaries of the 'the researchers' in Phillipson, *Astrology in the Year Zero*, London, Flare Publications, 2000.

References

Adorno, Theodor W. 1994, *The Stars Down to Earth and Other Essays on the Irrational in Culture*, Routledge, London.

Augustine. 1972, *City of God*, Penguin, London.

Berger, Helen A. 1999, *A Community of Witches: Contemporary Neo-Paganism and Witchcraft in the U.S.*, University of South Carolina Press, Columbia.

Bauer, Martin W., and Durant, J. 1997, "British Public Perceptions of Astrology: An Approach from the Sociology of Knowledge," *Culture and Cosmos*, Vol. 1, No. 1, Spring/Summer, 1997.

Bok, Bart J. "Objections to Astrology," *The Humanist*, September 1975.

Bryman, Alan. 1996, *Quantity and Quality in Social Research*, Routledge, London.

Campion, Nicholas. 2000, "Babylonian Astrology: Its Origins and Legacy in Europe," in *Astronomy Across Cultures: The History of Non-Western Astronomy*, ed. Selin, pp 509-554, Kluwer Academic Publishers, Norwell, MA.

Chapman, Allan. "Astrology on Trial: The Case Against," *Astronomy Now*, December 1990.

Cicero. 1929, *On Divination*, trans. W.P. Falconer, Harvard University Press Cambridge, MA.

Curry, Patrick. 1989, *Prophesy & Power: Astrology in Early Modern England*, Princeton University Press, Princeton, NJ.

_____,1992a, *A Confusion of Prophets: Victorian and Edwardian Astrology*, Collins & Brown, London.

_____,1992b, "Astrology in Early Modern England: the Making of a Vulgar Knowledge" in *Science, Culture and Popular belief in Renaissance Europe*, eds. Pumfrey, Rossi, & Slawinski, Manchester University Press, Manchester.

Davies, Owen. 1999, *Witchcraft, Magic and Culture 1736-1951*, Manchester University Press, Manchester.

Dawkins, Richard. 1995, "The Real Romance in the Stars," *The Independent on Sunday*, 31 December 1995.

Eysenck, Hans J., and David K. B. Nias. 1982, *Astrology: Science or Superstition?* Penguin, London.

Fischler, Edward, A. 1974, "Astrology and French Society: The Dialectic of Archaism and Modernity," in *On the Margin of the Visible: Sociology, the Esoteric, and the Occult*, ed. Tiryakian, Wiley-Interscience, New York.

Gauquelin, Michel. 1974, *Cosmic Influences on Human Behaviour*, Garnstone Press, London.

Greenwood, Susan. 2000, *Magic, Witchcraft and the Otherworld: An Anthropology*, Berg, Oxford.

Jung, Carl. 1933, *Modern Man in Search of a Soul*, Available at: http://www.marxists.org/reference/subject/philosophy/works/at/jung.htm

Luhrmann, Tanya M. 1994, *Persuasions of the Witch's Craft: Ritual Magic in Contemporary England*, Picador, London.

Kurz, Paul. "Objections to Astrology", *The Humanist*, September 1975.

Marshack, Alexander. 1972, *The Roots of Civilisation*, Weidenfeld and Nicholson, London.

Neugeberger, Otto. 1951, "The Study of Wretched Subjects," *Isis*, vol. 42, 1951, p. 111.

Orion, Loretta. 1995, *Never again the Burning Times: Paganism Revived*, Waveland Press, Illinois.

Phillipson, Garry. 2000, *Astrology in the Year Zero*, Flare Publications, London.

_____. 2001, "Self-defence for astrologers," *Astrological Journal*, Sept/Oct 2001.

Runkel, Philip J. 1990, *Casting Nets and Testing Specimens: Two Grand Methods of Psychology*, New York, Praeger

Stake, Robert E. 1995, *The Art of Case Study Research*, Sage Publications, London.

Tiryakian, Edward A., ed. 1974, On *the Margin of the Visible: Sociology, the Esoteric, and the Occult*, Wiley-Interscience, New York.

Zoller, Robert. n.d., *Fate, Freewill and Astrology*, Ascella, London.

Martyrs, Magic, and Christian Conversion

Patrick Maille

All would agree that martyrs contributed greatly to establishing the Christian community in Roman society. What is often overlooked is that the methods and the impact of Christian martyrdom successfully channeled beliefs related to magic into beliefs related to conversion to Christianity. A study of ancient Christian and non-Christian sources indicates that martyrs were seen as wielding, or claiming to wield, supernatural powers comparable to those associated with magicians. This supernatural power associated with Christian martyrs was not only surprisingly similar to the powers associated with ancient magicians, but it was also an essential element in stimulating conversions to Christianity.

Magic could lead to an increase in social status without going through conventional channels. The risk, however, is that those in power would punish such efforts. This made sense given that people with conventional power in society were challenged by those appearing to wield magical or supernatural power. This is a key theme in the rise of Christianity in Roman society. Christians claimed to have the ability to accomplish wondrous deeds and, therefore, earned respect and authority in society. Many people believed that Christian leaders did, in fact, demonstrate wondrous powers that seemed magical. Therefore, they converted. As the status of Christian leaders rose, the status of their opponents declined. Opponents to Christianity fought with all the sincerity of any social institution facing a threat. They also fought with a sincere belief that this pernicious threat made use of evil forms of magic.

This article examines Christian martyrs such as the Bishops Ignatius of Antioch, Polycarp of Smyrna, and Cyprian of Carthage in addition to female martyrs such as Blandina, Perpetua, and Felicitas. Additional background comes from the story of Peregrinus, a man who avoided martyrdom as a Christian but later died as a pagan martyr. Key elements in their stories indicate an important role for magic in how death was faced by martyrs and interpreted by Roman society. The ability to escape death is always asserted by the Christian sources, and it is evidently a concern of persecutors. An inability for persecutors to kill martyrs is claimed by Christian writers. The claims are narrated in a context familiar to Roman society as involving magic. The relics of martyrs were seen by Christians as possessing enormous power. Pagans saw this belief as closely related to established forms of sorcery. In short, both pagans and Christians believed that martyrdoms were related to a variety of supernatural powers that were clearly understood by contemporaries but interpreted in contrary ways. This fact is illustrated in a variety of ways by all the people who were willing to die as Christian martyrs.

One such person is the title figure in Lucian's *Death of Peregrinus* (Page 1936). Peregrinus allegedly gains influence and power among Christians while simultaneously undermining the reputation of Christianity in the pagan world. It might also be said that Lucian undermined the reputation of Peregrinus by associating him with Christians. Peregrinus was a figure of peripheral relevance for Christianity. He was a Christian for only a limited period, prior to converting to Cynic philosophy. What little we know of his relationship to Christianity comes mostly from the satirist Lucian. A small number of scattered sources, both Christian and pagan, suggest that Peregrinus was both admired and despised (Jones 1986, pp. 131-132). Lucian's characterization of him as a charlatan who takes advantage of ignorant people is similar to other critics of early Christianity such as Porphyry (Hoffman 1994). The willingness of Peregrinus to suffer and die was a quality admired by Christians and maintained by him even after he left them. His association with signs and wonders is indicated not so much in Lucian's *Death of Peregrinus*, but in other texts such as Athenagoras' *Legatio*, where his statue is said to have had the power to give oracles and heal the sick. The way in which Lucian portrays Christianity in relation to Peregrinus indicates the way in which Christianity was regarded within the society.

By the time of his death, Peregrinus had left the Christian religion for Cynic philosophy. His death is the main subject of Lucian's story. In the year 165, Peregrinus threw himself onto a giant fire in a pit at the closing of the Olympic Games. It is said that he wished to demonstrate his own disdain for life and to demonstrate to his followers that they should have contempt for life's misfortunes. His method for facing death has been compared to Indian Brahmins and the death of Heracles. But the concept of Christian martyrdom was the most influential factor.

The public spectacle of Peregrinus' death is at the center of *Death of Peregrinus*. Lucian attacks Peregrinus' reputation. To discredit Peregrinus, Lucian tells his readers a story in which Peregrinus is depraved and evil. He is said to have killed his wealthy father so that he could obtain money, to have committed adultery, and to have corrupted a young boy. It is at this point, Lucian says, that Peregrinus joined the Christians.

Lucian describes the Christians as ignorant people, easily duped because of their superstition and gullibility. He writes of Peregrinus:

> In a trice he made them all look like children; for he was prophet, cult leader, head of the synagogue, and everything, all by himself. He interpreted and explained some of their books and even composed many, and they revered him as a god, made use of him as a lawgiver, and set him down as a protector, next after that other, to be sure, whom they still worship, the man who was crucified in Palestine because he introduced this new cult into the world. (Lucian, *Death of Peregrinus* 11).

One may wonder what Christians saw in Peregrinus that made him so popular. Lucian suggests that Christians saw him as a prophet. Such a position could give rise to a possible charge of magic, given that prophecies were associated with magicians. Lucian's description of the Christian understanding of Peregrinus is that he was a cult leader (that is, one who leads worship). Further, Peregrinus is portrayed as something of an intellectual leader. He writes, interprets, and even is called a lawgiver. His flock supposedly places him just below Jesus. Already endeared to the heart of the Christian community in Palestine, Peregrinus seems to have moved from being loved as a community leader to being loved all the more as a prospective martyr.

It is interesting to contrast what Lucian had to say about Peregrinus being held in prison while awaiting death with what we know of the Christian bishop and martyr Ignatius of Antioch. Ignatius' death *circa* 107 C.E. has certain revealing parallels. Peregrinus would have been imprisoned as a Christian about halfway through the second century (fifty years or so after Ignatius). There are six letters associated with Ignatius that indicate he was visited by numerous delegations from various churches scattered around the Eastern Empire. The letters are from churches in Ephesus, Magnesia, Tralles, Rome, Philadelphia, and Smyrna. Efforts were made by leaders of these Christian communities to release him. Yet Ignatius is portrayed as desiring martyrdom. When Christian prisoners were in custody, admirers tried to comfort them through whatever means were available. In this context, Ignatius is portrayed as facing death with a "stoic" resolve while Peregrinus is portrayed as reveling in circumstances of which he can easily take advantage. The two are obviously different figures. However, the background given in Ignatius' letters to his fellow Christians and Lucian's description of Peregrinus' Christian admirers are strangely consistent. Lucian describes the Christians during Peregrinus' confinement:

> Proteus [the name Peregrinus would later take for himself] was apprehended…and thrown into prison, which itself gave him no little reputation as an asset for his future career and the charlatanism and notoriety-seeking that he was enamored of. Well, when he was imprisoned, the Christians, regarding the incident as a calamity, left nothing undone in the effort to rescue him. Then, as this was impossible, every other form of attention was shown him, not in any casual way but with

assiduity; and from the very break of day aged widows and orphaned children could be seen waiting near the prison, while their officials even slept inside with him after bribing the guards. Then elaborate meals were brought in, and sacred books of theirs were read aloud, and excellent Peregrinus—for he still went by that name—was called by them "the new Socrates."

Indeed, people came even from the cities of Asia, sent by the Christians at their common expense, to succor, and encourage, and defend their hero. They show incredible speed whenever any such public action is taken; for in no time, they lavish their all. So it was then in the case of Peregrinus; much money came to him from them by reason of his imprisonment, and he procured not a little revenue from it. The poor wretches have convinced themselves, first and foremost, that they are going to be immortal and live for all time, in consequence of which they despise death and even willingly give themselves into custody, most of them. Furthermore, their first lawgiver persuaded them that they are all brothers of one another after they have transgressed once for all by denying the Greek gods and by worshipping that crucified sophist himself and living under his laws. Therefore they despise all things indiscriminately and consider them common property, receiving such doctrines traditionally without any definite evidence. So if any charlatan or trickster, able to profit by occasions comes among them, he quickly acquires sudden wealth by imposing upon simple folk. (Lucian, *Death of Peregrinus*, pp. 12-13).

In spite of the fact that Peregrinus is portrayed as a charlatan and Christians are portrayed as simpletons, it is clear that Lucian's description of the circumstances related to Peregrinus have much in common with those of Ignatius of Antioch (*c.* 35-*c.* 107).

Ignatius was taken to Rome where he became a martyr. Along the way, he was met by a number of representatives from various Christian communities. The Roman guards allowed Ignatius to receive these visitors who treated the bishop as a heroic leader and offered to intervene with the Roman authorities on his behalf. According to the letters such as Ignatius' *To the Romans*, and to other Christian communities, he was determined to face the death penalty even though it seems possible that he could have avoided that fate with the help of the Christian community (Holmes 1992).

Lucian notes that Peregrinus was freed after the Syrian governor decided against making a martyr of him. From Lucian's own writing, it seems clear that Peregrinus was in fact quite willing to die as a Christian martyr. The ability to avoid prosecution was available to Ignatius but, he wanted martyrdom. In both cases, the attention paid to the Christian witness to the faith (which is what the word "martyr" means) is the same. Lucian, like other ancient critics of Christianity, portrays the Christians as ignorant, and yet, as he makes clear and as Ignatius' death illustrates, some Christians faced death with a sense of certainty and even optimism.

Another important element about Christian communities, revealed in both Lucian's passage quoted above and in Ignatius' letter *To the Romans* (Holmes 1992), was their tendency to have a network of rapidly acting communicators who were involved in representing Christianity to society. In spite of being viewed as ignorant, and in spite of being the target of capital punishment, both accounts portray the Christians as developing a strong sense of community and loyalty to leadership, even when faced with violence and ridicule. The willingness to die and the intense admiration attached to the martyrs are characteristic of the Christian faith.

If one defines faith as a confidence in something that cannot be verified in advance, martyrdom stories profoundly illustrate both the faith of the martyrs themselves and of the Christian communities that rally behind them. The type of faith being described in the examples of Peregrinus and Ignatius might, at first glance, seem to have little connection to magic. Nonetheless, it remains significant in establishing a social context. For example, Christian martyrs were seen as capable of wielding supernatural power in a number of ways by both their admirers and their opponents. Further, martyrs were powerful figures after their deaths by virtue of the fact that their relics were understood to be capable of accomplishing miraculous deeds.

The power associated with martyrs awaiting death while in the custody of pagan officials is significant. It is evident that magic was seen as a relevant factor in the minds of both the martyrs' captors and their admirers. An interesting case involves Perpetua, an early third-century Carthaginian noblewoman who, along with her slave and fellow Christian, Felicitas, and several others, was arrested and sentenced to be killed in the arena by wild animals (Salisbury 1997). Perpetua's execution was scheduled to be held on the birthday of the son of the emperor Septimius Severus. While awaiting their sentence, the prisoners underwent an obviously dreadful experience, moderated by the occasional opportunities for their admirers to aid and comfort them with food, companionship, and assurances that they were suffering for the worthiest possible cause.

The martyrs' reputations grew among the Christian community of Carthage. They were heroic figures before they died in the arena and they became even more greatly admired afterward.

Perpetua's story was written down (probably by the theologian Tertullian *c.* 160-*c.* 225) and is thought to include a portion made from her diary during her prison stay. In this document we find an interesting reference showing the government's concern with magical power associated with Christians:

> While they were treated with more severity by the tribune, because, from the intimations of certain deceitful men, he feared lest they should be withdrawn from the prison by some sort of magic incantations, Perpetua answered to his face, and said, "Why do you not at least permit us to be refreshed, being as we are objectionable to the most noble Caesar, and having to fight on his birthday? Or is it not your glory if we are brought forward fatter on that occasion?" The tribune shuddered and blushed, and commanded that they should be kept with more humanity, so that permission was given to their brethren and others to go in and be refreshed with them; even the keeper of the prison trusting them now himself. (Shewring 1931, p. 16).

The passage raises as many questions as it answers in terms of associating magic and martyrs. For example, while stating that the tribune and some "deceitful men" believed Perpetua could escape by using magic, there is no position taken by the Christian writer. Could she have escaped? Did Perpetua think that God could free her from captivity? It seems likely if one presumes that Perpetua believed in an all-powerful God. Surprisingly, Perpetua does not deny such a magical ability, given that she had been "treated with more severity" because of the tribune's belief. The passage portrays her as trying to convince the tribune to lessen the harsh treatment. She succeeds by playing upon his desire for a proper show in the arena rather than by relieving his concerns about magical powers.

The tribune's anxieties, aroused by the "deceitful men," do not seem attributable to anything Perpetua had done. She did not have the reputation of a magician. Far from that, she was a respectful Roman matron who had somehow fallen in with Christians, a subversive sect. But this subversive sect was associated with magic in the minds of Roman officials. Christians claimed the ability to perform countless feats of what their critics would call magic. Christian literature before and during Perpetua's time refers to prison escapes through supernatural means. Ordinary Christians would have been familiar with such stories and there is no reason to doubt that pagans would have been familiar with such stories.

The most prominent example of a Christian escaping from prison with supernatural assistance is found in the New Testament, in *Acts* 12, where the apostle Peter breaks free when an angel appears in prison to help him. The case is not unlike Perpetua's. Peter is arrested by the Roman client-king, Herod, for being a Christian in a move that meets with popular approval. Herod had already executed James, the brother of John, by the sword. An angel appears in the prison and the chains magically fall off Peter's hands, the doors open, and Peter walks away. *Acts* 12: 2-19 says the guards are put to death for allowing this to happen.

The point of the story is more than an assertion that Christians can do wonders or that powerful figures cannot thwart God's ability to defend his people. This story illustrates the inevitability of the spread of Christianity and the divine support of the Christian community in the face of earthly opposition. As if to accentuate the futility of Herod's efforts at punishing the Christian leader, and his *hubris* in failing to recognize Jesus as God, the very next passage tells of Herod's death. We are told that he spoke so eloquently that the bystanders credited him with being a god. Since he did not reject the praise, he was punished with instant death. He fell to the ground and was "eaten by worms" (*Acts* 12: 21-23).

The story about Peter's escape from prison may have entered the minds of those, like Perpetua, awaiting a death sentence. At the same time, the belief that they were being called upon by God to die as witnesses for their faith would have given martyrs the resolve to continue facing an upcoming death sentence even as they could hold out hope of divine intervention. We shall see how, in the case of Polycarp (*c.* 69-*c.* 155), bishop of Smyrna, stories of martyrdom would maintain both of these seemingly contradictory positions, that on the one hand Christians could not be harmed because of their divine protection while on the other hand Christians were willing to face death as martyrs. Let us consider how these stories would shape the thinking of the pagan captors of Christian martyrs.

The first point of which one must be aware is that the ability to escape from prison is not associated with Christians in any exclusive sense. That is, it was believed Christians, pagans, or Jews might escape from prison by marvelous means. This belief was held not just by the legal authorities but also by those on the other side of the law. Put differently, the belief that "magic" could be used to escape from jail was a fixed part of ancient society. While the term magic implies a value judgment, just as the term miracle does, the common denominator of belief is that supernatural power was thought to be potentially available for those seeking to escape from jail.

In the case of the apostle Peter, the term miracle may be used to reflect the Christian disposition. However, Christians would be disinclined to use the term miracle when comparable tales are told within a pagan or heretical context. For examples, one might turn to the texts of Greek Magical Papyri (referred to as *PGM*) collected by Hans Dieter Betz. These texts claim to teach a variety of magical processes: how to turn invisible—something that could aid in an escape from prison (*PGM*, pp. 247-262); how to open doors (*PGM*, pp. 327-334); how to win a court case regardless of guilt or innocence (*PGM*, pp. 35-68); and even how to loosen bonds or unshackle fetters. Consider this example of a spell that breaks shackles while invoking the name of Christ:

> Say, "Hear me, O Christ, in torments; help, in necessities, / O merciful in violent hours, able to do so much in the world, who created compulsion and punishment and torture." Say it twelve times by day, hissing thrice eight times. Say the whole name of Helios beginning from Achebykrom.

> "Let every bond be loosed, every force fail, let all iron be broken, every rope or every strap, let every / knot, every chain be opened, and let no one compel me, for I am"—say the Name (*PGM*, pp. 289-297).

A similar spell (possibly a variant of the one just noted) is found in Georg Luck's *Arcana Mundi*:

> "Hear me Christ [or, Helpful One] in my torture. Help me in my predicament, for you are compassionate in the hour of violence and the most powerful in the universe, and you have created Pressure and Punishment and Torture."

> For twelve days whistle three times and say the whole name of Helios eight times, beginning with the Achebykrom: Let every fetter be opened…let all irons break, every rope, every leather strap, every knot, every shackle be opened and let no one restrain me, because I am…(Luck 1985, pp. 98-99).

Both forms of the spell are found in an interesting context. The papyri on which they appear also contain magical elements that have a strong association with Christian belief and practices and would be appealing to non-Christians for the same reasons that they would appeal to Christians. The list of spells from which the above is taken includes instructions on how to perform exorcisms and raise the dead. Reports of both of these phenomenons are found in every genre of Christian writing, both canonical and apocryphal. The reference to Christ implies a Christian element or influence on the spell. It is not, however, a definite Christian reference. Perhaps it means anointed (which is what "Christ" actually means) in some sense unrelated to the Messiah Jesus. Whether the spell is an instance of syncretism, coincidental use of similar terms, or a direct borrowing from Christianity is irrelevant. The references to other gods are a solid indication that, even if Christians used these spells, such Christians were not sufficiently orthodox to reject other gods.

A more significant point in the present context is that magic could be used as a means of escape from the law. If one considers the point of view of a Roman judicial official who was imprisoning a convicted Christian until such time as a proper occasion for execution arrived, the following considerations would be troublesome: 1) Christians claim they can perform wondrous deeds such as exorcisms and resurrecting the dead; 2) magicians are known to be able to do these things as well as turn invisible, open locked doors, and break fetters of all sorts; and 3) the literature of the Christians features episodes that involve escaping from prison through supernatural means. Given these circumstances, one would be surprised if Perpetua's jailers and the tribune had not feared that she might use magic to escape. Any citizen that pointed out these issues to the tribune would have reason to do so, and, since a fellow Christian would not be so inclined, it is understandable that the Christian author of Perpetua's story (and Perpetua herself) would refer to such people as "deceitful men." It is just as likely that these men would have seen themselves not as being deceitful but rather as concerned, even fearful, that members of a subversive cult might use magic to escape justice.

Returning to the picture of Perpetua in her prison cell, she is suffering because of her Christian belief, steadfast in her convictions, and consequently persecuted by Roman society, which fears she is capable of using magic to thwart the justice system. She is judged deserving of death. At the same time, she is not immediately executed because of the importance of the emperor's son's birthday on which prisoners are to be executed as part of public spectacles. Perpetua pointed to the importance of the spectacle as a way of getting the tribune to back away from the torture he would have imposed on her, partly in order to prevent her and other imprisoned Christians from using magic to escape. The tactic evidently worked. Perpetua suggests that she must be allowed to be "refreshed" and to have the help of her Christian friends so that she can prepare for her execution. The tribune allows Perpetua to be a little more comfortable (a little less miserable, really) because he wants her to look decent and be relatively healthy when she is put to death in the arena. Even as Perpetua negotiated better treatment from her jailers and the judicial authorities, she was said to be facing death with pride and resolve. Her faith did more than make death tolerable. It made it honorable and desirable. To be a martyr was a privilege she welcomed. Just as with other martyrs, then, Perpetua did not see her circumstances as having been determined by the Roman government. It was an opportunity granted her by God.

Those who wrote about the Christian martyrs often wrote as if the judicial authorities were able to carry out their sentences only after divine intervention (one might say, supernatural or magical forces) had demonstrated that the martyrdom was part of God's will. This was often done by narrating a failed effort to kill the martyr, followed by the martyr's expression of desire to fit into God's plans or to emulate Christ's death. The actual death scene occurs only after the *passio* has established God's power and plan and simultaneously asserted mankind's inability to resist it. The death of Polycarp, bishop of Smyrna, in 155 C.E. is an excellent case in point. Polycarp was martyred a full generation before Perpetua. The *Martyrdom of Polycarp* is the oldest extant written account of

Christian martyrdom outside of the New Testament (Holmes 1992, p. 222). It serves in some ways as a model for other writings about martyrs. It may also be said to generally reflect established and developing attitudes about Christian martyrdom. Both of these circumstances relate to the role of magic in martyrdom.

It is the understanding of the writers and the sympathetic readers that, while supernatural forces were at work during the martyrs' experience, non-Christians either could not grasp the true meaning or remained unaware that God intervened to thwart pagans and protect Christians. However, the Christian belief that magical properties were related to the martyr's relics was very well understood by the pagans. In fact, pagan authorities made efforts to deny Christian communities access to the remains of martyrs. While pagans found it quite easy to dismiss the Christian belief that God was entirely in control of the martyrdom, they certainly would have a certain amount of concern and fear regarding the relics. The bodies of the dead, particularly those who died violent deaths, were generally thought to possess qualities that sorcerers could manipulate for evil purposes (Graf 1997, pp. 198-200). Christians denied pagans control over the martyrs' executions, adding to the pagans' fears. The death of Polycarp offers an example of just such Christian denial. The capture of Polycarp is said to have occurred after he dreamed of becoming a martyr. The dream was prophetic, symbolic, and therefore subject to interpretation. Before arrest, Polycarp is described as having the opportunity to escape but refusing it. When at last his capture is imminent, he is shown treating the soldiers in the manner one would treat houseguests. That is to say, Polycarp is compliant, but he also controls the situation (Holmes 1992, pp. 229-233). He goes to trial and prison not because he is compelled by the secular authorities but rather because he wants to do so in order to please God and imitate the example of Christ.

After being convicted of refusing to honor the gods and to sacrifice to the emperor, of participating as a leader of a religion deemed to be subversive to Rome, and of being a threat to humanity, Polycarp is led into a stadium where he is, as he knew from his earlier vision, sentenced to be burned to death. The crowd, which contains gentiles and Jews, asks for Polycarp to be thrown to the lions, but the proconsul, who had earlier threatened Polycarp with this very fate, explains to the people that the time for that type of execution has passed. "Then it occurred to them to shout out in unison that Polycarp should be burned alive. For it was necessary that the vision which he received…be fulfilled" (Holmes, 1992: 235-237). Thus, according to the narrative, the entire event is controlled directly by the Christian God even though the mob and the Roman authorities believe they are in charge.

What happens next demonstrates both the Christian control over circumstances and the supernatural forces that can prevent an execution by fire:

> The materials prepared for the pyre were placed around him; and as they were also about to nail him, he said; "Leave me as I am; for he who enables me to endure the fire will also enable me to remain on the pyre without moving, even without the sense of security you get from the nails."
>
> So they did not nail him, but tied him instead. Then he, having placed his hands behind him and having been bound,

like a splendid ram chosen from a great flock for a sacrifice, a burnt offering prepared and acceptable to God, looked up to Heaven and said: "O Lord God Almighty, Father of your beloved and blessed Son Jesus Christ, through whom we have received knowledge of you….May I be received…in your presence today…

When he…finished his prayer, the men in charge of the fire lit the fire. And as a mighty flame blazed up, we saw a miracle (we, that is, to whom it was given to see), and we have been preserved in order that we might tell the rest what happened. For the fire, taking the shape of an arch, like the sail of a ship that is filled by the wind, completely surrounded the body of the martyr; and it was there in the middle, not like flesh burning but like bread baking or like gold or silver being refined in a furnace. For we also perceived a very fragrant odor, as if it were the scent of incense or some other precious spice.

When the lawless men eventually realized that his body could not be consumed by the fire, they ordered an executioner to go up to him and stab him with a dagger. And when he did this, there came out a large quantity of blood, so that it extinguished the fire; and the whole crowd was amazed that there should be so great a difference between the unbelievers and the elect. (Holmes, 1992: 232-237).

For the Christian hearing this story, several important points are made that would have been either rejected by non-Christians or else interpreted in far less flattering terms. First, Polycarp is presented not as an executed criminal but as a willing sacrifice to God. Although the execution is formally carried out by the state, its power is seen by the Christians as impotent rather than ultimate. The means and manner of death are described as if the Christians controlled them and were directing the civil authorities, rather than the other way around. The author does not see the inconsistency in saying that an executioner went up and stabbed him and then the fire was doused with blood. Would the executioner be expected to walk through flames to stab Polycarp? Even the horrible smell of burning flesh is replaced with the pleasing odor of incense, furthering the sacrificial symbolism.

While Polycarp is not seen by the pagans as a practitioner of magic, the entire narrative is woven through with a supernatural thread. All of the key themes referred to in the previous paragraph can be interpreted as relying on the supernatural. Without them, the story cannot be interpreted in the positive way its author intended. Only through the application of elements that would appear magical to outsiders can the story of Polycarp be seen as a Christian victory.

Those who heard the story in a Christian setting and those who witnessed the event as Christians no doubt were as impressed as the author hoped they would be. This is certainly not a story designed to deceive an audience by claiming magical abilities for the protagonist and his admirers. Rather, the story reveals the lens through which a persecuted Christian community viewed its world. It tells us how, with a definite sense of the miraculous and a firm belief in their God, these Christians interpreted the persecutions which they endured. Martyrs became the object of veneration in all senses, including the literal. The remains of their bodies were venerable objects.

Relics constitute a link between magic and martyrdom. Tertullian's famous remark that the martyrs are "seed for the Church" was profound at several levels (*Apologetic Works* 50, p. 12). The physical remains of the martyrs (relics) evoked religious awe. They functioned in ways that the Church and its members would have called miraculous and that the persecutors of the Church would have labeled magical. Consequently, while Tertullian was correct in his assertion, it may have been equally true that persecutors of Christians felt justified in their actions when they saw Christians using relics to perform healings or to exorcise demons. W. H. C. Frend's major study of martyrdom in the early Church reached a conclusion that relates to the present topic: "Atheism and black magic, these provided the fuel to the sporadic outbursts of anti-Christian feeling" (Frend 1967, p. 196). As more Christians became martyrs and their remains became more commonly used by Christians, the use of those relics for healings, exorcisms, and protection from harmful supernatural forces would have come to the attention of civil authorities, thus further fueling the flames of persecution.

The use of body parts as talismans was well known to the ancients, as was their use in magical formulas. For example, a spell for invisibility involved the use of an ape's eye which is not, obviously, a *human* body part, but the same formula allows the substitution of an eye from "a corpse that has died a violent death." (*PGM*, pp. 247-262). A corpse that died in a violent fashion, such as by an execution, has significance in magical contexts. When a corpse was magically revivified it was referred to by Greek speakers as a *parhedros*. A *parhedros* could be used by a sorcerer as an assistant demon that aids the sorcerer in his evil practices. The use of the dead as elements in magic was a serious concern in Roman popular culture. Authorities involved in the punishment of Christians would have felt the need to address this issue. It is no surprise, then, that Polycarp's Jewish opponents wanted to deprive the Christians of the martyr's remains.

There are many comparable examples where relics are used as objects capable of producing the miraculous and, consequently, capable of maintaining faith or inspiring conversions. A strong tradition of martyrs and their relics serving as focal points for conversions runs through early Christianity as a central thread in the fabric of the Church. The early examples of martyrdom such as Stephen in *Acts* or Ignatius of Antioch are not connected to the cult of relics. Somewhat later by the 150s or 160s when Polycarp of Smyrna was martyred, there is still only indirect evidence. As noted already, there was an effort to prevent the Christians from obtaining his remains. Alternative explanations are certainly plausible. His followers may have wished simply to give him an honorable burial. Such honors were not always granted convicted criminals, be they Christian, pagan, or Jew.

Yet, by the summer of 258 C.E. when Cyprian, the bishop of Carthage, was executed, there were Christians anxious to obtain relics at the scene of his impending death. The description of the incident by Robin Lane Fox, which includes quotations from the *Acts of Cyprian*, is instructive:

> As [Cyprian] prepared for his execution, he was watched by crowds, some of whom had climbed the trees for an unimpeded view. Before kneeling, Cyprian asked that his executioner be given twenty-five pieces of gold. The deacons helped him to remove his outer tunic, and, "almost the last

thing Cyprian saw was a little pile of cloths," thrown by the crowd "to catch the martyr's blood and become relics for the faithful." No pagan notable had ever looked down on such a sight. His body was left lying until nightfall, "because of the pagans' curiosity," before it was escorted to a prominent cemetery, a magnet for future Christian burials (Fox 1986, p. 16).

Fox concludes that "Before long, Church leaders were digging up corpses and breaking them into fragments, a type of grave robbery which pagans had never countenanced." Relics had to be interpreted, as with any new phenomenon, through the lens of prior experience. To their critics, Christians seemed to be providing evidence of bizarre behavior connected to sorcery. Not only did Christians seek to obtain the bodies and blood of their heroes (who were, in fact, convicted of capital crimes), but they also used these remains in activities that were understood as sorcery or witchcraft (such as those related to a *parhedros*, an exorcism, or healing).

The incidents which occurred in Lyons in 177 C.E. are also relevant. A young Christian woman named Blandina, along with a number of other Christians, was martyred after refusing to acknowledge the pagan gods and renounce Christianity. According to Irenaeus of Lyon, the tortures that Blandina underwent were, if not unusual for a martyr, nonetheless, horrific:

> But the blessed Blandina, the last one left, having, like a noble mother, encouraged her children and sent them on before her victorious to the King, endured herself the same

conflicts....After she had been scourged and exposed to the wild beasts, and roasted in the iron chair, she was at last enclosed in a net and cast before a bull. She was tossed by the bull. But she didn't feel the things which were happening to her. This was because of her hope and firm hold of what had been entrusted to her and her communion with Christ. Thus, she also was sacrificed. The heathens themselves confessed that never among them did a woman endure so many and such terrible tortures (Irenaeus of Lyon, *Letter from the Church of Lyon*, p. 17).

The story resembles others told about Christian martyrs in this period. Blandina's faith remains resolute, no matter how harshly the pagans torture her. The pagans' efforts result in her death, and yet the Christians interpret this as a victory. Blandina becomes a heroine for her community.

But then something happens that is different from earlier accounts of martyrdom. The Christians have a desire to lay claim to the body. The pagans are well aware that the Christians will want the body. Wishing to punish the Christians further, they deny them access to the martyr's remains:

> But our state was one of deep sorrow that we could not bury the bodies. For night did not help us in this matter; money failed to persuade; and entreaty did not move them to compassion. But they kept up the guard in every way, as if they were to gain some great advantage from the bodies of the Christians not receiving burial...The bodies of the Witnesses, after having been maltreated in every way and exposed in the

open air for six days were burned. Their ashes were swept by the wicked into the river Rhone, which flows past so that no trace of them might be visible on earth. They [the Roman authorities] did all this as if they had been able to overcome God. They thought they could deprive them of their second birth in order, as they said, that "they [the Christians] may not have hope in a resurrection. Through the Christians' trust in the resurrection they bring to us this foreign and new religion. They despise dangers and are ready to even go to death with joy. Now let us see if they will rise again and if their God can help them and rescue them out of our hands." (Irenaeus of Lyon, *Letter from the Church of Lyon,* p. 19).

The pagan community clearly wished to deny the remains to the Christians. The pagans also are presented as attempting to prevent the resurrection of the martyrs. However, as any Christian would attest, pagans did not even believe in the resurrection, which means that they had another motive for denying the Christians access to the remains. Why would they be so thorough in disposing of the Christian remains? One possible answer is that the pagans simply wanted to add insult to injury. Another is that they desired to demonstrate that belief in the resurrection was not only misleading, but also subject to their control. These are not mutually exclusive possibilities and the likelihood is that they were both strong motivations for the anti-Christian behavior.

The practice of denying burial to convicted criminals who suffered capital punishment was by no means uncommon. Civic behavior associated with punishment included mockery of the body and, it is safe to say, the worse the punishment was, the worse the mockery associated with the convicted person's body. John Dominic Crossan has explored this issue and reached conclusions that are as controversial as they are simple (Crossan 1995). He argues that because Jesus was crucified by the Romans (had "the Jews" been responsible for his death, the form of execution would have been stoning) his body would likely have been treated like those of other crucified individuals. Crossan notes that if the Romans had allowed his body to be taken for burial (in accordance with Jewish custom), they would have been certain he was already dead. However, it is unlikely that the Romans would have allowed such a thing because it was not *their* custom.

Further, the gospel accounts clsim that Joseph of Arimathea took possession of the body. Joseph's role in the gospels raises suspicions, however. He was supposed to have been part of the Jewish council that convicted Jesus, yet he is shown to be one of Jesus' followers. Joseph is said to have asked Pilate for the body, yet the gospel narrative also describes Jesus' followers as having fled or "gone underground" after the execution. A comparison of the gospel accounts of Joseph of Arimathea shows consistently that he is credited with obtaining the body of Jesus from Pilate. Although it is strange that Pilate would consent to such a request, none of the gospel writers explains this irregularity. In fact, far from the more obvious concern about getting in trouble with the Roman authorities, John's gospel has Joseph *secretly* taking Jesus' body "for fear of the Jews" (*John*, 19: 38). According to Crossan,

> If the Romans did not observe the Deuteronomic decree [that Jesus be buried in accordance with a Jewish custom] Jesus' dead body would have been left on the cross for the wild

beasts. And his followers, who had fled, would know that. If the Romans did observe the decree, the soldiers would have made certain Jesus was dead and then buried him themselves, as part of their job. In either case, his body left on a cross or in a shallow grave barely covered with dirt and stones, the dogs were waiting. And his followers, who had fled, would know that, too....The horror of that brutal truth is sublimated through hope and imagination into its opposite (Crossan 1995, p. 154).

Regardless of one's opinion about Crossan's conclusions, certain features emerge which are relevant not only for Jesus but also for the martyrs. Both Christians and pagans thought that it was important for their group and their opponents to know what became of the body. This issue grew in significance with the passing of the years. Both sides wanted their opponents to feel as though they had no control in the matter. That is, Christians wanted pagans to feel as if they ultimately could not harm the bodies of Christian holy people while pagans wanted to demonstrate an absolute control over Christian holy people not only by killing them but also by mocking them and then obliterating their remains.

In their essential elements, pagan and Christian sources are not very different. They do differ in interpreting the significance of the events. If we return to the role of magic as it relates to this issue, a few points may be reiterated. Ancient culture attached significance to dead bodies that involved supernatural power. For the pagans, who were concerned about their entertainment and the execution of "justice," killing Christians was necessary in the fight against a superstition that could cause the gods to withdraw their favor and, consequently, lead to any number of cultural and social problems. More importantly for the issue of magic, executed people and their remains were connected to the practices of sorcery and necromancy.

For Christians, the bodies of executed people had even more significance. They would one day be resurrected just as Jesus had been. Perhaps more significantly, their remains had a power beyond human understanding. Not only could they heal, exorcise demons, protect from harm, and work an infinite variety of miracles (or magic from another view), but relics were also key in legitimizing the authority of those who controlled them, especially the bishops whose honor was assured, at least in part, by the presence of relics in their churches. The more prestigious the church, the more prestigious were the relics and *vice versa*. This was yet another reason that pagans regarded Christianity as a superstition rather than a religion and that Christians were so frequently treated with contempt and suspicion.

The leading apostles of the early Church, Peter and Paul, had their remains kept in Rome. While the importance of the eternal city itself made its church community more significant than others, the fact that the relics of Peter and Paul were interred there gave it an even higher status. Rome had what Paul Johnson calls "an *embarras de richesse*" because of its possession of the remains of both Peter and Paul (Johnson 1976, p. 60). Further, Rome collected an almost infinite number of relics that reflected its long and eminent Christian history.

Early Christians developed a fascination and profound respect for relics, while at the same time these riches provided another reason for persecutors and critics to find fault. It requires no leap of imagination whatsoever to link magic and relics. This is true from the viewpoint of pagans as much as from the viewpoint of Christians. The only significant difference is that the former would see sorcery or a perverse mistreatment of the body while the latter would see the miraculous and profound effects of sanctity. The differences, in fact, are even less than I have suggested. For, just like pagans, Christians would certainly not approve of the use of dead bodies for the practice of sorcery. They would see the use of a body or a *parhedros* as witchcraft. But Christians would make an exception if the wonder was worked by God. No surprise, then, to read in Crossan's (1995) that "Jesus uses magic, or thaumaturgy, if you prefer a euphemism, but the only objective distinction between magic and religion is that *we* have religion while *they* have magic" (Crossan 1995, p. 104).

References

Athenagoras. 1956, *Embassy for the Christians* and *Resurrection of the Dead*, ed. Johannes Quasten and Joseph C. Plumpe, Trans. and annotated by Joseph Hugh Crehan. In *The Works of the Fathers in Translation*, volume 23, The Newman Press, Westminster, Maryland.

Crossan, John Dominic. 1995, *Jesus: A Revolutionary Biography*, Harper, San Francisco.

Fox, Robin Lane. 1986, *Pagans and Christians*, Harper Collins, San Francisco.

Frend, W. H. C. 1967, *Martyrdom and Persecution in the Early Church*, Anchor Books, Garden City, New York.

Graf, Fritz. 1997, *Magic in the Ancient World*, Harvard University Press, Cambridge, Massachusetts.

Greek Magical Papyri in Translation. 1986, ed. Betz, H. D., University of Chicago Press Chicago.

Holmes, Michael W., editor. 1992, *The Apostolic Fathers: Greek and English Translations of Their Writing,.* (Originally edited by J.B. Lightfoot and J.R. Harmer), second ed., Barker Book House, Grand Rapids, Michigan.

Holy Bible. Revised Standard Version.

Irenaeus of Lyon. 1952, *Proof of the Apostolic Preaching*, ed. Joseph P. Smith, trans. Joseph P. Smith, Newman Press, Westminster, Maryland.

_____. 1992, *Against the Heresies*, trans. and annotated Dominic J. Unger, Paulist Press, Mahwah, New Jersey.

Johnson, Paul. 1976, *A History of Christianity*, Atheneum, New York.

Jones, C. P. 1986, *Culture and Society in Lucian*, Harvard University Press, Cambridge.

Lucian. 1936, *The Passing of Peregrinus*, in *Lucian*, ed, T. E. Page *et. al.*, Trans. A. M. Harmon, volume 5, Loeb Classical Library, Greek edition, Harvard University Press, Cambridge, Massachusetts.

Luck, George, ed. 1985, *Arcana Mundi: Magic and the Occult in the Greek and Roman Worlds*, Johns Hopkins University Press, Baltimore.

Porphyry. 1994, *Porphyry's Against the Christians: The Literary Remains*, ed. R. Joseph Hoffman, Prometheus Books, Amherst, New York.

Salisbury, Joyce E. 1997, *Perpetua's Passion: The Death and Memory of a Young Roman Woman*, Routledge, New York.

Shewring, W. H., trans. 1931, *The Passion of Perpetua and Felicity*, London.

Tertullian. 1950, *Apologetic Works*, ed. Joseph Deferrari, *et. al.*, trans, Rudolph Arbesmann, *et. al.*, Fathers of the Church, vol. 10, New York.

"Worshiping the Devil in the Name of God" Anti-Semitism, Theosophy and Christianity in the Occult Doctrines of Pekka Siitoin

Kennet Granholm

Introduction

In Finland, the neo-Nazi politician Pekka Siitoin became (in)famous throughout the country for his curious mix of radical racist political activism and satanic magical practice, both of which he championed since the early 1970s. In the few studies of the man, the focus has been on his political activism, whereas the occult dimension has not been deemed worthy of serious attention (see Kalliala 1999a; 1999b; 1999c; Kaplan 1999; 2001). The short discussion of Siitoin in the postscript of the Finnish translation of Gary Valentine Lachman's *Turn of Your Mind* (Vil 2003) is one of the few texts where the occult aspect is given primary attention. This article is an attempt to remedy the situation by providing insight into the very interesting and, indeed, highly disturbing occult teachings of Pekka Siitoin, while contextualizing them within his racist political philosophies. I seek to understand his highly unorthodox politics and occultism through the lens of the political and social history of post-World War II Finland. As my aim is to first and foremost focus on the occult dimensions of Pekka Siitoin's life, certain artificial divisions will be made. As the radical political philosophies of Siitoin easily over-shadow his occult practices, my discussion of Siitoin's life history will make a division of these two aspects. In practice, these two fields of Siitoin's life were intrinsically linked, which will be apparent in my more detailed discussion of Siitoin's theories regarding magic.

Pekka Siitoin: Biography and Legend

Pekka Siitoin was born in Varkaus, Finland, on 29 May 1944 and lived his early years with his parents in Loimaa, in southeastern Finland. Later on, however, Siitoin came to claim that he was adopted. His real parents were supposed to be the German officer, or *obersturmbannführer*, Peter von Weltheim, and a Russian-Finnish whore[1] and/or nurse. Consequently, Siitoin sometimes referred to himself as Baron von Weltheim and would actually publish some of his books under the pseudonym Peter von Weltheim. Siitoin's childhood was generally happy and normal although there are some indications that his father may have had an inclination towards alcoholism. At age fifteen or sixteen, Siitoin and his mother moved to Turku, Finland, following some monetary arguments between his parents, according to Siitoin (Kalliala 1999a, p. 258; Nordling & Koskela 2006, pp. 37-38).

In the early 1960s Siitoin took up photography and video filming as hobbies, something of which he later came to make a profession of (Kalliala 1999a, p. 258; Nordling & Koskela 2006, p. 45). In the mid 1960s he founded the photography firm *Siitoin-filmi oy* in Turku. At age twenty-two, he married and eventually had four children with his wife. Two of these children later died, and Siitoin conceived two more children with other women after his wife's passing away (Nordling & Koskela 2006, pp. 182-183).

In 1973 Siitoin and his family moved to Naantali, a town near Turku, and it was here that most of Siitoin's political and metaphysical activities would be centred. In 1997 Siitoin moved to Vehma, also near the city of Turku (Nordling & Koskela 2006, pp. 52-53). On 8 December 2003, Siitoin died of cancer (Nordling & Koskela 2006, p. 161).

Political Activities

It is his controversial, extreme right-wing politics that Siitoin is most known for, and he claimed to have become interested in Nazism at the age of four (Nordling & Koskela 1999, pp. 35, 40). Siitoin's political activism and career can be divided into three main eras: political awakening and direct action in the 1970s, stagnation in the 1980s, and a re-awakening and in the 1990s.

Siitoin's political activities started in the late 1960s with sympathies for the bourgeois party, *Kokoomus*. Quite soon, however, Siitoin's political interests started to take on a more radical flavour. In the early 1970s Siitoin started to publish populist writings in local newspapers, and he was even a candidate for *Suomen maaseudun puolue* (SMP, The Finnish Rural Party) in the 1972 municipality and church elections in Turku, albeit without much success. He was also a member of the *Suomen kansan yhtenäisyyden puolue* (SKYP, The Party for The Unification of the Finnish People), an offshoot of SMP. As the 1970s progressed Siitoin's political ambitions started taking an increasingly right-wing turn. In the mid 1970s he started to use his metaphysical society, *Turun hengentieteen seura* (THS, Turku Occult Society), as a forum for his right-wing, nationalistic politics. The small journal, *Nationalisti-pasuuna* (The Nationalist-Bassoon), published on a weekly basis, served this interest, as did several books published by the society. At the end of 1975 Siitoin started to wear black shirts and blue ties in his public appearances, a style of clothing borrowed from the 1930s Finnish fascist organization *Isänmaallinen kansallisliitto* (IKL, Patriotic People's Alliance). He also sported an Adolf Hitler-styled moustache, which he claimed to have grown per request of the members of his political party (Nordling & Koskela 2006, p. 182). The *Isänmaa ja vapaus* (Fatherland and Freedom) group was founded in early 1976, and the more organized *Isänmaallinen kansallisrintama* (IKR, Patriotic People's Front) in late 1976. For IKR the main enemy consisted of the Soviet Union and communism, and rhetorical devices used were derived from German Nazism. The Soviet Union was argued to be the "product of a Jewish communist conspiracy" (Kalliala 1999a, pp. 259-265).

After the mid 1970s, Siitoin's political interests led him to organize coups against communist media personalities. He admits to having staged several instances of threat-calls to what he perceived to be communist journalists, as well as a smoke-bomb attack on the offices of communist newspaper *Kansan uutiset* (The People's News) (Nordling & Koskela 2006, p. 13, 61, 175-176; Kekkonen 2004, p. 225). However, it was the arson of the communist-owned printing house *Kursiivi* which led Siitoin to be incarcerated. In late 1977 the ministry of internal affairs made the decision to disband all of Siitoin's unregistered organizations as contrary to the 1944 (Paris) and 1947 (Moscow) peace treaties, which outlawed fascist organizations (Pekonen et al. 1999, p. 37). Less than a week later, an arson attempt at *Kursiivi* occurred. An individual close to Siitoin was arrested for the deed, and Siitoin was found guilty of incitement. He received a jail sentence of five years on 13 November 1978. (Kalliala 1999a, pp. 274-275). Siitoin himself consistently argued his innocence and thought he had been the victim of political conspiracy on the part of Finnish president Urho Kekkonen (Nordling & Koskela 2006, p. 13).

When Siitoin was released from jail in 1981, the political atmosphere of Finland had changed, and so had the public and media views on Pekka Siitoin. The era of political activism was over, and Siitoin appeared hopelessly outdated. As a convicted felon, he was now deemed dangerous and the media portrayals of him reflected this. His background as a felon also attracted the criminal element to his politics, something which he disliked. Increasingly he started to figure in porn magazine articles to further his cause[2] although he did appear in other media as well (Nordling & Koskela 2006, pp. 31, 182-183). Siitoin's new political party, *Kansallis-Demokraattinen Puolue* (KDP, the National-Democratic Party), was mentioned for the first time in 1978, and was officially announced after Siitoin's release from jail in 1981. The party published the newsletter/magazine *Rautaristi* (Iron Cross). The death of Siitoin's oldest son in 1985 led him to greatly decrease his public appearances, and he spent the rest of the 1980s mostly in correspondence with his foreign contacts in the neo-Nazi and neo-Fascist milieus (Kalliala 1999a, pp. 277-279).

The rise of neo-Nazism and the White Power movement in the 1990s brought Siitoin to the front anew. The circulation of the KDP newsletter *Rautaristi* increased, and it now included translated texts from the global right-wing radical scene. Instead of the anti-communist politics, which had been at the absolute centre during the 1970s, a shift towards White Power ideologies occurred. In 1993 Siitoin appeared with other leading neo-Nazis in the documentary *Sieg Heil Suomi*, which depicted the foundation of *Kansallinen rintama* [National Front][3] (Stenros 1994). Amidst all of this, Siitoin expressed rather negative sentiments about the Skinhead movement, which he saw as being more focused on mindless violence than on political ideology (Nordling & Koskela 2006, pp. 180, 185-186). However, Siitoin was now regarded as a drunkard and a "Nazi-clown", not as a serious political or religious figure (see e.g. Kaplan 2001). He was a candidate in both the 1992 and the 1996 city council elections in Naantali, and actually received the sixth most votes, 141 in total, in the 1996 elections. He was not elected, however, as he was nominated as an individual, and the D'Hondt system used in Finland favours political parties and coalitions (Kalliala 1999a, pp. 280-282; Nordling & Koskela 2006, pp. 171-172).

Metaphysical Career

In later retellings, Pekka Siitoin's metaphysical journey appears to have started early. He claimed to have met a friend of his father who was clairvoyant at a young age (Nordling & Koskela 2006, p. 39). He also claimed that a gypsy woman foretold that the young lad would grow up to be a famous man (Nordling & Koskela 2006, pp. 40, 188-189). However, Siitoin's actual career in magic and metaphysics can be regarded to have started in 1971 when he contacted the famed Finnish fortune-teller Aino Kassinen due to some financial troubles (Nordling & Koskela 2006, pp. 50-51, 172).

Aino Kassinen (1900-1977) was something of an "official fortune-teller" of Finland from the 1930s onwards. Kassinen claims to have been consulted by, among others, Risto Ryti, the president of Finland between 1940 and1944 and Marshall Mannerheim, a marshall in the army, (Kassinen 1972, pp. 49-52, 57). Kassinen seems to have been largely self-taught in fortune-telling and esoteric philosophy, but she did come into contact with at least the Theosophical Society and some of its Finnish offshoots, as well as the writings of Rudolf Steiner (Kassinen 1972, p. 47). It is highly likely that she would have been influenced by these contacts. In her autobiography Kassinen mentions Siitoin as one of her two most promising students in the occult (Kassinen 1972, pp. 64-65). Siitoin would throughout his life stress his initial contacts with Kassinen (e.g. Siitoin 1973, p. 21; 1985, p. 88), and claim that he was baptized into Satanism by her (Nordling & Koskela 2006, p. 192).

In 1971, Siitoin founded *Turun Hengentieeteen Seura*, mentioned above (Kalliala 1991a, p. 261). Aino Kassinen was in contact with this group, which she claims had about thirty members in the early 1970s (Kassinen 1972, p. 64). Siitoin's association held meetings and lectures in Turku, offered long-distance spiritual healing, and published and sold books (Ultra 1974b, p. 36; Kalliala 1999a, p. 261). Later, two sister organizations, *Föreningen Veronica* (The Veronica Organization) and *Pegasos-seura* (the Pegasus-Society), formed in order to market and sell occult material outside the borders of Finland (Kalliala 1999a, p. 261). According to Mari Kalliala, Siitoin was fairly popular in the occult milieu of Finland in the early 1970s and did receive plenty of contacts from people seeking spiritual guidance. In the mid-1970s, however, this changed as his political sentiments and activism caused resentment.

Aino Kassinen, who had earlier praised Siitoin, warned people to stay away from him (Kalliala 1999c, p. 92; Nordling & Koskela 2006, pp. 50-51), and the only alternative spiritual magazine in Finland, *Ultra*, refused to print Siitoin's articles and advertisements from the summer of 1974 onwards[4] (Kalliala 1999a, p. 260-261). In November 1977, when the Finnish ministry of internal affairs discontinued all of Siitoin's societies and political parties, THS was discontinued as well (Kalliala 1999a, pp. 274-275). The new organization *Kansallis-mytologinen seura* (National-Mythological Society) was formed in 1981 after Siitoin's release from jail (Kalliala 1999a, p. 277), and it was under this organization that Siitoin published his remaining books.

Although Siitoin wrote books under his given name, most of his books on metaphysical subjects were published using pseudonyms. Most were also published before his imprisonment. The following books dealing with magic were written by Siitoin and published by his societies:

* *Yhteys ufoihin ja henkimaailmaan* [Contacts with UFOs and the Spirit World], originally published in 1973 under the pseudonym Hesiodos Foinix. Also published in Swedish as *Kontakt med ufos och andevärlden*, parts one and two.
* *Musta magia, osa 1* [Black Magic, part 1], originally published in 1974 under the pseudonym Peter Siitoin. Also published in Swedish as *Svart magi, del 1*.
* *Uuden ajan unikirja* [Dream-Book for the New Age], originally published in 1974 under the pseudonym Cassius Maximanus. Also published in Swedish as *Nya tidens drömbok*.

* *Ufot, uskonto ja paholainen* [UFOs, Religion, and the Devil], originally published in 1974 under the pseudonym Jonathan Shedd.

* *Musta magia, osa 2* [Black Magic, part 2], originally published in 1975 under the pseudonym Peter Siitoin. Also published in Swedish as *Svart magi, del 2*.

* *Paholaisen katekismus* [The Catechism of the Devil], originally published in 1977.

* *Kohti uutta uskoa* [Towards a New Faith], originally published in 1989 under the pseudonym Peter von Weltheim.

Besides the books written by Siitoin himself, his societies also published and sold books such as a translation of the grimoire *The Sixth and Seventh Books of Moses*[5] (Siitoin 1986), a book on witchcraft by Ray Isaksson (1985), and various works by persons connected to the Theosophical/Anthroposohical-milieu such as H. P. Blavatsky, Rudolf Steiner, and Pekka Ervast.

Aino Kassinen had instructed Siitoin to read works by the founder of the Anthroposophical Society, Rudolf Steiner (Kalliala 1999a, p. 260), and it is indeed apparent that Siitoin was indebted to this writer for much of his occult philosophies. As Siitoin began to increasingly combine his unorthodox political views with his occultism, while continuing to recommend Anthroposophical literature to his correspondents, the Finnish members of the Anthropological Society started to become concerned. In 1972, the president of the Anthropological Society in Finland and Siitoin discussed the issue publicly on the pages of *Ufoaika*, the precursor to the earlier mentioned alternative spiritual magazine *Ultra* (Kalliala, 1999a, 260).

Metaphysical Worldview and Magical Practice

The Heavenly Hierarchy

In Siitoin's view of the cosmos, the world was created by an impersonal and all-powerful being, or electro-magnetic force-field (Siitoin 1974, p. 14). Although this being is thought to be impersonal, it is often referred to in the masculine as Father. This creator-being does not in any way participate in worldly events since it has created several subordinate beings who have taken this role. In the book *Ufot, uskonto ja paholainen* these subordinate beings are identified as Kether, Chokmah, Binah, Chesed, Geburah, Tiphereth, Netzach, Hod, Yesod, and Malkuth (Siitoin 1974, p. 15). These divine beings, or "gods," have their negative counterparts in another ten beings: Saatan-Moloch, Beelzebub, Lucifer, Ashtaroth, Asmodeus, Belphegor, Baal, Adrammalech, Lilith, and Nahema (Siitoin 1974, p. 15). In the book *Svart Magi del I*, the divinities, now called arch-angels and Zefiroths,[6] get slightly different names: Eheje-Eleie-Ether Elion (Metatron), Jrhowah (whose "class is Chochma"), Tetragrammaton Elohim (whose "class is Bizah"), El (whose "class-number is Aesed"), Elohim (whose "class-number is Geburah"), Eloha (whose "class-number is Tipheret"), Tetragrammaton Zebaoth (whose "class-number is Nezaed"), Elohim Sabaoth (whose "class-number is Hod"), Sadai (whose "class-number is Jesod"), and Adonay Melech (whose "class-number is Malchat") (Siitoin 1985, pp. 46-51). Although the existence of "shadows" to these Zefiroths is mentioned, they are not named. Siitoin does, however, write that the "angels of light" are led by Mikael and the "angels of darkness" are led by Lucifer, and that the Creator-Father does not interfere in their operations (Siitoin 1985, pp. 51-52).

In connection to these divine beings, a nine-level hierarchy of spiritual attainment is described (Siitoin 1985, pp. 41-45). Jesus Christ is mentioned as the only being to have attained the sufficient degree of spiritual evolution to reach the highest level, and thus is the highest personified divine being in cosmos. Lucifer is described as having attained the next highest spiritual evolutionary level and Satan as having attained a stage under this (Siitoin 1974, p. 104). Jesus Christ is also described as the reincarnation of Zoroaster who at the request of the Creator-Father, left his material body and manifested as the Christ (Siitoin 1974, p. 29). However, it is not Jesus Christ who is the most important deity for Pekka Siitoin; this is reserved for Satan and Lucifer. As mentioned earlier, Lucifer is identified by Siitoin as the ruler of the "angels of darkness." This does not mean, however, that Lucifer is deemed an evil being. In *Ufot, uskonto ja paholainen*, Lucifer is described as one of the highest beings on the spiritual planes and the one who created the material world. He is also said to have severed his ties to the heavenly host by refusing to leave earth when human beings had been created (Siitoin 1974, pp. 11-13). Lucifer is also said to support the development of physical beings into "great personalities" through the use of technology and material luxuries, but love and emotive behaviour stands in the way (Siitoin 1985, p. 55). According to Siitoin, it is important to accept both "Christ-consciousness" and "Lucifer-consciousness" in our existence as they are both necessary forces that balance each other (Siitoin 1973, p. 145). Satan, then, is regarded as a being separate from

Lucifer, and as the divinity of material and physical indulgence. This being is said to value material lusts, animalistic orgies, the amassment of monetary wealth, heavy drinking, and all other kinds of over-indulgence (Siitoin 1985, pp. 55-56). Satan-Moloch is also identified as the current ruler of the material world while Lucifer has chosen to dwell on the spiritual planes (Siitoin 1974, p. 24). The last central deity in Siitoin's metaphysical system is Jehovah. This being is not identified as the Creator-Father, but rather as a divine being comparable to Satan and Lucifer, and the creator of the Jewish people. In Siitoin's mythology Jehovah is the spiritual being most closely identified as "evil." He is described as having a competitive relationship with Lucifer and Satan and as striving for dominion over the world.

Cosmogony, Anthropogony and Misogyny

Pekka Siitoin displays a very unorthodox view of the creation of the world and of man. The "electromagnetic force-field," the Creator-Father in Siitoin's metaphysical system, is the original source of everything. However, the process of creation was performed by the subordinate divine beings mentioned above. One of these beings, Lucifer, was responsible for the creation of our solar system (Siitoin 1974, pp. 12-13). The creation of our world was a seven-stage process, in which each stage was assigned a responsible creator from among Lucifer's servants. When reaching the fourth stage, Earth was ready for population. However, human beings were created on other planets through selective breeding, and were transported to earth using spacecrafts (Siitoin 1974, p. 17). The technologically advanced society of Atlantis was founded about 90,000 years ago, and Lucifer severed his ties to the Heavenly Host in order to become the overlord and god of the Atlanteans. The Atlanteans were more spiritual in nature than modern humans, and they eventually divided into seven sub-races (Siitoin 1974, pp. 17-21). When the Atlanteans started to abuse their spiritual powers, their gods destroyed their island in a flood (Siitoin 1973, p. 21). The fifth sub-race of Atlanteans, the Semites, had come to develop the capacities of morality and individual thought, but this development of independent thought diminished man's occult powers. It is from the Semitic race that modern humans, the Aryans, descend (Siitoin 1973, p. 20).

Although Siitoin's focus is on the Atlanteans, he does not consider them to be the first root-race of human beings. Instead, the Atlanteans were preceded by the Lemurians, which where in turn preceded by two other root-races (Siitoin 1974, p. 17). Here Siitoin's account takes an overtly racist turn. The Lemurians procreated with animals and thus "cave-men" were created. According to Siitoin, the Africans and gorillas are the result of cross-species procreation of these "cave-men," animals, and Atlanteans (Siitoin 1974, p. 23). Thus, the African people are, in Siitoin's view, comparable to primates and are less human than "the Aryans."

When Lucifer created the world, the divine being, Jehovah, was part of his "team" (Siitoin 1974, p. 26). However, Jehovah was a jealous and power-hungry being, and secretly plotted against Lucifer and his people. He created Adam and Eve in his own image, and thus the Jewish people were born. At the same time, he created the notion of sin in order to gain control over the people he had created. Siitoin describes Jehovah as a being that constantly seeks to dominate others, and these characteristics are transferred to the Jewish people as well (Siitoin 1974, pp. 26-27).

The Japanese and Chinese are a curious anomaly in Siitoin's mythology. Siitoin explains the advanced and alien culture of the Asian peoples by placing their origin on an alien planet (Siitoin 1974, pp. 23-24). According to Siitoin, the Japanese and Chinese destroyed their home planet in an atomic war and a handful of them escaped using spacecrafts. UFOs are central to Siitoin's philosophy. This can probably be attributed at least partly to the alternative spiritual milieu of Finland in the 1970s, which was strongly focused on UFO beliefs. For example, the only real alternative spiritual magazine of the time was the 1972 launched *Ufoaika* (UFO Age), which focused heavily on UFOs (*Ultra* 1974a; 1974b). Many of Siitoin's publications from the 1970s feature the word UFO in the title (i.e. Siitoin 1973; 1974). In Siitoin's mythology, UFOs are the vehicles of higher spiritual beings. The answer for these peoples having an advanced, but not extraordinarily advanced, culture is that all the scientists and scientific knowledge were destroyed in the war. Siitoin does not seem to dislike Asians, and values them much more highly than he does people of Jewish and African origin.

In addition to being racist in his accounts of non-European cultures and people, Siitoin is also explicitly misogynistic. In his mythology and philosophy women have no real substance. In esoteric contexts, highly evolved spiritual beings are commonly described as androgynous, but in Siitoin's account they are strictly male. Women can only evolve on a high spiritual level once they are reborn as men (Siitoin 1976, p. 63). In several of Siitoin's books the ideal roles and natures of women are described. A woman should ideally get married at an age between fourteen and sixteen to a man twenty to thirty years her senior. The reason for this is that she can then easily be "taught" by her man and become subordinate and eager to please her man, and thus the marriage would be a "happy" one (Siitoin 1976, pp. 59-61; 1985, pp. 102-103). Siitoin regards it "a pity that women fast become spoilt after the age of sixteen," presumably because adult women are more independent. (Siitoin 1985, pp. 102-103). Furthermore, a woman should be monogamous while a man can have several wives (Siitoin 1976, pp. 59-61). Interestingly, but hardly surprisingly, Siitoin seems to regard all women as having loose sexual morals (e.g. Siitoin 2000, pp. 22), and this also applies to his imagined birth mother (Nordling & Koskela 2006, pp. 37-38).

The Practice of Magic

Magical practice for Pekka Siitoin entails "speaking with God in his own language." The use of this "mystery-language," which entails the use of symbols, incantations and ritualistic practices, grants the magician power over the natural world (Siitoin 1985, pp. 10-11). Even though two of Siitoin's books are named Black Magic, he seems unsure of how to define this "black" magic. In some regard he adheres to the classic distinction of white magic being benevolent in nature and black magic being malevolent. However, only violence is regarded as truly evil and is, as such, something which Siitoin does not condone in his books (Siitoin 1985, pp. 10-12). Generally he is very strict in pointing out that the goal of metaphysical studies should first and foremost be the evolution of mankind and the world (Siitoin 1974, p. 95). However, what is most likely meant by mankind is "the Aryan race" and males only, since Siitoin's views of what is beneficial for the world probably differ greatly from common sentiments.

Of Siitoin's books, *Svart magi del I* (Siitoin 1985) and *del II* (Siitoin 1976) contain the most detailed instructions for magical practice, largely consisting of an amalgam of Theosophical notions and folklore material. The classic grimoire, *The Sixth and Seventh Books of Moses*, often named "The Black Bible" in Finland, was a central piece of magical literature in Siitoin's system. Siitoin's translation of the book (Siitoin 1986) was published in several printings from the 1970s and is often referred to in his other books (e.g. Siitoin 1976, pp. 5-6; 1985, pp. 14-18). In *Svart Magi del I*, two ways of making a pact with Satan are described, both involving ceremonial sacrifice. The first involves the ceremonial sacrifice of a black cat. The cat should be boiled alive during a midnight with a full moon (Siitoin 1985, pp. 60-63). During the cooking, the would-be magician is to read the following phrases aloud, eight times at the different cardinal points: *"I call to You Oh Prince of Darkness Lucifer, In Your name I ask Satan to take me as his servant"* (Siitoin 1985, p. 62). When the cat is cooked, its flesh is burnt, and the bones are collected for keeping under one's mattress. Three months after doing this ceremony the magician is to contact Satan through the use of an Ouija-board and hope for a positive answer from the Prince of Darkness. However, in a television interview, Siitoin says that he is very fond of cats and has never performed a sacrifice comparable to the one described in his book (Youtube 2007[7]). The second way of gaining the favour of Satan is reserved for men only and is an indication of Siitoin's misogynistic tendencies. The would-be magician is to find a young woman who has not yet lost her virginity. He should then seduce her, and when he sleeps with her for the first time, he should mentally focus on the following incantation: *"Here, oh Prince of Darkness, You have a humble gift so that Satan in your name may take me as his pupil"* (Siitoin 1985, p. 63). Most of the practical magic described in *Svart Magi del I* and *del II* are based on folkloristic sources and deal with the mundane: for example, spells and rituals for causing the haunting of an enemy's home, the humiliation of and victory over antagonists, the cessation of bleeding, the calming down of an angry dog, and the curing of warts, ear infections, and sleeplessness (Siitoin 1985, pp. 70-73, 89-93, 121-129). However, Siitoin also includes a quite elaborate ceremony for waking the dead (Siitoin 1985, pp. 78-86).

Siitoin attributes great importance to sexuality as an avenue of magical practice (Siitoin 1976, pp. 58-60). The earlier example of a pact with Satan includes the ritual use of sex, and sexual magic is also described as a part of other ceremonies as well. A peculiar ritual, again in order to seek the approval of Satan, is described in *Svart magi del I*. Here the practitioners are divided into groups of four women and four men. These individuals should undress and stand so that the men and the women are opposite each other, staring at each others' genitalia. The participants who are sexually aroused, indicated with an erect penis for men and vaginal secretion for women, are suitable to be servants of Satan (Siitoin 1985, pp. 108-110). Another sexually explicit ritual described involves the sacrifice of semen. In this ritual the oldest woman of the group, attributed the role of priestess, has her genitalia smeared in olive oil by the youngest man in the group and her behind smeared in olive oil by the oldest man in the group. At the same time the participants proclaim: *"Demon est deus Inversus, hallow and blessed be You oh holy snake"* (Siitoin 1985, p. 112). Hereafter the rest of the women in the group are to sexually stimulate the men and collect their semen in coffee cups. While this occurs, the Priestess circles the group and repeatedly incants, *"Legich, Legich, Legich, come and witness our loyalty to Satan"* (Siitoin 1985, p. 112). Finally the priestess blesses the semen, which has been poured into a big jar, and it is then burnt and the smoke inhaled (Siitoin 1985, pp. 111-113). No descriptions as to what specific effects these sexual rituals are thought to have are given, other than that they are enjoyable to Satan and that the participants may ask Satan for general favours after having performed a ritual of sexual nature (Siitoin 1985, p. 113).

Sources of Inspiration

Pekka Siitoin self-identified as a Satanist, but his particular brand of Satanism is very different from most common forms of contemporary satanic philosophy. The advent of modern Satanism can be attributed to Anton Szandor LaVey (1930-1997). In 1966, LaVey founded the Church of Satan in San Francisco, USA, and in 1969 his *Satanic Bible* (LaVey 1969), which was to become the holy book of a great number of contemporary Satanists (see Lewis 2002), was published for the first time. Pekka Siitoin, however, does not seem to have been particularly influenced by LaVey. The former was aware of the existence of the latter, and expressed a willingness to translate his works into Finnish (Nordling & Koskela 2006, p. 103). However, he did not regard LaVey as the instigator of Satanism (Nordling & Koskela 2006, p. 191). There are significant differences between the satanic philosophies and doctrines of Siitoin and the main strands of contemporary Satanism. When comparing LaVey's "Nine Satanic Statements" (LaVey 1969) with Siitoin's "Ten Satanic Commandments" as found in Siitoin's *Paholaisen Katekismus* (Siitoin 2000), the differences are apparent. Pekka Siitoin's

Ten Satanic Commandments are the direct reversals of the ten biblical commandments. In contrast, LaVey's Nine Satanic Statements are presented in a manner which implicitly refer to the biblical Ten Commandments, but cannot be regarded as simple reversals. Also, whereas the Church of Satan was essentially an atheist organization, the Satanism of Pekka Siitoin is metaphysically grounded.

Pekka Siitoin's brand of Satanism and Devil Worship is also unorthodox in its interesting take on traditional Christian concepts and figures. In Siitoin's system, it is fully acceptable to worship any of the higher divine beings. However, this worship must be performed in the name of God! Also as discussed above, Siitoin's view of Christ is very positive, and his Satanism can therefore not be regarded as anti-Christian *per se*. When taking Siitoin's extensive use of Christian mythology and his positive view of Jesus the Christ into account, his philosophy could, in a loose sense, be termed "Christian Devil Worship." It goes without saying that Siitoin's doctrines are very far removed from any forms of traditional Christianity. My use of the term Christian in the description of Siitoin's philosophy should be understood in a comparison to organizations such as Church of Satan. Most forms of contemporary Satanism are very far removed from any Christian context, and rarely make use of Biblical figures other than Satan (the use of whom is heavily detraditionalized). It should be noted that Siitoin did express sentiments that the true teachings of Christ had been distorted by the Church (e.g. Siitoin 1973, pp. 156; 1974, 105-107; 2000, 24-27), and his doctrines can therefore be seen as anti-Church.

Siitoin actually has a peculiarly inclusive view of who is to be regarded a Satanist, as he mentions H.P. Blavatsky, Merlin the Magician, Christian

Rosencreutz and emperor Caligula as such (Nordling & Koskela 2006, p. 191). In the same context, Siitoin also mentions Manly Palmer Hall's book *The Secret Teachings of All Ages* (Hall 2001) as a work in which famous Satanists are named. This book has indeed influenced him a great deal. The Theosophical Society, mainly through the books of H.P. Blavatsky, and the Anthroposophical Society, through the texts of Rudolf Steiner, were extremely influential for Siitoin. Siitoin's doctrines on cosmogony and anthropogony are to a large extent derived from Theosophical sources. The notions of seven root-races, the seven souls of man, and the seven stages of creation are found both in Blavatsky's and Siitoin's books, as are the mythological continents of Lemuria and Atlantis. Blavatsky similarly assumed a rather positive view of Lucifer, even naming the magazine of her London-based Esoteric Section of the Theosophical Society after this entity. Lucifer was here not equated with the Biblical Satan, but instead was imagined as a being who could illuminate the spiritual path of the occultist. Rudolf Steiner, in turn, based much of his speculations on the nature of reality on his notion of The Akashic Chronicles – the past, present and future history of creation as recorded in astral realms. The notion of the Akashic Chronicles is frequently mentioned in Siitoin's books as well and is featured as one of the main legitimising factors of his speculations. Siitoin probably first came across these sources in the early 1970s when his mentor, the fortune-teller Aino Kassinen, suggested that he should read works by Rudolf Steiner (Kalliala 1999a, p. 259). Another book which Siitoin himself names as influential on him is Trevor Ravenscroft's *The Spear of Destiny*, a book which Nicholas Goodrick-Clarke identifies as essentially derived from Anthroposophic doctrine (Goodrick-Clarke 2001, pp. 120-121). In the book, Hitler's military and political success is attributed to him having had the mythical Spear of Longinus in his possession (Ravenscroft 2000). The legend of the spear is that it was the one used to pierce Jesus' abdomen during his crucifixion. A person in possession of it will hold the destiny of mankind in his hands. The book was first published in 1972, and it is very likely that Siitoin learned of it early on. Clearly then, Siitoin's use of Blavatsky's, Steiner's, Hall's and Ravenscroft's works consists of rather radical reinterpretations, in which the latent seed of racism is utilized to its fullest possible extent.

Anti-Semitism and Magic

Anti-Semitism has a long and profound, although not uniform, history in West. During the Alexandrian and Roman occupations of Israel, the Jewish religion was regarded as a potential source of rebellious uprising. In the early Christian writings of Paul, the Jewish people were seen as overwhelmingly sinful, and in the later Middle Ages, official Christian sentiments towards Jewry were explicitly negative (Chazan 2005, pp. 398-399). It was, however, with the rise of nationalism in the nineteenth and twentieth centuries that anti-Semitism as we know it today emerged. Jews were then perceived as foreign elements in otherwise homogenous national cultures (Chazan 2005, p. 402). *The Protocols of the Elders of Zion* (see Marsden 2006), from the turn of the nineteenth century, expressed the anti-Jewish sentiments of the time and have continued to exert influence to this day. The text was produced in 1897 by Philip Petrovich Stepanov as the manuscript *Subjugation of the World for Jews*, and was first published in 1905 as an appendix to the second edition of Sergei Nilus' book *The Great in the Small* (Ben-Itto 2005, pp. 21-25) The Protocols were presented as the authentic proceedings of a meeting arranged by King Solomon in 929 BCE (Ben-Itto 2005, p. 21). The protocols of the meeting, which were arranged in order to devise a way for the Jews to conquer the world without bloodshed, contained numerous examples of the perceived sinister nature of the Jewish people (Ben-Itto 2005, p. 21). Divided into twenty-four protocols, the text deals with subjects such as economic and military control, brainwashing and re-education of the gentile, and control of the press, all in order to keep the world under Jewish control (Marsden 2006). Phrases of the following nature are plentiful in the protocols:

* "The ruler who is governed by the moral is not a skilled politician" (Marsden 2006, p. 19).

* "Whether a State exhausts itself in its own convulsions, whether its internal discord brings it under the power of external foes – in any case it can be accounted irretrievably lost: IT IS IN OUR POWER" (Marsden 2006, p. 18).

* "Without an absolute despotism there can be no existence for a civilization which is carried on not by the masses but by their guide" (Marsden 2006, p. 22).

* "In order to incite seekers after power to a misuse of power we have set all forces in opposition one to another" (Marsden 2006, p. 32).

The Protocols were conclusively proven to be falsifications as early as 1921, but they have nevertheless been used for anti-Semitic purposes throughout the twentieth century (Ben-Itto 2005, p. 67). Famous examples are Adolf Hitler's and Henry Ford's propagandist use of them (Ben-Itto 2005, p. 58-73). Marc Levin's documentary film *The Protocols of Zion* (2005) provides a number of examples of the anti-Semitic use of the Protocols in the contemporary world.

For Pekka Siitoin, *The Protocols of the Elders of Zion* were the truth. He published the text, and refers to them in several of his books. It is, however, interesting to note that his view of Jews was somewhat ambivalent. Moses is identified as the person who rebelled against the will of the evil god Jehovah, and strived to convey the secrets of magic to non-Jews (Siitoin 1985, pp. 14-16). Siitoin's sentiment seems to be that Jews have the chance to reform, just as long as they abandon Jehovah and aspirations of world domination. However, at other times Siitoin seems to regard Jews as utterly irredeemable and flawed on a racial level.

It is fascinating that a man who holds extreme, anti-Semitic views and actively pursues an anti-Semitic agenda would base his magical philosophy on Jewish mysticism. For anyone even faintly familiar with Jewish Kabbalah the god-names of Siitoin's Heavenly Hierarchy, as mentioned earlier, should be familiar. They are of course the names of the different *Sefirot* on the Kabbalistic Tree of Life (see Idel 2005). The counterparts are in turn named after the arch-demons of *Kelipoth*, the shadow-side of the *Sefirot* (see Pick 1974, pp. 77-78; Scholem 1991, pp. 73-77, 232-244; Giller 2001, pp. 49, 148-149; Idel 2002, pp. 465-467; Granholm 2005, pp. 22-23). It is very unlikely that Siitoin would have borrowed these names directly from Kabbalistic sources. Instead the likely source is Manly Palmer Hall's *The Secret Teachings of All Ages*, which Siitoin himself names as a book which has inspired him (Nordling & Koskela 2006, p. 192). In Hall's book both the *Sefirot* and the *Kelipothic* arch-demons are named, albeit slightly differently than in Siitoin's books[8]

(Hall 2001, pp. 120-122). Another author who treated the *Kelipoth* in the 1970s is the British magician Kenneth Grant (see Evans 2007, pp. 284-344), whose "Typhonian Trilogies" contain ample reference to the night-side of Kabbalah (See Grant 1994a; 1994b). It is, however, unlikely that Siitoin would have been familiar with these works, and it should be noted that Grant's works do not contain the blatant racism which is infused in Siitoin's books.

Political Climate in Finland

When treating Pekka Siitoin's anti-Semitism, the political climate of Finland in the 1970s must be taken into consideration. The political atmosphere of Finland after World War II was affected deeply by the country's close proximity to the Soviet Union (see Allison 1985). Finland had waged war against the Soviet Union in 1939-1940 and 1941-1944 and had received aid from Nazi Germany. Finland, of course, lost the war, and, while maintaining its independence, fears of a Soviet retaliation were embedded in the collective consciousness of the people. During the 1930s, fascist political parties and groups had a presence in Finland, as elsewhere in Europe. The peace treaties of 1944 (Moscow) and 1947 (Paris) outlawed fascist organizations, and these laws were quite strictly enforced in Finland (Pekonen et al. 1999, p. 33). Furthermore, the Soviet Union exercised pressure to silence anti-communist and anti-Soviet sentiments (Singleton 1998, p. 134), which were indeed strong in Finland (Kalliala 1999b, p. 73). In short, the major concern of Finnish post-World War II foreign policy, and of Finnish politics in general, was to maintain peaceful relations with its eastern neighbour (Pekonen et al. 1999, pp. 33-34). The major political parties of the era were in general agreement on this condition, and thus no real room for radical right-wing parties to grow and prosper existed (Pekonen et al. 1999, p. 34). Indeed, radical right-wing and racist political parties have never been particularly successful in Finland (Kestilä 2007, pp. 33-34).

It was in this political climate that Pekka Siitoin was born and raised. Anti-communist and anti-Soviet sentiments were widely spread, but they could not find expression. The sentiments towards Nazi Germany were mainly positive for quite a long time. Hitler's regime had been regarded as the only force powerful enough to withstand the "evil" Soviet empire, and, while the terrors of the holocaust were known in Finland as elsewhere, it took a long time before the subject received any substantial discussion in the country. Thus, it was not before the 1970s that the mostly positive view of Nazi Germany started to change. It is within this context that Siitoin's anti-Semitic sentiments must be examined. Siitoin had strong anti-communist and anti-Soviet sentiments and came to see communism as part of a Jewish conspiracy. As detailed above, Siitoin was well familiar with *The Protocols of the Elders of Zion*, and in these a section entitled "We support communism" can be found (Marsden 2006, pp. 33-37). Basing his anthropogony on the writings of Helena Petrovna Blavatsky, which are infused with the racism of the late nineteenth century, an anti-Semitic worldview was easy to formulate. Before the 1990s, there is an apparent lack of articulated racist sentiments towards non-Jews in Siitoin's written production. While the genealogy of African people provided in *Ufot, uskonto ja paholainen*, as discussed above, is obviously racist, it is not an articulation of *reflected* racism *per se*. It should be interpreted more as an expression of utter unfamiliarity and orientalism. Before the 1990s the number of people of foreign origin in Finland was almost non-existent (see Pekonen 1999, p. 52), and it is really with the increasing number of asylum seekers in the 1990s that the neo-Nazi movements and racism directed towards non-Caucasian people took hold (Pekonen 1999, p. 37-39). As Siitoin wrote most of his books before the 1990s, not much of an expressed racism towards people of color is to be found in them. He did, however, express radical racist sentiments in, for example, television interviews (see Youtube 2007).

Conclusion

During my youth, in the 1980s and 1990s, Pekka Siitoin was most commonly regarded a joke. A rather representative example of this is a television show from the 1990s, in which Siitoin is called a "Nazi-clown" to his face by the interviewer (Youtube 2007), a comment which he dismissed but did not seem all too bothered by. Having familiarized myself with the occult productions of Siitoin, I believe that the outrageous comments made by him are better understood when put into the context of his magical worldview and life-philosophy. In short, Siitoin was not simply a "Nazi-clown," and his quite elaborate metaphysical worldview, a synthesis of both occult and political sources, demonstrates that he was not simply a moron. Rather, he led his life in accordance to the "will of Satan" in his magical system. This is also what makes his political sentiments more disturbing. Pekka Siitoin was a true nihilist, and had he ever attracted any significant following, the results could have been devastating.

Although the search for *Philosophia Perennis*, the eternal and infallible teaching which is beyond time, is a common trait of esoteric philosophies (see Faivre 1998, pp. 114-115), esoteric teachings are as firmly grounded in their history as are all other human endeavours. The books by H.P. Blavatsky were imbued by popularized understandings of one of the most influential scientific theories of the nineteenth century: evolution. Thus, the notion of a succession of more and more advanced human races, as expressed in her *The Secret Doctrine* (Blavatsky, 2007a; 2007b), is a consequence of late Nineteenth-Century preferences. Pekka Siitoin's unorthodox appropriation of Theosophically grounded material also needs to be understood in the historical and societal context of his time. The racist ideologies inherent in early Theosophist materials were easily fitted together with the anti-Semitism of *The Protocols of the Elders of Zion*, the fear of the communist Soviet Union, the admiration of Nazi Germany as the antagonist of this "Evil Empire," and the view of Adolf Hitler as a master occultist as expressed in Trevor Ravenscroft's *The Spear of Destiny*.

Notes

1 Siitoin tended to regard all women more or less as whores.

2 Siitoin had, however, appeared in a porn magazine article as early as 1976 (Kalliala 1999a, pp. 267-268).

3 Part of this documentary can be viewed on the Internet, on URL: http://video.google.com/videoplay?docid=-3697974924756747358&q=Pekka+Siitoin.

4 Issues one and two of *Ultra* do, however, contain material related to Siitoin. Issue one contains a review of Siitoin's book *Ufot, uskonto ja paholainen* (*Ultra*, 1974a, p. 32) and issue two contains an advertisement for the aforementioned book (*Ultra*, 1974b, p. 35), as well as an announcement regarding the activities of Turun Hengentieteellinen Seura (*Ultra*, 1999b, p. 36).

5 The Sixth and Seventh Book of Moses was published in several printings since the 1970s, and was, according to Siitoin, his bestseller (Nordling & Koskela 2006, pp. 50-51). The book was, of course, not

authored by Siitoin. The oldest published version of the grimoire was printed in Germany in the mid 1800s. It is unknown when the text was originally written.

6   In Kabbalah, Sefirot is the plural whereas Sefira is the singular, thus no form of writing such as Sefirot*s* exists. However, Siitoin appears to use *Zefiroth* as singular and *Zefiroths* as plural, when discussing his archangels.

7   The name of the interviewer and the TV-program are unknown. There are indications that the show would have aired in 1998, although this is unsure.

8   Hall's Adam Belial is termed Beelzebub, Lucifuge is changed into Lucifer, and Baal Chanan is simply shortened to Baal. The spelling is a bit different as well.

References

Allison, Roy. 1985, *Finland's Relations with the Soviet Union 1944-1984*, Macmillan, London.

Ben-Itto, Hadassa. 2005, *The Lie That Wouldn't Die. The Protocols of the Elders of Zion*, Vallentine Mitchell, London.

Blavatsky, Helena Petrovna. 2007a, *The Secret Doctrine. Volume 1: Cosmogenesis*, available at: http://www.theosophy.org/Blavatsky/Secret%20Doctrine/SD-I/SDVolume_I.htm.

_____. 2007b, *The Secret Doctrine. Volume 2: Anthropogenesis*, available at: http://www.theosophy.org/Blavatsky/Secret%20Doctrine/SD-II/SDVolume_2.htm.

Chazan, Robert. 2005, "Anti-Semitism, Revision of Alan Davies' original article from 1987," in *Encyclopedia of Religion*, 2nd edition, ed. Lindsay Jones, Macmillan, Detroit.

Evans, Dave. 2007, *The History of British Magick after Crowley: Kenneth Grant, Amado Crowley, Chaos Magic, Satanism, Lovecraft, The Left Hand Path, Blasphemy and Magical Morality*, Hidden Publishing, London.

Faivre, Antoine. 1998, "Renaissance Hermeticism and the Concept of Western Esotericism," in *Gnosis and Hermeticism from Antiquity to Modern Times*, ed.Roelof van den Broek & Wouter J. Hanegraaff, State University of New York Press, Albany.

Granholm, Kennet. 2005, *Embracing the Dark: The Magic Order of Dragon Rouge – Its Practice in Dark Magic and Meaning Making*, Åbo Akademi University Press, Åbo.

Grant, Kenneth. 1994a (1975), *Cults of the Shadow*, Skoob Books, London.

_____. 1994b (1977), *Nightside of Eden*, Skoob Books, London.

Giller, Pinchas. 2001, *Reading the Zohar, The Sacred Text of the Kabbalah*, Oxford University Press, Oxford.

Goodrick-Clarke, Nicholas 2001, *Black Sun: Aryan Cults, Esoteric Nazism and the Politics of Identity*, New York University Press, New York.

Hall, Manly Palmer. 2001, *The Secret Teachings of All Ages: An Encyclopedic Outline of Masonic, Hermetic, Qabbalistic and Rosicrucian Symbolic Philosophy*, available at http://www.sacred-texts.com/eso/sta/index.htm.

Hanegraaff, Wouter J. 1996, *New Age Religion and Western Esotericism. Esotericism in the Mirror of Secular Thought*, Brill, Leiden.

Idel, Moshe. 2002, *Absorbing Perfections: Kabbalah and Interpretation*, Yale University Press, New Haven.

_____. 2005, "Qabbalah," in *Encyclopedia of Religion*, 2nd edition, ed.Lindsay Jones, Macmillan, Detroit.

Isaksson, Ray. 1985, *Mustan magian salaisuudet*, Kansallis-mytologinen yhdistys, Naantali.

Kalliala, Mari. 1999a, "Radikaalioikeisto – tapaus Pekka Siitoin," in *Isänmaan puolesta, Suojeluspoliisi 50 vuotta*, ed. Matti Simola and Tuulia Sirvio, Gummerus, Jyväskylä.

_____. 1999b, "Traditions of the Radical Right in Finnish Political Culture," in *The New Radical Right in Finland*, ed Kyösti Pekonen, Jyväskylä, The Finnish Political Science Association, Jyväskylä.

_____. 1999c, "Pekka Siitoin – A Representative of the Cultic Milieu," in *The New Radical Right in Finland*, ed. Kyösti Pekonen, The Finnish Political Science Association, Jyväskylä.

Kaplan, Jeffrey. 1999, "The Finnish New Radical Right in Comparative Perspective,"in *The New Radical Right in Finland*, ed. Kyösti Pekonen, The Finnish Political Science Association Jyväskylä.

_____. 2001, "Radical Religion in Finland?," in *Nova Religio*, vol. 5, no.1, pp. 121-142.

Kassinen, Aino. 1972, *Sierskan*, Larson, Täby.

Kekkonen, Urho. 2004, *Urho Kekkosen päiväkirjat*, in *Osa 4 '75 – '81*, ed. Juhani Suomi, Otava, Helsinki.

Kestilä, Elina. 2007, *Radikaalioikeistopuolueet länsi-euroopassa. Tutkimuksia vaalikannatuksen vaihteluun vaikuttavista kysyntä- ja tarjontateoreettisista tekijöistä*, Turun yliopisto, Turku.

LaVey, Anton Szandor. 1969, *The Satanic Bible*, Avon, New York.

Lewis, James R. 2002, "Diabolical Authority. Anton LaVey, *The Satanic Bible* and the Satanist 'Tradition'," *Marburg Journal of Religion* vol. 7, no.1, pp. 1-16 available online at: http://web.uni-marburg.de/religionswissenschaft/journal/mjr/pdf/2002/lewis2002.pdf.

Levin, Marc. 2005, *Protocols of Zion*, Documentary film, HBO/Cinemax Documentary.

Marsden, Victor E. 2006, *The Protocols of the Elders of Zion*, Filiquarian Publishing, n. p.

Nordling, Iiro and Olavi Koskela. 2006, *Suomen Führer. Valtakunnanjohtaja Pekka Siitoin*, self-published, Tampere. (ISBN 952-92-0509-0)

Pekkonen, Kyösti, Pertti Hynynen, and Mari Kalliala. 1999, "The New Radical Right Taking Shape in Finland," in *The New Radical Right in Finland*, ed Kyösti Pekonen, The Finnish Political Science Association, Jyväskylä.

Pick, Bernhard. 1974, *The Cabala: Its Influence on Judaism and Christianity*, Open Court, La Salle, USA.

Ravenscroft, Trevor. 2000, *Pyhä keihäs*, Gummerus, Jyväskylä.

Scholem, Gershom. 1991, *On the Mystical Shape of the Godhead: Basic Concepts in the Kabbalah*, Schocken Books, New York.

Siitoin, Pekka (as Hesiodos Foinix). 1973, *Yhteys ufoihin ja henkimaailmaan*, Turun hengentieteellinen seura, Turku.

_____ (as Jonathan Shedd). 1974, *Ufot, uskonto ja paholainen,* Turun hengentieteellinen seura, Turku.

_____ (as Peter Siitoin). 1976, *Svart magi del 2,* Pegasos-club, Turku.

_____ (as Peter Siitoin), 1985 (1974/5), *Svart magi del 1.* Turku, Pegasos-club

_____, trans. 1986, *Kuudes ja seitsemäs Mooseksen kirja eli Mooseksen taika- ja henkioppi ja selityksiä ihmetöistä joita tekivät vanhat ja viisaat heprealaiset,* Kansallis-mytologinen yhdistys, Naantali.

_____(as Peter von Weltheim). 1989, *Kohti uutta uskoa.* Kansallis-mytologinen yhdistys, Naantali.

_____. 2000, *Paholaisen katekismus,* Kansallis-mytologinen yhdistys, Naantali.

Singleton, Fred. 1998, *A Short History of Finland,* revised and updated A. F. Upton, Cambridge University Press, Cambridge.

Stenros, Nina. 1994, *Sieg Hail Suomi,* Documentary film, Oblomovies oy, Helsinki.

Ultra, 1974a, issue 1, November 1974.

Ultra, 1974b, issue 2, December 1974.

Vil, Ike. 2003, "Suomentajan jälkisanat. Ex boreus lux," in *Tajunnan alkemisti, Kuusikymmentäluvun mystiikka ja vesimiehen ajan pimeä puoli,* (Gary Valentine Lachman), Like kustannus, Helsinki.

Youtube, 2007, "Interview with Pekka Siitoin on Finnish TV," available at: http://www.youtube.com/wtach?v=e5P2n1UOMtA.

"The Witching Hour: Sex Magic in 1950s Australia"

Marguerite Johnson

> You don't know what your long letters mean to me; understanding and eloquent they are and happily satisfying to my nature, occult, obscene, and of other worlds and beings.
>
> Eugene Goossens to Rosaleen Norton
> Incomplete Letter. Undated

> ... the truth can only enhance his reputation by revealing him as a radical spiritual / sexual explorer many years ahead of his time.
>
> Drew Crawford
> "Dialogue," *Sydney Morning Herald*
> 25 February 2002

On 9 March 1956, Sir Eugene Goossens (1893-1962), the first permanent conductor of the Sydney Symphony Orchestra and Director of the New South Wales State Conservatorium, was apprehended at Sydney's Mascot Airport and subjected to a customs' inspection of his luggage. This unearthed alleged indecent material, namely books, photographs, and film. He was subsequently charged under Section 233 of the Customs Act with importing prohibited goods. At Martin Place Court of Petty Sessions on 21 March, Goossens pleaded guilty *in absentia* and was fined the maximum penalty of £100. He resigned from his positions as Chief Conductor of the Sydney Symphony Orchestra and

Director of the New South Wales Conservatorium of Music and returned to England on 26 May. The events that led to the charges against Goossens were initiated by the discovery of a series of letters he had written to Rosaleen Norton (1917-1979), the "notorious" Witch of Kings Cross, an occultist and esoteric artist, which detailed his practice of sex magic with her and her companion Gavin Greenlees (1930-1983). The correspondence, which can be dated between *c.*1953-*c.*1955, had been stolen from Norton and Greenlees' flat in September 1955 by Joe Morris Senior, a crime reporter for *The Sun*. Morris handed over the letters to the police who subsequently placed the unsuspecting Goossens under surveillance prior to and during his time abroad.

Detective Sergeant Bert Trevenar of the Sydney Vice Squad, the chief investigator of the events of 1956, kept a copy of the correspondence in his Ashfield home until his death in 2003.[1] The originals were lost, possibly destroyed by the police, when they failed to gain permission to prosecute Goossens on an additional charge of scandalous conduct. The latter charge was dropped because of the intervention of the Attorney General and Minister of Justice, Mr R. R. Downing, who, according to Carole Rosen (1993):

> ... instructed the Commissioner of Police to take no further action against him on the grounds that the evidence did not disclose any criminal offence with which he could be charged. Premier Cahill, when questioned as to his future, emphasised that he had been fined under a Federal Act. The Crown law authorities had examined the police report of the case and decided to take no further action against him. (p 357)

A historical and cultural study of these events, which saw the public disgrace of a man regarded as a cultural giant, a musical innovator and a champion of Australian classical music, has not been undertaken to any significant degree to-date. The apparent absence of scholarly discourse may be partially in response to the subject of sex magic and the esoteric in general that has until recent years remained as a subject worthy of enquiry only outside the academy (cf. Owen 1997). The trio's occult interests, particularly in sex magic, have, however, been treated in three separate genres: the print media, creative works and documentaries. In most instances, the letters have been utilized to varying degrees ranging from direct quotation to artistic interpretation.

David Salter, in his 1999 lead article for the *Sydney Morning Herald*, "The Strange Case of Sir Eugene and the Witch," discussed the letters and quoted from them. In the research for the 1990 fictionalized account of the relationship between Goossens and Norton for the novel *Pagan*, Inez Baranay accessed the correspondence and utilized it, particularly in Chapter 28 entitled "The Letters." There have been four plays: Barry Lowe's *Rosaleen – The Wicked Witch of the Cross* (1983), Timothy Daly's *Complicity* (1998), *The Witch of Kings Cross* directed by Jocelyn McKinnon (2003), and Louis Nowra and Mandy Sayer's *The Devil is a Woman* (2003).[2] The latter was promoted as a documentary-drama based on extracts from diaries, letters, poems, fiction and non-fiction although the authors later claimed that references to the letters were removed owing to legal threats over alleged breach of copyright. In 2004 two documentaries were screened: Geoff Burton's *Fall of the House* and Salter's "Sir Eugene Goossens: Sex, Magic and the Maestro." The quotations in Burton's film were loosely based on the letters and Salter's ABC documentary included direct passages from them.³ Finally, Act I ("Disgrace") of *Eugene and Roie*, an opera-in-progress by Drew Crawford, premiered on 17 January 2004 at the Riverside Theatre, a premier venue in the Sydney suburb of Parramatta. Partially inspired by the letters, Crawford was also threatened with a legal injunction, but, as with Nowra and Sayer's play, the show went on.⁴

It is the subject of Goossens' letters – his practice of sex magic with Norton and Greenlees – that constitutes the theme of this essay. Far from contributing to the scandalous reputation of the three individuals involved, it is anticipated that this research will augment the limited academic material available on magic in Twentieth Century Australia. It is an exegesis of a personal experience and represents Goossens, Norton, and Greenlees as serious adherents to an occult system that has been, and sometimes remains, quintessentially misunderstood. It also makes use of Norton's writings and artwork to augment the examination of her life as an occultist and to complement Goossens' descriptions of sex magic with her and Greenlees.

The analysis begins with a survey of the practices of Aleister Crowley (1875-1947)⁵ whose multitudinous writings (seldom read by his detractors) reveal another side to the man popularly regarded as wicked (cf. Sutin 2000). This paper does not seek to defend Crowley's ethics and certain ritual activities but aims to discuss his philosophical systems, particularly sex magic. This will provide a basis for the assessment of the rites of Goossens, Norton, and Greenlees, whose magical practices paid significant deference to Crowley's work.

Crowley and Sex Magic

Hugh Urban (2003) notes that "[Crowley] stands out as one of those remarkably enigmatic characters who has had a tremendous impact on contemporary new religious movements, esotericism and occultism, even as he has been almost entirely ignored by academic scholarship." (p 139). Indeed, it is Crowley, as opposed to, for example, Gerald Gardner, who served as the major influence on Norton, Greenlees and Goossens when it came to sex magic.

Crowley is exceptionally well-known among scholars and practitioners of magic and related traditions and is usually regarded as infamous, immoral, if not terrifying by those among the general public even vaguely familiar with his name. Arguably, Crowley's most significant contribution to western esotericism was the theory and practice of sex magic, a complicated system that was partially developed in 1904 as a result of several visits he and his wife, Rose, made to the Boulak Museum in Cairo, during which they experienced communications with an entity called Aiwass (or Aiwaz), a messenger of Horus. A well-documented episode in the life of Crowley, the Cairo experience led to the *Liber Al vel Legis* (1936), a text in which he chronicled and analysed the significance of the encounters, the result of which was the beginning of his philosophies on sex magic:

> Now ye shall know that the chosen priest and apostle of infinite space is the prince-priest The Beast, and in his woman called The Scarlet Woman is all power given. They shall gather my children into their fold: they shall bring the glory of the stars into the hearts of men. For he is ever a sun and she a moon ... (I.15-16)

Crowley dedicated the rest of his occult life to the art of sex magic and the pursuit of the ultimate Scarlet Woman with whom he could perfect his system of Thelemic "Will." Through his encounters with the Scarlet Woman, Crowley believed he was demonstrating his powers as the Lord (or the Great Beast) of the New Aeon through serious acts of ceremonial "magick" (Crowley's variant spelling). Sex magic was intended to not only bring about the conception of "a child mightier than all the kings of the earth" (Crowley 1936, III.44-45) but also to lead to the attainment of absolute consciousness.

The intrusion of Karl Theodor Reuss (1855-1923), founder of the *Ordo Templi Orientis* (O.T.O.), into Crowley's London apartment in May 1912 is sometimes regarded as the unofficial – and unceremonious – revelation of a deeper significance of sex magic to Crowley (for a discussion of this event and its chronological problems, cf. Kaczynski 2002, pp. 202-3; Sutin 2000, pp. 225-26; and Owen 1997). According to Richard Kaczynski (2002), Reuss ranted about Crowley's unauthorised use of "[t]he magic secret of sex" (p 202) contained in the secret documents of the O.T.O. Crowley was bemused until Reuss placed a copy of Crowley's *The Book of Lies* (1913) before him. The text contained the "The Star Sapphire," a ritual that included the following: "Let the Adept be armed with his Magick Rood [and provided with his Mystic Rose]" and "Let him drink of the Sacrament and let him communicate the same." For the first time Crowley became aware of the sexual symbolism inherent in his writing as it applied to the IX° initiation of the O.T.O. (a level Crowley had not yet reached). Reuss interpreted the rood and the rose as terms for the male and female genitalia respectively, and the second passage as reference to the sexual congress between the priest and priestess as the culminating ritual of the IX° initiation. Crowley was astonished (he had, for example, taken the rood as the cross) – not so much about the allegations of plagiarism and breaking the code of silence of the O.T.O. – but by the revelations Reuss' arrival had heralded. According to Lawrence Sutin (2000), the two spent the following hours in intense discussion, resulting in Reuss conferring upon Crowley the IX° and, later, the X° along with the title of "Supreme Rex and Sovereign Grand Master General of Ireland, Iona, and all the Britains" (p 226).

Crowley assumed the magical title Baphomet, an idol believed to be worshipped by the Order of the Knights Templar, to whom the O.T.O. claimed occult lineage. The origin of the name is uncertain: a corruption of Mahomet (Mohammed); a combination of the Greek words *baphe* and *metis* ("absorption of wisdom'); or, in the system devised by Eliphas Levi (1910), a symbol of the "Universal Agent," the all-powerful force in "Nature" that the adept can adapt and guide. Levi's artistic interpretation of Baphomet, entitled *The Sabbatic Goat*, clearly inspired some of Norton's work. For example, there is a photograph printed in the *Sydney Truth* on 7 September 1952 that shows Norton's mural of Baphomet on the office wall of her publisher, Walter Glover. Likewise, Nevill Drury's "Introduction to the Second Edition" of *The Art of Rosaleen Norton with Poems by Gavin Greenlees* (1982) notes that "There were other major deities too [besides Pan]: Lucifer, Baphomet, Hecate, Jupiter" (p.8).

Crowley had experimented with sex magic prior to this revelation, as exemplified by the Cairo sojourn and also the time he spent in the North African desert in 1909. Accompanied by his novice Victor Neuburg (1883-1940), Crowley performed a series of rites, spiritually terrifying and dangerous, which involved crossing the thirty Aethyrs (or Aires) – metaphysical spirit spheres surrounding the earthly plane. Kaczynski (2002) states that Crowley had attempted this in Mexico in 1900 but could not "pass through or comprehend any Aethyrs beyond the first two" (p 71). Crowley understood the meaning of the Aethyrs in terms of the system of magic practised by the Elizabethan scholar and occultist Dr John Dee (1527-1608) and his diviner Edward Kelley (1555-c.1593) and the adaptation thereof by the Hermetic Order of the Golden Dawn, of which Crowley had been a member (1898-1900). This involved angel magic based on the Kabbalistic tradition as adapted by Henry Cornelius Agrippa (1486-1535), which Dee had modified to develop his Enochian system: a cosmology of angels and demons as well as thirty otherworldly realms, which he called Aethyrs.

In 1909 Crowley aimed to regress through the thirty Aethyrs over a period of several days with Neuburg assisting and recording the visions (as a Kelley to his Dee). During his attempt at contemplating the fourteenth Aethyr, however, he experienced an obstacle in the form of an angel who ordered him to depart (Crowley 1911). On descent from Mount Dáleh Addin, where the rite had been attempted, Crowley was inspired to build an altar to the god Pan and offer a sacrifice. This sacrifice took human form: to experience the fourteenth Aethyr the magus sacrificed himself via submission to Neuburg in the form of homosexual passivity.

The theme and concept of offering oneself for sacrifice, an ancient Mediterranean tradition, was a keystone of anthropological works that inspired Crowley, such as James Frazer's *The Golden Bough*. The practice permeated the occult revival as epitomized by Rosicrucianism and the

Golden Dawn, as well as featuring in Masonic rites, which in turn had inspired the aforementioned magical societies. Crowley's experience in the North African desert, where he attempted to enter Dee's fourteenth Aethyr, exemplifies the magical connections he made between accessing various esoteric planes, encountering angelic and demonic entities therein, and negation of the conscious self through sexual ritual in order for this to be achieved.

After the sexual ritual with Neuburg, Crowley again embarked on his Enochian quest and encountered Chorozon (the Dweller of the Abyss). The Abyss is connected with *Da'ath*, the so-called eleventh sephirah on the Tree of Life. Alex Owen (1997) describes Crowley's understanding of the term, after the time in the desert: "It represented Dispersion: a terrifying chaos in which there was no centre and no corresponding consciousness." (p. 111).

The episode of 1909 is a salient example of Crowley's understanding of sex magic. What he and Neuburg experienced in the desert "prefigured his elaboration of the techniques of sex magic" (Owen 1997, pp. 99-100), which he was to consciously pursue – especially after Reuss' arrival on his doorstep in 1912. The quest for heightened imagination and power through self-sacrifice and the subsequent obliteration of the ego came to underline Crowley's system of sex magic. The rites that evolved, which included autoeroticism and homoeroticism in addition to heterosexual sex, became a significant component of Crowley's reworking of the various degrees of initiation in the O.T.O. under his leadership (which he assumed in 1922 and held until his death in 1947) and the main focus of his own order, the *Argenteum Astrum* (Silver Star), established in 1907.

Crowley's legacy, most notably sex magic, has had a profound impact on practitioners of magic, quite often through direct means via his writings or through the conveyance of his work via interpreters. Crowley's famous mantra, as quoted below, was to inspire occultists into the Twentieth Century and beyond:

> I personally believe that if this secret [of sexual magic], which is a scientific secret, were perfectly understood, as it is not even by me after more than twelve years' almost constant study and experiment, there would be nothing which the human imagination can conceive that could not be realized in practice. ([1929] 1969, p 767)

Norton, Greenlees, and Goossens - magical experiences

Norton remains one of the outlaws of Australian bohemian culture. Born in New Zealand in 1917, she and her family moved to Lindfield on Sydney's North Shore in 1925. Despite her adult poverty, living in squats and impoverished flats in Kings Cross and other inner-city suburbs, Norton's family was well-off and she lived a comfortable, middle-class childhood until she chose to leave it behind and make her own way in the world at the age of 16. While working in an assortment of jobs in the city, then hitch-hiking along the north and south coasts of Australia, Norton developed her artistic talents and read various occult texts. On returning to Sydney, Norton dedicated her time to her art and burgeoning magic activities. Her pictures were published in the alternative journal *Pertinent* during the early 1940s and her first exhibition in 1949, held at the Rowden-White Library at The University of Melbourne, suggested a promising start to a public career had it not ended in a court case for obscenity (cf. Drury 2002, pp. 39-40). Undeterred, she continued to paint and draw, and in 1952 *The Art of Rosaleen Norton with Poems by Gavin Greenlees* was released to extensive media coverage for its alleged vile nature. Another court case ensued.

After the drama of Goossens' arrest in 1956, Norton continued to be interviewed by various tabloid journalists and her life was extensively chronicled, almost always in an exaggerated, voyeuristic manner for the prurient interests of the Australian public. During the late 1960s and until the early 1970s, however, she tended to shun publicity, living quietly near her beloved sister, Cecily, surrounded by an assortment of animal companions. She left the earthly plane on 5 December 1979, her departure the result of colon cancer. Greenless followed her, four years later to the day.

Norton was clearly influenced by Crowley's work, most notably his *Magick in Theory and Practice,* although she also refers to the writings of Eliphas Levi (1810-1875), Helena Blavatsky (1831-1891), Alice Bailey (1880-1949) and Dion Fortune (1890-1946).[6] Norton's determination not only to explore and develop her belief system, but also to publicly acknowledge it, occurred at a time when witchcraft was still illegal in Australia (cf. Hume 1997, p. 224). Although dubbed a "witch" by the tabloids and eventually embracing the title herself, Norton's religion was far from stereotypical witchcraft (for example, Satanism, gross forms of sacrifice and other related inversions of Christianity). Her worship and beliefs were intense, complex, and eclectic; in addition to the aforementioned authors, her system of magic drew on the Kabbalah,

Theosophy, and world mythology articulated through her readings and interpretations of Sigmund Freud and, more significantly, Carl Jung.

In contrast, Greenlees' early occult experience is not documented although his precocious poetic talent reveals an early interest in surrealist literature and visionary or mystical poetry. The major influences on Greenlees included Comte de Lautréamont (1846-1870), Arthur Rimbaud (1854-1891) and Peter D. Ouspensky (1878-1947). Lautréamont's work was characterized by its overtly obscene imagery, which created visionary, nightmarish scenes peopled by blasphemous characters intent on evil. Rimbaud, like Lautréamont, was regarded as a precursor to the Surrealists and experimented with free verse and *synethesia* (the representation of one sense experience in terms of another). He urged fellow poets to become seers by the submission of the self to a total derangement of the senses. Ouspensky was also an experimenter in alternative states of consciousness and promoted the occult teachings of the Armenian mystic Gurdjieff (1878-1947). These sources of inspiration are present in the poems Greenlees was writing by the age of thirteen, as evidenced in his work for *Pertinent*, which included the dreamscape pieces entitled *Poem* (May 1944) and *The Square* (June 1944). As Norton's artwork was also published and reviewed in *Pertinent* (for example, October 1941), the pair may have sought out each other as a result of a perceived "connection." Drury (1988) suggests that it is "likely that Roie and Gavin first met one another in the last year of the war, when Beresford [Norton's husband at the time] was away in New Guinea and Roie was living in the stables in Bayswater Road [inner Sydney]. Cecily [Norton's sister] remembers seeing him there" (p. 48).

Norton and Greenlees worshipped Pan and conducted rituals to this god (and others) in their shared accommodations in Kings Cross during the late 1940s and throughout the 1950s. In a letter to C. S. Lewis dated 14 November 1952, Norton referred to Pan as "the unfallen one who expresses Itself through" the "powers of Earth:" "geological activity," "animals, vegetation, [and] place intelligences" (Norton in Drury 1988, p. 76).[7] Her definition of Pan was closely aligned to her interpretations of Gnosticism and the Kabbalah in particular: she worshipped the god, "the Elemental," (Norton in Drury 1988, p. 76) who functioned as a "neutralising power" (Norton in Drury 1988, p. 79) juxtaposed to Adam Kadmon (the archetypal human; the body of God), "the fallen ... the one who expresses itself through the human race" (Norton in Drury 1988, p. 76). Norton articulated her system, beginning with Pan:

> A being whose state has been supreme delight and harmony, who has expressed nothing but goodwill – and knew of no other – and who had reached for still higher forms of manifestations ... Adam K. would have destroyed all his creation ... and any other under his influence, except for the neutralising power of Pan the Elemental. (Norton in Drury 1988, p. 79)

Norton and Greenlees' worship of Pan may have been partially influenced by Crowley, whose rituals to the god played a significant role in the workings in 1919. In *Magick* (1929 [1973]), Crowley included an elaborate hymn to the god prefaced by an excerpt from the Greek tragedy *Aias* by Sophocles (496-406 BC). Owen's work on Neuburg and Crowley's time in the desert references Crowley's *Confessions*, in which Crowley defines the god as "All devourer, all begetter" (1997, p. 130).

For Crowley, to understand Pan is to understand "Panic," and "to know "Panic" is to experience both ecstasy and terror at the hand of the god" (Owen 1997, p. 130). Owen goes on to write:

> Pan, representative of a pagan Greece that had special significance for Victorian homosexual men, and long associated in the Christian imagination with the devil, was a powerful signifier of the sexualized magic initiated by the two men. When Crowley and Neuburg speak of Pan, the imagery is redolent with heat and violence; a god, half man, half beast, who rapes and ravishes men and women alike. (Owen 1997, p. 130; cf. also Newman 2004, pp. 36-61).

In addition to Crowley's profound experiences of the god, and his narratives elucidating these, Fortune's work, particularly her 1936 novel *The Goat Foot God*, "did honour to Pan as the prime symbol of a paganism needed to heal the modern world" (Hutton 1999, p. 85). Here we detect an alternative comprehension of Pan in comparison to Crowley's experiences of the god; an understanding which, nevertheless, was of interest to Norton:

> Some occult theories hold the stars and planets to be the bodies of great beings and so do I. I think the God Pan is the spirit whose body – or such of it as can be seen in these four dimensions (the fourth being time) – is the planet Earth, and who, therefore, in a very real sense, is the ruler and god of this world. Perhaps that is why he was given the name 'Pan, which in Greek means 'All', for he is the totality of lives, elements and forms of being – organic, 'inorganic' and otherwise,

> comprising the planet as a whole: much as an animal body is a totality of myriads of cells, bacteria etc, in which ordered whole these live and function, having their own forms of "intelligence" and perception, according to type. *Such a body would be the "world" to any of its micro-organisms*, and the integrated consciousness of the body's owner would exist in another "world", and on a different plane from theirs. (Norton 1957, p. 15)

Norton's understanding of "different plane[s]" is highly relevant to an appreciation of the magical content of the letters she received from Goossens. Her practice of self-hypnosis as a means of artistic enlightenment (begun in *c.*1940) was the beginning of a process that indeed carried over into the realm of astral travel (mentioned by Goossens in several correspondences).

Her development of trance art techniques, partially inspired by the practices of the Surrealists, notably Salvador Dali and Yves Tanguy (cf. Drury 1994, p. 106), had a profound effect on her art and life. As means of example, the following is an extract from an account she wrote to psychologist L. J. Murphy in 1949:

> Eventually I decided to experiment in self-induced trance; the idea being to induce an abnormal state of consciousness and manifest the results, if any, in drawing. May aim was to delve down into the subconscious and, if possible, through and beyond it. **[A description of the trance process follows.]**

The drawings were quite different in form from previous ones, and full of symbols, many of which were previously unknown to my conscious mind ... prominent symbols being crescent, fish, ram-headed mask, cornucopia, swastika, 6-pointed star, triple sign, tower, etc.

Each of the drawings at this period were compositions having another significance not realised until much later, since they prophesied in symbolic form a future subjective experience for myself.

Numerous other things took place which I need not record here: my consciousness, however, was extremely exalted over the entire period–about five months in all. I seemed, while experiencing a great intensification of the intellectual, creative and intuitional faculties, to have become detached in a curiously timeless fashion from the world around me, and yet to be seeing things with a greater clarity and awareness than normally. I was working day and night, having very little sleep or rest, yet a supply of inexhaustible power seemed to flow through me. (Norton in Drury 1988, p. 30)

As the following passages from the same account reveal, the practice that enabled astral communication with higher beings involved more complex magic, of which Norton became an adept:

I had heard that it was possible to achieve transition to a different Realm of existence and live consciously the type of life that is generally experienced after physical death. **[There**

follows passages describing Norton's preparations for this event, her various experiences leading up to it, an early experience and finally an explication.]

I doubt if any impression of the actual initial experience could be conveyed in words, so I shall not attempt to describe it, beyond saying that there was a sensation of ecstasy, during which my entire being seemed to dissolve and disintegrate, then gradually re-form into a new whole. **[The description continues, and then Norton describes the physical sensations.]** Far from being devoid of sense enjoyments, a plasmic body of this type contains the very essence of sensuousness to a degree that renders the physical sensory organs utterly negligible by comparison. **[This is elaborated.]** 'There,' the body is completely a reflection of the mind, so that any type of pleasure, whether emotional or intellectual, engenders as part of itself a corresponding sensuous enjoyment. **[This is elaborated.]**

Contrary again to the usual idea of such states, sexual sensation still exists in an equivalently more advanced and intensified form.

I have been asked how a purely intellectual activity such as abstract thought could be attended by sensual enjoyment. It is, nevertheless, for instead of feeling interested one 'becomes' an embodiment of Interest itself. It is rather difficult to explain what I mean by this since a sense or state of Consciousness peculiar to the other realm is concerned. To begin with, 'thought' in those realms is very different from that which is normally understood by the word. There, 'thought' or rather the energy generated by such is felt as a tangible thing, a current of living force which assumes palpable or visual form. I had been told, earlier, that 'entities in the Plane assumed form at will'. This is literally true; one actually changes shape very frequently, since the new 'sense' referred to is that which could be described as 'being'. (Norton in Drury 1988, pp. 34-35)

Norton's descriptions of her psychic travel through inner and outer worlds or planes of consciousness are, as she noted, difficult to describe in written form. Her letter to Murphy, nevertheless, raises some key interpretations, particularly when juxtaposed to her artistic representations of these experiences.

Prior to meeting Goossens in 1952/1953, Norton (with Greenlees) was also a practitioner of sex magic. The work entitled *Witches' Sabbath*, included in Norton's 1949 exhibition at the Rowden-White Library at The University of Melbourne, exemplifies her experience with such rites – albeit in exaggerated form (the rituals did not include bestiality, for example). Here a demonic animal and witch embrace in an ecstatic moment of joyful lust while a crucified, naked nun (top left) and a sensuous, winking Virgin Mary (top right) look on. Police confiscated this picture, along with *Lucifer*, *Triumph* and *Individuation*, after two officers attended the exhibition in response to alleged complaints.

Norton explained to one of them, Detective John Olsen, that *Black Magic* (another name for *Witches' Sabbath*) "was a 'symbolistic' drawing: the female figure depicted was a witch, the panther personified the powers of darkness, and their embrace represented the initiation of the witch into the 'infernal mysteries.'" (Norton in Drury 1988, p. 40).

Despite the fact that Norton was charged under the Police Offences Act of 1928 and appeared before a court hearing while the remaining works were still being exhibited, she included a revised version of the work, re-entitled *Black Magic* (Plate I) in the 1952 publication, *The Art of Rosaleen Norton with Poems by Gavin Greenlees*. This confident decision may have been motivated by the fact that the court case was resolved in her favor. Such confidence, however, was misplaced, as the artistic collaboration between Norton and Greenlees was to cause another obscenity charge.[8]

In the book (p. 42), *Black Magic* was accompanied by one of Norton's poems, which elaborates on the theme of the piece and points to her erotic sacred rites; an excerpt follows:

> Light's Black Majesty: Midnight Sun: Lord of the wild and living stars:
> Soul of Magic and master of Death;
> Panther of Night … enfold me.
> Take me, dark Shining One; mingle my being with you,
> Prowl in my spirit with deep purring joy
> Live in me, giver of terror and ecstasy
> Touch me with tongues of black fire.

1. Black Magic

Through the practice of magical travel to alternate realms of existence Norton was able to encounter esoteric forces in a visceral sense, mingling her "being" with the entity encountered. Her experiences therefore differed from the standard Jungian interpretation of the Collective Unconscious that entailed an interpretation of other-wordly beings as "projected thought forms" (Drury 1994, p. 109); she believed that the deities and demons of these planes were real and could be contacted. In view of her statements concerning her earlier experiences of trance techniques, which inspired her art and supplied her with "inexhaustible power," the more highly developed practice of astral communication may be interpreted as enabling her to access a more exalted level of consciousness and creativity.

Norton's artwork remains the best expression of her experiences, as further demonstrated by the work entitled *At Home* (Plate 2) included in *The Art of Rosaleen Norton with Poems by Gavin Greenlees*. This piece combines a comfortably comic home setting with a figure depicting the artist experiencing a psychic visitation from a range of beings. The accompanying essay has the bracketed heading "From an episode by Rosaleen Norton." This may suggest that despite the many beings depicted, the work is a representation of an actual "episode." Yet the number of figures, combined with the text, establishes a playful ambiguity that suggests alternatively an artificial depiction of one or, more likely, many astral experiences. Nevertheless *At Home*, like many of Norton's artworks, if not possibly the majority, pays deference to her trances and astral travels. Here the beings are shown in the presence of a human figure (Norton) that sits semi-upright and alert as a witness

2. *At Home*

to the event(s). The text opens with a passage on Asmodeus who also features in the picture (top right-hand corner):

> Meet the Monk – alias Jannicot, alias Brother Hilarian, alias Frater Asmodeus – who, as Familiar Spirit-in-Chief is President and Master of Ceremonies. He wears the cowl and habit of a mediaeval monk, and his subtle, rather cryptic face generally shows traces of a lurking secret amusement. His feet are curious, for if you look closely, you will notice that they are actually neat, cloven hooves. Brother Jannicot also has other names known only to his most intimate friends; and it is believed that he is an extremely important Personage. Certainly he is to me since he manages most of my occult activities, supervises trances, escorts me into other planes of Being, and sometimes assists the Sphynx in selecting visions for me. (p. 74)

Asmodeus, the chief conveyor of Norton to her astral planes, referred to as Abaddon in The Apocalypse (ix.11), features in a narrative in the apocryphal Book of Tobias (iii.8) and is also mentioned in the Testament of Solomon. In *The Goetia: The Lesser Key of Solomon the King*, translated by S. L. MacGregor Mathers with an essay by Crowley, Asmodeus (called Asmoday or Asmodai) is the thirty-second spirit of the seventy-two listed:

> He is a Great King, Strong, and Powerful. He appeareth with Three Heads, whereof the first is like a Bull, the second like a Man, and the third like a Ram; he hath also the tail of a Serpent, and from his mouth issue Flames of Fire. His Feet are

webbed like those of a Goose. He sitteth upon an Infernal Dragon, and beareth in his hand a Lance with a Banner. (Mathers and Crowley 1904 [1980], p. 32)

In Mathers' *Sacred Magic of Abramelin the Mage* (Crowley had worked with this text for several years prior to his visit to Egypt in 1904, using it to attempt to summon his Holy Guardian Angel), Asmodee (Asmodeus) is described accordingly: "Some Rabbins say that Asmodeus was the child of incest of Tubal-Cain and his sister Naafrfah. Others say that he was the Demon of impurity." As Goossens' letters show, Asmodeus was to play a part in their rites.

Goossens had occult interests and possibly practical experience prior to meeting Norton and Greenless. Born in England to a musically gifted family, Goossens came to Australia in 1947 to become the first permanent conductor of the Sydney Symphony Orchestra and assume directorship of the Conservatorium. He wrote to Norton in response to the publication released in September 1952, which he had purchased at the Notanda Gallery; Norton subsequently invited him to tea. This suggests a meeting sometime late that year or during the following year.

In addition to being well-versed in occult writings, particularly those of Crowley, Goossens' circle of friends in England included composer and pianist Cyril Scott (1879-1970) and Philip Heseltine (1894-1930), composer, critic, and editor, better known as Peter Warlock.[9] Scott, described by one his teachers, Iwan Knorr, as "brilliant and revolutionary," (cited by Rowena Pearce) and by Goossens as the "father of British modern music," (Tame 1984, p. 264) was an occultist who published extensively on Theosophy, theology, philosophy, and various

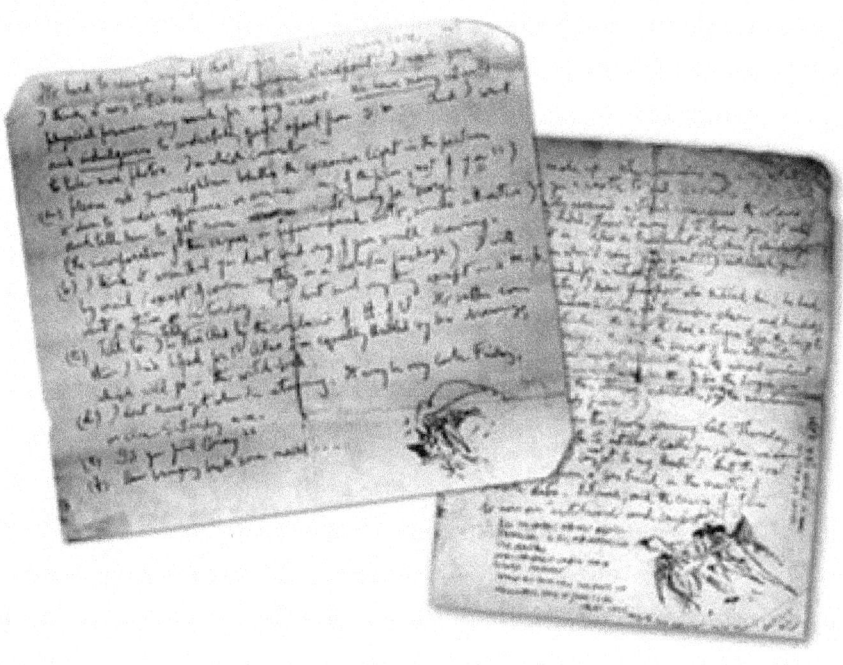

3. Examples of Goosens' Letters

other esoteric matters. The series of works known collectively as The Initiate Books, penned under a pseudonym, reveals Scott's active involvement with Theosophy, expressly the work of Blavatsky and her philosophy of the "Great White Brotherhood," an assembly of Himalayan masters who possessed the mystical powers to connect humans with the masters of the divine cosmic hierarchy.

Scott actively explored occultism, particularly the connection between esotericism, music, and literature although, unlike Heseltine and Goossens, he openly articulated his research and practices. In *Music: Its Secret Influence Throughout the Ages*,[10] Scott expounded his Theosophical beliefs in a discussion of the "two types of composers; those we may refer to as the inspired ones, in that they possess qualities which permit of their being used by the Higher Powers, as opposed to these, the uninspired ones, who, lacking such qualities, cannot be used as mediums" (1933 [1958], p. 28). In turn, it is not only the esoteric forces that inspire great works; great works inspire humanity and its spiritual awakening. As with Heseltine, the direct influences of Scott on Goossens in terms of occultism cannot be traced owing to the absence of direct communication between the men on the subject. Goossens' circle of close friends, which clearly included these men, nevertheless point to a friendship not only based on music and composition, but also on a shared personal philosophy despite its different manifestations.[11]

According to Goossens' younger sister, the celebrated harpist Dame Sidonie Goossens-Millar, her brother's interest in the occult can be dated from the time of his friendship with Heseltine (cf., Rosen 1993, p. 339 and also Smith). Goossens and Heseltine were close companions during their youth, and in his autobiography released in 1951 Goossens records a summer spent in the company of Heseltine in 1915:

> Sometimes Philip and I, on a decrepit motor-cycle, would explore together the neighbouring countryside for old parish churches and hostelries: the former to sketch, and the latter to sample the local Cotswold brew. Twice we encountered staid friends of mine on these trips ... Later we sustained a puncture opposite Marie Corelli's home during a tea-party on the lawn, which we were promptly invited to join – and did. The charming, rather eccentric authoress of *The Sorrows of Satan*, whom I had previously met professed little love for contemporary music or musicians. (Goossens 1951, pp. 111-12; cf. also Rosen 1993, p. 45)[12]

Extant letters from Goossens to Heseltine reveal an intense relationship of shared intimacies:

> I miss you muchly – on your return we must have many evenings at the Savoyard – or elsewhere. There's lots I really want to talk about – as you're quite the most 'understanding' person where I'm concerned. (Goossens to Heseltine, undated in Rosen 1993, p. 46)

Prior to the summer of 1915, Heseltine had become increasingly absorbed in occult matters. His meeting with musician and composer Frederick Delius (1862-1934) in 1911 was to prove significant in relation to this interest, as the latter was experienced in astrology and the casting of horoscopes and was a collaborator on *Anatomie et physiologie de l'orchestre*

(1894) with renowned French occultist Dr Gèrard Encausse (1865-1916), better known as 'Papus' (cf. Smith 1996, p. 117). This pamphlet placed the four instrumental groups into a Kabbalistic system thus: strings: God, the head, the nervous system; brass: man, the chest, arterial system; woodwinds: woman, the chest, the venous system; percussion: nature, the abdomen, the lymphatic system (cf. Jensen 1994). Although in later years Delius made light of his occultism, passing it off as the folly of youth, Heseltine's biographer writes: "It is more than likely that at some stage he would have discussed his opinions and experiences [on occultism] with the young and impressionable Philip" (Smith 1996, p. 118).

Heseltine's friendship with the unorthodox composer Bernard van Dieren (1887-1936), whom he met in 1916, has also been cited as having an influence on him. Of the latter, Heseltine's son, Nigel, wrote: "Of his own Satanism we know little except by inference and analogy. But we do know that he captured and held Philip" (Heseltine 1992, p. 81).[13] Yet Heseltine, by his son's own admission, already knew Crowley in London (c.1914):

> ... it was Aleister Crowley who had the most immediate effect and who no doubt (to quote Augustus John) 'held me by his glittering eye as any bore is apt to do,' arousing in Philip a curiosity for the history and practice of magic, which he pursued for several years, and which eventually destroyed him. (Heseltine 1992, p. 75).

Heseltine continued his study of the occult, meeting and striking up a friendship and literary partnership with Neuburg in 1922 after the latter had ended contact with Crowley.

The associations between the occult and music influenced Heseltine, as revealed in the following letter of 22 August 1918 to Colin Taylor (1881-1973):

> ... in my view individuals in artistic matters (as elsewhere) are but tools of certain tendencies and forces. One is given certain talents, certain forces in order that one may play a particular part in the general operations. ... One allies oneself with a certain force or direction and the more one effaces oneself, the more strongly can this force operate through one ... For years now I have been led by some power stronger than myself along strange paths or preparation for the work that has now clearly revealed itself to me. I have travelled in the dark, often ignorant of the end of my journey, often ignorant of the very fact that I was travelling at all. During the last few months the light has begun to break: I have had experiences which have brought me to the realization of things which seemed before incredible ... when we meet I shall tell you of experiences which will astonish you, which you will probably be unable to believe at first. ... It is not for no purpose that I have been drawn to the study of the things that lie beyond the confines of our narrow sensuous world: and I will tell you, in strict confidence, that I have already received very definite and detailed communications *concerning music* from sources which the ignorant and unheeding would call supernatural: and that

there is unlimited power behind these sources. (Smith 1996, p. 155).

In view of the fact that 1918 was the year in which Heseltine produced "the songs that made him,"[14] the letter to Taylor appears to be an acknowledgement of the power of occult practice in the production of great works.[15]

While Goossens' friendship with both men was more than likely influential on his own belief systems, Salter refers to an earlier fascination with the occult: "Even as a child, Goossens seems to have had an almost compulsive interest in pagan symbolism. Sidonie remembers the fixation emerging through young Eugene's talent for drawing: 'When he was 11 years old, he was doing etchings which were quite beautiful. Little caricatures and things. He always loved to draw pictures with gargoyles. He had a sort of mania about gargoyles.' "(Salter 1999, p. 17). As an adult his private reading on witchcraft and related matters were alleged to have disturbed his third wife, Marjorie (cf. Rosen 1993, p. 339). If one considers Goossens' musical output there is an additional indication of his fascination for and familiarity with the occult. According to the family biographer, these interests "had inspired the magical atmosphere he conjured up in the First Violin Sonata and *Don Juan de Mañara*; an extreme sensuality of sound expressed in constantly changing chromaticism and a shimmering orchestral palette." Rosen continues: "His was the world of *Faust* and *The Tempest*; his search was for the secret formula that would enable him to reconcile his Catholic conflict between desire and conscience and engender perfect harmony between body and mind." (Rosen 1993, pp. 239-40).

But it was *The Apocalypse*, Goossens' masterwork that best represents his attempts to combine the esoteric, the religious and the occult; it is his exploration of the musical coalescence of the sacred and the profane. Its world premier was at the Sydney Town Hall on 22 November 1954 after some eleven years of contemplation and writing. Based on The Revelation of St John the Divine, the concluding book of the New Testament, the opera chronicles the eschatological visions of the saint including the deliverance of the New Jerusalem. Rosen posits that the opera even popularised magic for a while: "Since the performances of *The Apocalypse*, interest in the occult had become far more widespread amongst the fashionable circles of Sydney's prominent citizens. A little indulgence in Pantheism with sexual overtones made a welcome contrast to barbecued ribs on the North Shore or cocktails in Katoomba." (1993, pp. 364-65).[16]

The Letters

There are eleven extant letters written by Goossens to Norton and Greenlees although one takes the form of instructions in the use of an unguent, which suggests it may have been included in one of the other letters or in a lost piece of correspondence; one is incomplete with only page three intact. Each of the letters extends to approximately two-and-a-half handwritten pages; they had been composed in Australia and overseas; seven open with a greeting to Norton; four either refer to and / or send greetings to Greenlees (one is actually a postcard from Lord Howe Island addressed to Greenlees);[17] three are signed with Goossens' magical name, "Djinn" (discussed below); five include references to caution and anonymity; six contain small sketches, two of which are sex magic images (cf. Plate 3 for reproductions of Letters I and II). The letters are not dated, although one has an intact envelope stamped 4 June 1953 with a Canberra postmark. Another includes a series of potential meeting times, which suggest four possible dates: March 1952 (too early), August 1953, May 1954 or January 1955. Each letter deals with magic and sex magic is expressly mentioned in all of them, with two particularly lengthy descriptions, which begin the following analysis.

In one letter Goossens describes an erotic magical experience with both Norton and Greenlees:

> … as promised, you came to me early this morning (about 1.45) and when a suddenly flapping window blind announced your arrival, I realised by a delicious orificial tingling that you were about to make your presence felt in a very real sense! Seriously you were very definitely here, and you were doubtless enjoyably aware of what took place. I was in the middle of a rite with A. and he had just asked for the "osculum infame" (which I was about to administer) when you took advantage of my position and administered it to me. A strange hoofed creature was in the room with us – upper and middle parts female, lower centaur, and a pretty crustacean creature with large milky breasts also appeared. I will draw it for you when I see you. All night I was in s.m. delight, and my offerings were, by results, more acceptable to the beings … More of this later.
>
> Your description of the triple s.m. rite (you, G. and me) was curious because I was aware of you both as female (G. always

comes to me as a female,) and I was fully present, also in changing form. **[Letter One]**

It is evident that Goossens believed in astral travel and it appears that he understood this occult experience in a similar way to Crowley, namely that astral travel "was conducted within … [one's] own mind" (Owen 1997, p. 106). Crowley had perfected astral travel and was in the process of instructing Neuburg in the practice during his sojourn in the desert. What Crowley had experience with, and so too it appears did Goossens, was a form of psychic travel akin to that studied by the Golden Dawn, namely accessing "Astral Light," "separate planes or orders of existence which interpenetrate the world of earthly perceptions." (Owen 1997, pp. 105-106).[18] Here we also detect the influence of Norton whose experiences (as described above) would have been discussed with Goossens.

Earlier in the letter Goossens refers to travelling to Norton via "aerial coven," which establishes an appropriate tone for the description of psychic or astral sex magic that follows. Goossens states that prior to the "arrival" of Norton he was preparing to perform the "osculum infame" (the obscene kiss) to "A." The abbreviation could refer to Asmodeus, named in full in another letter and discussed in some detail by Norton (as quoted previously). As the "Demon of impurity," Asmodeus is an appropriate guide to the realms involving sex magic rites. The "osculum infame" that Goossens was about to administer to "A." refers to the standard practice accused witches in the early modern European age were believed to perform on the devil, namely the kissing of his anus. Within the rites as practised by the trio, however, the act may well have been fellatio and cunnilingus. The reference to Norton's "arrival" and her performance of the same act on Goossens is indicative of the sex magic they shared. This may be comparable to Crowley's offering of himself to Pan (Neuburg): the submission of the self as the necessary ritual in order for an esoteric experience and subsequent enlightenment to manifest.

The reference to Norton's "description of the triple s.m. rite (you, G. and me)," clearly refers to the trio's shared participation in magical sex on the aforementioned alternate plane. Goossens notes that Norton's words were "curious" because he experienced both partners as "female." The theme of shared correspondence is a feature of the letters, and the exchange of ideas and events that occurred to each writer during the other's physical absence is common. In this context, Norton's description of a rite involving the three of them, in Goossens' physical absence, is indicative of an active communication about sex magic rites. Norton's non-extant correspondence, in view of Goossens' response, appears to have indicated she came to him in both male and female form (note his reference to "I was fully present, *also* in changing form" [my italics]). The mutability of both gender (male "becomes" female and female "becomes" male) and sexual roles (active becomes passive and vice-versa) is another feature of such rites as R. J. Stewart articulates:

> In magic the relationships or exchanges made are undeniably sexual; polarised energies are exchanged, entities react with one another. But they are not sexual in the commonly accepted illusionary sense of personal gratification, or of the basic breeding drive that perpetuates the species. Magical psychology does not limit sexuality to gender-oriented interaction; ultimately it emphasises the balanced androgyny

or total being reflected through mankind (Stewart in Hume 1997, p. 75).

Norton understood the sexual philosophies penned in Goossens' letter. She was aware of (what Stewart refers to as) "balanced androgyny" through her extensive readings of Jung in particular whose theories on Individuation she had represented in her artwork, including one of her best known pieces that bears the Jungian term as its title (cf. Plate 4). Drury writes of the work, *Individuation*, that it is "a work which was intended to demonstrate a universal mystical principle: the cosmic union of opposites. The title itself presents the key, for 'individuation' was Jung's term for psychic unity or inner wholeness" (Drury 1988, pp. 121, 124; cf. also Jung 1968). As Crowley interpreted the philosophy of the union of opposites, so did Norton, as this excerpt from one of her journals reveals:

> *Individuation* – The unified Self which contains all the opposites (such as the conscious and unconscious minds, masculinity and femininity, the animus and the anima etc.) in polarisation symbolised by the Hermaphrodite figure. Whenever the Hermaphrodite is shown it indicates polarisation (unity of opposites) and/or equilibrium. (Norton in Drury 1988, p. 124).

In another letter, written on an aeroplane, Goossens refers to "a pleasant unguent" that he procured from "one familiar with these things" in Paris "where they are by no means uncommon." The instructions on the use of the unguent is described on a single page and written in uppercase. It reads as follows:

4. Individuation

> USE HALF LEVEL TEASPOONFUL, MASSAGE CREAM INTO SKIN OVER WIDE AREA ON INNER FACE OF THE THIGH (BETWEEN CROTCH AND KNEE) OR ON ABDOMEN. USE ON UNWASHED SKIN. DON'T BATHE ANOINTED AREA ONE HOUR BEFORE OR THREE HOURS AFTER. DON'T USE DURING MENSTRUAL PERIOD. NO MAN MUST USE THIS UNGUENT. IT WOULD BE MORE THAN DANGEROUS. **[Space]**. DJINN. **[Space]**. BASE CREAM D'EGYPTE PREPARED BY ANNA (PARIS). **[Space]**. HERB OINTMENT – BLOOD BASE. **[Space]**. APPLY ONCE A DAY FOR 3, 4, OR 5 DAYS.

The purpose of the potion was to augment "mutual physical evocation," which suggests a rite with Goossens again *in absentia*, similar to the activity described in the correspondence above but with Norton and Greenlees simultaneously aware of the events.

This is followed by a passage on Crowley:

> Thanks ... also for retaining the A.C. writings. I re-read them again recently. So far, they merely touch on the future sequel of operations which culminate in what A used to term "il magico della s-x" (or what may be referred to as s.m.). His dual nature and build well equipped him to deal with its every manifestation ... consumingly, and with results – [In this connection in your last letter, I wanted you to mount this "favourite hobby horse" of yours still further (Dualism). It is also mine!] **[Letter Two]**

This description of Crowley and his "dual nature and build" in the context of his "il magico della s-x" continues the theme of gender and role fluidity. While the words here are somewhat coded, the meaning may be interpreted as Goossens' desire to be "mount[ed]" by Norton in a "s.m." rite in keeping with his understanding of the term "Dualism." Basically defined as "twofold," dualism seems to be associated by Goossens with the merging of male/female identities in the context of sex magic. Crowley interpreted dualism in the context of the "three main principles of the Universe: Dualism, Monism and Nihilism." (1929 [1973], Part III.O). The destruction of Dualism, right and wrong, good and evil, male and female, was the aim of high magic according to Crowley:

> Any idea that is thus in itself positive and negative, active and passive, male and female, is fit to exist above the Abyss; any idea not so equilibrated is below the Abyss, contains in itself an unmitigated duality or falsehood, and is to that extent qliphotic and dangerous. (1929 [1973], Part III.VIII.I)

On the term "qliphotic" Crowley writes: "Qliphoth generally suggest the vice characteristics of the Sephira" ([1912] 1973, p. 58). The word literally means "husk" or "empty shell."

Norton, in recorded psychological records penned by Murphy in 1949, discusses her bisexuality and fantasies of penetrating women. She also spoke of her encounters with male homosexuals: "These men are soft and rounded, and they let me do what I like with them" (Norton in Drury 1988, p. 47). Indeed, her understanding of sexual/gender fluidity is associated with her interpretation of the Jungian concept of Individuation.

Despite Norton's public reputation as a witch that has maligned her and cast her as the initiator and malevolent influence on Goossens in the material to-date, the letters occasionally reveal *his* role as the occult educator. This is best illustrated in a third piece of correspondence:

> Yes, I'll instruct you in the grimoire. The diagrams are necessarily crude but none the less effective, being all from unimpeachable sources. You will be my best – and only – pupil, and I shall appoint you keeper of the seals. (You nearly / really **[?]** hit the nail on the head in your bit about A.C. and self in letter).
>
> Unfortunately, I didn't bring the book, but shall bring it next week for lesson one. **[Letter Three]**

The composition of a grimoire, a handbook of magic, has an ancient tradition as illustrated by the Greco-Roman material collectively known as the *Greek Magical Papyri* discovered in Egypt in the Nineteenth Century and covering a history of beliefs and practices dating from the First Century BCE to the Fifth Century CE. Such manuscript traditions were continued during the Early Modern and Renaissance ages. The co-production of the aforementioned *Goetia: The Lesser Key of Solomon the King* by Mathers and Crowley in 1904, attributed by them to the legendary ruler, exemplifies the extension of the tradition into the Twentieth Century. Goossens' reference to the "grimoire" appears to define it as a personal record of the practices that he devised from his own studies (note the somewhat self-deprecating line: "[t]he diagrams are necessarily crude." The reference to "A.C." (Crowley) that immediately follows the discussion of the grimoire points to him being one of Goossens' "unimpeachable sources."

In the first letter quoted, there is also attention paid to the creative output of the three practitioners:

> Tell G I'm thrilled by the conclusion of the H. of U. It's better than I had hoped for!! Also I'm equally thrilled by his drawings, which will go in the witch book. **[Letter One]**

This alludes to the planned opera, *The Fall of the House of Usher*, based on the short story by Edgar Allan Poe: Goossens would write the musical score and Greenless the libretto, while Norton would provide the artistic design. It appears that the sex magic had paid off.[19] On this theme, one is reminded of Crowley's mantra (previously quoted) that points to one of the prime reasons for such practice, namely the attainment of imaginative, indeed artistic, epiphany that would lead to the production of master works of illumination. As Urban (2003) writes: "Sex magic, particularly in its transgressive, non-reproductive forms, can thus unleash the supreme creative power: the power to create not an ordinary fetus, but a magical child of messianic potential" (p. 166). It was most probably with this aim in mind that Goossens, a conductor and composer, Norton, an artist, and Greenlees, a poet, combined their magical forces to enhance their creative ones.

The use of magical names is consistent throughout the letters. Goossens' magical name, Djinn, has a long history in mysticism, theology and magic and features predominantly in the Koran. The *djinni* were created from the flame of a smokeless fire (Koran 15:27), and it was believed they could be summoned by an Arab magician (*muqqrribun*) to attain knowledge and acquire power. According to the Islamic scholar Ibn Taimiyah (b.1263 CE), the *djinni* also possessed humans, notably those inclined to be wrongdoers, those who indulge in lust, and interestingly, musicians (cf. al-Ashqar). In Arab myth they were also associated with inspiring artistic powers, again through possession or madness. Crowley also mentions the *djinni* and refers to them as beings an adept magician is able to summon and as forces able to copulate with humans, which aligns them to incubi, vampires, and similar sexual entities.

Magical practices performed by Goossens independently of Norton and Greenless are also noted, including a reference to his experiment with Crowley's Cakes of Light:

> I LEFT THE SECONDHAND COPY OF THE "G.B." PROPPED AGAINST YOUR DOOR, AND HOPE YOU FOUND IT SAFELY THERE ON YOUR RETURN. I FOUND IT AT THE OFFICE AFTER LEAVING YOU THE OTHER DAY; HAVE SINCE READ IT AND CONFIRMS ALL I KNEW OF A.C. THOUGH EXAGGERATES CERTAIN THINGS OVERMUCH. I EXPERIMENTED ON ONE OF THE CAKES OF LIGHT (PG 64) (NOT SUCCESSFULLY) HOPE YOU WILL HAVE BETTER LUCK WITH THE UNGUENT ... **[Letter Four]**

This excerpt is revealing on a number of levels, especially Goossens' reference to the book confirming all he knew of Crowley, suggesting that at some time in his pre-Australian life he had either got to know the man or, as discussed above, associated with those who did. The book referred to may be John Symonds' biography of Crowley, *The Great Beast: The Life of Aleister Crowley*, which was released in 1951.

The Cakes of Light were a delicacy of Crowley's, and a recipe was included in *Liber Al vel Legis*:

> 24 For perfume mix meal & honey & thick leavings of red wine: then oil of Abramelin and olive oil, and afterward soften & smooth down with rich fresh blood.
>
> 25 The best blood is of the moon, monthly: then the fresh blood of a child, or dropping from the host of heaven: then of enemies; then of the priest or of the worshippers: last of some beast, no matter what.
>
> 26 This burn: of this make cakes & eat unto me. This hath also another use; let it be laid before me, and kept thick with perfumes of your orison: it shall become full of beetles as it were and creeping things sacred unto me. (III)

Crowley intended the cakes to be used in the "Mass of the Phoenix ... mixed with the blood of the Magus" (1929 [1973], Part III.XX.I). The Cake or Eucharist, consumed daily, enabled a magus to replace matter with spirit, the human with the divine, thereby becoming capable of any task. As the letter indicates, it is uncertain in what context Goossens used the formula, except that the process was unsuccessful.

Goossens composes his supersensual experiences within the clear, unadulterated vocabulary of reason and realism. The accounts of sex magic within the realms of astral planes are juxtaposed to everyday observations, updates on Goossens' travels, and requests for updates from Norton, such as the enquiry concerning her cat, Gray, who apparently went missing **[Letter One]**. Amid these commonplace snippets are some fascinating pieces of information, which conclude this analysis.

Goossens reveals his contact with Heseltine in one brief note, clearly in response to an inquiry by Norton:

> Yes I knew P.H. in both phases:- remind me to tell you about our doings together! **[Letter Five]**

The reference to "both phases" may indicate his friendship with Philip Heseltine *and* Peter Warlock, while the allusion to "our doings together!" suggests several possibilities: their time in the summer of 1905, a same-sex relationship, and / or the practice of magic together. As lovers of music, particularly the classical repertoire as the reference to "P.H." indicates, Norton and Greenless had yet another passion to share with the conductor and composer. Goossens in fact, as several letters show, invited them to dress rehearsals and performances and Norton "was often to be seen on guest tickets at his concerts in the Town Hall." (Rosen 1993, p. 341).

Goossens also reveals the extent of the friendship with the pair, which involved the exchange of family histories and anecdotes. For example, Goossens refers to the family nickname for him, Zenny (Rosen 1993, p.

119), which in reference to Norton's slight lisp in its pronunciation, entices him:

> I see your argument about changing over from Djinn, but anonymity is still best served by sticking to it ... than the more familiar family name. Yet let it serve you in our private speech, if you will, but never in written. It would sound wonderful from your little tongue – the hiss of the Z would be intoxicatingly perverse. **[Letter Six]**

He writes of his acquaintance with Yusapov, the Russian noble who killed Rasputin **[Letter Seven]**, his love of castles **[Letter Seven]** and his delight in Norton's gift of the infamous *Black Magic* painting **[Letter Five]**.

It seems superfluous to note that the activities of Goossens, Norton, and Greenlees were decidedly against the normative sexual practices and values of Australia during the 1950s, a reality not lost on Goossens:

> And how I agree with you about all that normality "pap"! Let's "piss it out" of existence (as A.C. used to say). It would be intolerable if the conventional set-up of "social sex" fastened even a shadow on our transpirings – of all kinds!! **[Letter Seven]**

Despite this defiant tone, Goossens consistently pleads that all the correspondence be destroyed. Homosexuality or more specifically sodomy was illegal[20] and the 1950s saw "the sharp increase in the number of people charged and convicted for what was officially labelled unnatural offences" (Willett 2000, p. 10). This increase was a result of the intensification of policing ordained at "the highest level" (Willett 2000, p. 10). The New South Wales Commissioner of Police at the time of Goossens' apprehension at Mascot Airport, C. J. Delaney, was a committed campaigner against homosexuality, "calling it in 1958 'the greatest social menace' facing Australia" (Willett 2000, p. 10). Delaney's rhetoric is in keeping with that "directed against homosexuality during the Cold War" that connected it with "disease, decadence or security risk" (Murphy 2000, p. 62). While gays and lesbians were obviously a presence during the 1950s, they were an invisible and silent one, represented in the meagre media coverage usually in the context of court cases concerning sexual misconduct. In this environment the sexual relations between Goossens and Greenlees, which a more sophisticated reading would reject as equating to homosexuality, were against the male hegemony that characterised Australian society, culture, and sexual mores at this time.

Bisexuality was, like sex magic, unfamiliar to the average Australian. Indeed the very concept of sex magic was almost unheard of, and when Norton was covered in the newspapers of the day, her beliefs and art were not only regarded as Satanic but also perverted and pornographic. Norton's individuality and personal independence – let alone her sexuality – were also at odds with the traditional female role that was essentially confined to the idealized image of the homemaker or the "career" nurturer such as teacher or nurse. The expression of female sexuality was not absent or necessarily repressed in the 1950s, but it was predominantly confined to marriage and marriage that was preferably sanctioned by the Christian Church. As John Murphy has recorded, approximately nine out of ten Australians identified themselves as Christian in the census of 1954 and that for "a growing number of Australians, particularly women, religion continued to provide a frame of moral reference in the 1950s" (2000 pp. 64-65). In this context, Norton, an artist, bohemian, divorcee and witch who lived intermittently with a male who was, for all intents and purposes, identified as homosexual, was the antithesis of the widely held stereotypical image of "woman." Such an image of Norton was consistent in the multifarious reports on her in the print media as summarised in the memoirs of crime reporter Bill Jenkings (1992):

> I'd encountered her on many occasions and I reckoned she was on the lowest rung of humanity. She was the epitome of depravity, but she must have had some sort of diabolical charm, because she had a large circle of devoted worshippers around her. Norton was a self-styled high priestess of black magic, who led a coven of witches and warlocks in the bohemian Kings Cross area. She exuded evil – I used to feel like sprinkling holy water whenever I was in her presence. (pp 221-22)

Jenkings was at the airport the day Goossens was arrested (his memoirs also detail this event), and while his words may strike the modern reader as hyperbolic, they do encapsulate the media's representation of Norton during the late 1940s and 1950s. One is here reminded of the similar reception of Crowley, particularly in the English press, the most infamous description of him as "the wickedest man in the world," as described in London's *John Bull* magazine on 24 March 1923.

Goossens' letters to Norton and Greenlees speak of sex magic but of many other things besides. Contained herein is a documented friendship between three practitioners that broke social and class barriers not only in the pursuit of sex magic but of the achievements it promised. Goossens came to Australia as a prominent musician and composer with a world reputation. He also came as an experienced occultist who found in Norton and Greenlees a partnership of equals, two individuals who could match his knowledge and were prepared to explore the possibilities of artistic genius. The rituals never reached the ultimate aims the practitioners sought; potential rites were unrealised and *The Fall of the House of Usher* remained unfinished. After Goossens' public humiliation in 1956 and his subsequent return to England, the letters stopped.[21]

Notes

1   Copies of the letters came into my possession through contact with filmmaker Geoff Burton in 2003. Burton obtained copies from Trevenar during a series of interviews with him for the documentary entitled *Fall of the House*. As the letters are now in the public domain and the incorporation herein is selective, the use of them is regarded as fair dealing. For the sake of convenience, the letters quoted have been artificially numbered for easier cross-referencing.

2   *Rosaleen – The Wicked Witch of the Cross* (unpublished script) was performed at the Tom Mann Theatre in Sydney and directed by Roddie Thomas. *Complicity* debuted at Sydney's Marian Street Theatre. *The Witch of Kings Cross* (unpublished script by the ensemble cast) premiered at The Hangar, The University of Newcastle (Ourimbah Campus, New South Wales). *The Devil is a Woman* (unpublished script) premiered on 1 November 2003 at the Aussie Rules Club, Kings Cross. The venues for the plays are informative as they represent the small, select interest in Norton; the Tom Mann Theatre in the inner-city suburb of Surry Hills caters for amateur and professional groups

and regularly showcases non-traditional, non-mainstream productions; Marian Street Theatre, on Sydney's North Shore, was a small operation with its performance space in a community hall (it ceased trading in 2001); The Hangar, a student performance space at the small campus of Ourimbah (Central Coast, New South Wales) was a run-down building, off-campus, along a quiet street;* the Aussie Rules Club, Kings Cross is a somewhat rough-and-tumble club, with a performance space upstairs for the culture-vultures of inner-Sydney, while downstairs club members play the 'pokies' and watch sport on cable television.

* I was honoured to be a member of the group that wrote, staged and performed *The Witch of Kings Cross* at The Hangar in 2003. The venue, then the only performance space for drama students at this small campus, a satellite of The University of Newcastle, was closed several years ago owing to its state of ill-repair. The production was staged for three nights and had full-capacity crowds in its small space (seating roughly 60 people) - a triumph considering the cold winter nights and the demography of the region (albeit most of the attendees were connected to the university in some capacity).

3 Burton's film was first screened at the Sydney Film Festival on Sunday 20 June 2004. The ABC (Australian Broadcasting Commission) documentary "Sir Eugene Goossens: Sex, Magic and the Maestro" aired on Sunday 5 September 2004 on *Rewind*.

4 Pamela Main, Goossens' companion in later years and the beneficiary of a will he wrote 11 days before his death, threatened legal action. No official proceedings eventuated.

5 Prior to the work of Aleister Crowley, Paschal Beverly Randolf (also spelt "Randolph") (1825-1875) developed and practised a form of sex magic (cf. Deveney 1996). In addition to Randolf, Karl Kellner (originator) and Karl Theodor Reuss (founder) of the *Ordo Templi Orientis* (O.T.O) organized initiations (the seventh, eighth and ninth degrees), based on sex magic.

6 Cf. Drury (1988, pp. 136-37) and Richmond (2000, p. 2). Drury concludes: "Rosaleen's main occult sources, books one could actually *use*, were the occult manuals prepared by writers like Dion Fortune and Aleister Crowley" (p. 137).

7   Interestingly, Drury has claimed: "As far as we know, Rosaleen received no reply to her letter" (p. 80). There was, in fact, a reply, which as been preserved in a private collection. Lewis' reply is rather short, distanced and clearly intended to curb any further correspondence Norton may have been contemplating.

8   As a result of the book, Wally Glover was charged with producing an obscene publication and appeared at Central Court on 25 November 1952. The prosecutor Mr D. J. Vine-Hall singled out *Black Magic*, *Esoteric Study* and *Individuation* as particularly offensive. Glover was found guilty and fined £5 plus costs. Two works from the book, *Fohat* and *The Adversary*, were blacked out in remaining copies; for related details on the Post Office and Customs ban, cf. Drury (1988) and Coleman (1962, pp. 58-59). In September 1955 *Black Magic* was exhibited at the Kashmir Cafe, Macleay Street, Potts Point. The manager of the establishment, David Goodman, was charged with "a breach of the Obscene and Indecent Publications Act" and in the ensuing court case, Mr Dash SM described *Black Magic*, *Beelzebub* and *Belphagor* thus: "I deem that all three pictures emphasise matters of sex unduly and as tending to corrupt the morals of unsophisticated members of the general public, and, in consequence, they are obscene." *Black Magic* was further described by Dash as "lewd, lustful and erotic." (Anonymous 1955, p. 45). Goodman was found guilty and fined £5 plus costs (cf. also Drury 1994).

9   In November 1916, Heseltine published an article on Goossens' chamber music in *The Music Student*, which marked the first usage of Heseltine's pseudonym, Philip Warlock. Heseltine wrote to Goossens explaining that "for very important reasons" he had to conceal his identity from the editor of the journal, Walter Wilson Cobbett (cf. Smith 1996, p. 103). While it is unwise to accredit too much significance to what may be a coincidence, this nevertheless may point to a mutual understanding and sharing of occult beliefs that had developed during the previous summer.

10 Cf. also, Scott (1969) where he discusses his friendship with Percy Grainger (1882-1960), also a friend of Goossens. Grainger was a virtuoso pianist and innovative composer as well as a sexual adventurer (cf. Bird 1976). He and his wife Ella were among

11   One of the positive results of Goossens' return to England was his renewed closeness with Scott. When Goossens died, Rosen (1993, p. 387) reports that Scott telephoned his sister Sidonie and offered the following condolences: "'It's all right. Eugene's with Percy Grainger on the other side and they've already formed their own orchestra!'"

12   This summer of 1915 was not in its entirety as idyllic as Goossens recalls; cf. Smith 71-73. Novelist Jean Rhys (1890-1979) recorded the holiday in her short story 'Till September Petronella;' cf. Rhys 1960 [1987].

13   It is noteworthy that Nigel Heseltine equates magic with Satanism and his intense dislike for the occult is evident throughout this account of his father's life.

14   Taylor (cited in Smith 1996, p. 154). Taylor, Heseltine's piano teacher at Eton, remained a mentor and friend throughout his life.

15   Smith (1996, p. 154) also suggests the influence of the medium Hester Dowden at this time.

16   Rosen's reference to the North Shore is to the Goossens' residence at Wahroonga, a most well-appointed locale, and to Goossens' "getaway" in Katoomba in the Blue Mountains some 100 km N-W of Sydney. Goossens refers to his cottage in Mount Victoria in the Blue Mountains in Letter 3 and provides Norton with directions for getting there, writing: "Obviously a pied-à-terre is necessary, hidden and private …"

17   Lord Howe Island, off Australia's east coast, is the closest island resort to Sydney.

18   Cf. Crowley, *Magick* Part III.XVIII. Fortune's system was also in keeping with Crowley's; cf. Fortune (1935, pp. 180-81).

19   As noted by Rosen (1993, p. 341), there were sketches for *The House of Usher* found among Goossens' papers after his death, but these were for a ballet not an opera.

20   Australia had inherited its sodomy laws from the United Kingdom through colonization. During the Nineteenth Century, these laws were

Goossens' few supporters during the crisis of 1956 (cf. Rosen 1993, p. 361).

maintained in the criminal codes of colonial parliaments, and by the state parliaments in the post-Federation era. In response to the Wolfden Report in Britain (1957) that initiated change to the Sexual Offences Act (1967), the Dunstan government of South Australia introduced its "consenting adults in private" defence in 1972 and repealed the state's sodomy law in 1975. Between 1976 and 1990, with the exception of Tasmania, the other states and territories repealed the sodomy law. Tasmania did so in 1997.

21 I am grateful to Inez Baranay for permission to access her files held at the National Library of Australia; Geoff Burton for his generous attitude towards the sharing of information; Graham Stone for the collection of material from the late Jock McKenna; Timothy Daly for providing me with a copy of *Complicity*; a private collector for allowing me to use his extensive material on Norton; Colin Rosewell for formatting the visual material from the letters; Nevill Drury for comments on the paper and to the anonymous referee for insightful comments and suggestions.

Copies of the letters herein have been altered digitally in order for a clearer representation of the artwork without interfering with the integrity of the originals.

Norton's artwork is the copyright of the Glover Estate.

References

al-Ashqar, Umar S. 2003, *The World of the Jinn and the Devils in the Light of the Qur'an and Sunnah*, trans. Jamaal al-Din M. Zarabozo, International Islamic Publishing House, New Delhi.

Anonymous. 1955, "Art in Cafe 'Lewd'," *Truth*, December 4.

Baranay, Inez. 1990, *Pagan*, Collins/Angus & Robertson, Australia.

Bird, John. 1976, *Percy Grainger*, Paul Elek, London.

Coleman, Peter. 1962, *Obscenity, Blasphemy, Sedition: Censorship in Australia*, The Jacaranda Press, Brisbane.

Crowley, Aleister. 1911 [1972], *The Vision and the Voice*, Sangreal Foundation, Dallas.

_____. 1912 [1977], *777 and Other Qabalistic Writings of Aleister Crowley* Weiser Books, York Beach, Maine.

_____. 1913, *The Book of Lies*, [On-line], http://www.sacred-texts.com/oto/lib333.htm.

_____. 1929 [1969], *The Confessions of Aleister Crowley: An Autohagiography*, ed. John Symonds and Kenneth Grant, Hill and Wang, New York.

_____. 1929 [1973], *Magick*, ed., annotated, and introduced by John Symonds and Kenneth Grant, Routledge & Kegan Paul, London.

_____. 1936 [1997], *Liber Al vel Legis*, Weiser, York Beach, Maine.

Deveney, John Patrick. 1996, *Paschal Beverly Randolf: A Nineteenth-Century Black American Spiritualist, Rosicrucian, and Sex Magician*, intro. Franklin Rosemont, State University of New York Press, New York.

Drury, Nevill. 1982, "Introduction to the Second Edition," *The Art of Rosaleen Norton with Poems by Gavin Greenlees*, 2nd ed., Walter Glover, Sydney.

_____. 1988, *Pan's Daughter: The Strange World of Rosaleen Norton*, Collins Australia, Sydney.

_____. 1994, *Echoes from the Void: Writings on Magic, Visionary Art and the New Consciousness*, Prism Press, Dorset.

_____. 2002, *The Witch of Kings Cross*, Kingsclear Books, Sydney.

Fall of the House [Video] 2004, Kurrajon Films, Australia.

Fortune, Dion. 1935 [1987], *The Mystical Qabalah*, Aquarian Press, Northamptonshire, UK.

_____. 1936, *The Goat Foot God*, Aquarian, London.

_____. 1935 [1987], *The Mystical Qabalah*, Aquarian Press, Northamptonshire, UK.

Glover, Walter. 1952, "Introduction to the First Edition," *The Art of Rosaleen Norton with Poems by Gavin Greenlees*, Walter Glover, Sydney.

Goossens, Eugene. 1951, *Overture and Beginners: A Musical Autobiography*, Methuen & Co., London.

Heseltine, Nigel. 1992, *Capriol for Mother: A Memoir of Philip Heseltine (Peter Warlock)*, Thames Publishing, London.

Hume, Lynne. 1997, *Witchcraft and Paganism in Australia*, Melbourne University Press, Melbourne.

Hutton, Ronald. 1999, *The Triumph of the Moon: A History of Modern Pagan Witchcraft*, Oxford University Press, Oxford.

Jenkings, Bill. 1992, *As Crime Goes By ... The Life and Times of "Bondi" Bill Jenkings*, Ironbark Press, Randwick.

Jensen, Eric Frederick. 1994, "Sounds as Symbol: fin de siècle perceptions of the orchestra," *The Music Review*, W. Heffer, Cambridge, 55, 227-40.

Jung, Carl, 1968. *Alchemical Studies*, trans. R. F. C. Hull, Routledge & Kegan Paul, London.

Kaczynski, Richard. 2002, *Perdurabo: The Life of Aleister Crowley*, New Falcon Publications, Arizona.

Levi, Eliphas. 1910 [1995], *Transcendental Magic: It's Doctrine and Ritual*, trans. Arthur Edward Waite, Senate, Middlesex.

Mathers, S. L. MacGregor. 1898, *Sacred Magic of Abramelin the Mage*, available at http://www.esotericarchives.com/abramelin/abramelin.htm.

Murphy, John. 2000, *Imagining the Fifties: Private Sentiment and Political Culture in Menzies' Australia*, Pluto Press, Sydney.

Newman, Paul. 2004, *Aleister Crowley and the Cult of Pan*, Greenwich Exchange, London.

Norton, Rosaleen. 1957, "Witch Was No Class At School," *Australasian Post*, 24 January 15.

Owen, Alex. 1997, "The Sorcerer and His Apprentice: Aleister Crowley and the Magical Exploration of Edwardian Subjectivity," *Journal of British Studies*, vol. 36, no. 1, pp. 99-133.

"Papers of Inez Baranay," National Library of Australia, MS 8269, Series One.

Rowena Pearce, 'Cyril Scott', available at http://www.lib.unimelb.edu.au/collections/grainger/percy/cyril.html.

Rhys, Jean. 1960 [1987], *The Collected Short Stories*, intro. Diana Athill, W. W. Norton, New York.

Richmond, Keith. 2000, *The Occult Visions of Rosaleen Norton*, The Oceania Lodge of the *Ordo Templi Orientis* and the Kings Cross Arts Guild, Sydney.

Rosen, Carole. 1993, *The Goossens: A Musical Century*, Andre Deutsch, London.

Salter, David. 1999, "The Strange Case of Sir Eugene and the Witch," *The Sydney Morning Herald* ("Good Weekend") July 3, 16-21.

Scott, Cyril. 1920, *The Initiate, Some Impressions of a Great Soul*, Routledge, London.

_____. 1927, *The Initiate in the New World*, Routledge, London.

_____. 1932, *The Initiate in the Dark Cycle*, Routledge, London.

_____. 1933 [1958], *Music: Its Secret Influence Throughout the Ages*, The Aquarian Press, Northamptonshire, UK.

_____. 1969, *Bone of Contention: Life Story and Confessions*, Arco Publishing, New York.

Smith, Barry. 1996, *Peter Warlock: The Life of Philip Heseltine*, Clarendon Press, Oxford.

Sutin, Lawrence. 2000, *Do What Thou Wilt: A Life of Aleister Crowley*, St. Martin's, New York.

Symonds, John. 1951, *The Great Beast: The Life of Aleister Crowley*, Rider, London.

Tame, David. 1984, *The Secret Power of Music*, Destiny Books, Rochester.

The Goetia: The Lesser Key of Solomon the King. 1904 [1980], S. L. MacGregor Mathers, trans., with an Introduction by Aleister Crowley, The Aquarian Press, UK.

Urban, Hugh, 2003, "Unleashing the Beast: Aleister Crowley Tantra and Sex Magic in Late Victorian England," *Esoterica: The Journal of Esoteric Studies*, 5, 138-192.

Willett, Graham, 2000, *Living Out Loud: A History of Gay and Lesbian Activism in Australia*, Allen & Unwin, Melbourne.

Reviews

Andy Roberts, *Albion Dreaming: a popular history of LSD in Britain*, London, Marshall Cavendish, 2008, Hardback, 266pp, index, bibliography, illustrated, photographs. UK £18.99

Rather like Robert Conner's book reviewed elsewhere in this issue of *JSM*, this is a volume that would be unlikely to ever emerge from a British University due to the highly contentious subject matter. The author, Andy Roberts, is a well-known writer on various aspects of paranormal and otherwise "Fortean" matters—indeed he is a columnist for the *Fortean Times* in addition to being a more mainstream journalist—and, although not a tenured academic, he has here produced a work that is as brave as it is well-researched.

This book offers the many fruits of much stringent research, using diverse sources: mining the complexities of governmental archives to unearth arcane internal memos, trawling legal case transcripts, poring over tabloid newspaper sources, and conducting interviews with major players in the history of this much-disputed substance. The interviews were with those who would actually talk, at least, since some are now either in positions of power or respectability from which they would wish to distance themselves from a supposed disreputable past, or in the cases of some of the medical and military researchers, they have to maintain their silence in adherence to the *Official Secrets Act*. Faced with this awkward and annoying evidential void in places, Roberts has done well to fill in the gaps to produce a coherent and compelling narrative.

It would have been easy to produce a "take-the-money-and-run" slapdash historical overview of the impact of LSD in Britain, and such a work would doubtless have sold well in some circles. What Roberts has instead done is to expend considerable energies (and much time) trailing back the convoluted intertwined threads of research into a story that is far more complex than most readers would suspect. These cover the early psychotherapeutic uses of the drug in Britain, the lengthy (and ultimately abortive) attempts to find a military/battlefield use for the drug, the counter-culture explorations of the internal universes which were made accessible through this substance, the legal-political landscape in which all of these events unfolded, and much more. The voices of psychonauts, medics, lawyers, philosophers, politicians, clinical patients and the unwitting "guinea pigs" used in military experiments are all made audible and coherent here in a very well-balanced work. That a reputable publisher has taken up the book underlines the value of Roberts' contribution to modern British cultural history here and the understanding of the use of entheogenic substances.

Each chapter is usefully organised in a vaguely linear timeframe, and the chapters are split by subject. Thus we have a fascinating overview of the discovery of the drug (coincidentally the book emerged at almost the same time as Professor Hofmann, the creator of LSD, died aged over 100), the medical experiments and hope that LSD could be a magic bullet for treating mental illnesses, the military experiments, the counter-cultural uses, the criminal trials, and the current situation of research scientists and *ad-hoc* users (or perhaps we should call them freelance researchers…).

Albion Dreaming is not a pro-acid evangelical book; in fact, there is much content herein to dissuade many folk from experimenting with the drug, but it is certainly a pro-scholarship and a pro-understanding book, for which this reviewer offers enthusiastic applause. Roberts appears to have written a very sane and rational book about a contentious subject that is prone to evoke quite opposite reactions in mixed and supposedly intelligent company. It comes highly recommended to anyone interested in modern British history and is of significant value in conveying a broader picture of the free festival and counter-culture movement of the early 1970s (and onwards) from which a great deal of the "Green" ecology movement sprang, as well as a wide swathe of modern paganisms. Thus, it would be of great interest to many *JSM* readers. The use of drugs to approach religious states is covered well (the reader is also referred to the review of Andrew Letcher's *Shroom* in *JSM4*, another book that deals with some of the same green and pagan issues with regards to hallucinogenic mushroom use in culture).

Overall, Roberts offers a book that stands as a striking and powerful exemplar for independent scholarship being an important facet of academic study; it is a significant, informative, and thought-provoking summation of stringent research. [Dave Evans]

Greenwood, S. 2005. *The Nature of Magic: An Anthropology of Consciousness.* **Berg Publishers, Oxford, paperback, 288 pp., ISBN-10: 1845200950, $US36.95.**

In this, her second book, Susan Greenwood extends her earlier doctoral work (*Magic, Witchcraft and the Otherworld: An Anthropology*, Berg 2000) examining gender and identity issues in contemporary Western magical communities (see also e.g. Greenwood 1998, 2000), to offer a cognitive anthropological approach to "nature religion" and the concept of "magical consciousness," focusing on contemporary paganisms in Britain. In order to resolve some of the issues raised by scholarship on the topics of "magic," "consciousness," "nature/culture" and "nature religion," Greenwood tackles an impressive array of thinkers (concentrating on Gregory Bateson and David Abram), engaging with such issues as phenomenology, animism, shamanism and deep ecology – and of course the nature of magic and consciousness.

Greenwood suggests nature religion, of which magical consciousness is an essential part, "comprises a number of spiritual ontologies, all of which have different conceptions of nature, but most share the view that there is an interconnected and sacred universe…[t]his universe is usually viewed primarily in animistic terms" (p.ix). She indicates that the spectrum of magical consciousness is broad, encompassing her own life-threatening exposure to the elements on a Welsh mountain and one practitioner's experience of recognising plants as other-than-human-persons while walking in a vegetable garden. Greenwood expresses magical consciousness itself in terms of participation, consciousness expansion, and human cognitive consistencies: magical consciousness is "a participatory and expanded concept of consciousness awareness…an aspect of consciousness, a part of nature; it is natural rather than supernatural, and participatory rather than individual" (p.viii)…"[it is] a heightened awareness of an expanded connected wholeness" (p.47) – "common to all humans" (p.4).

Embedding her theory in context, Greenwood examines a number of contemporary pagan practices involving engagements with nature, principally of the shamanic and/or animist kind. Key informants include the environmental educator and shaman Gordon "the Toad" MacLellan and the Romany "chovihano" Patrick "Jasper" Lee. Studies on paganisms to date have increasingly adopted an experiential, participatory and in some cases "insider" approach, and Greenwood's methodology offers a number of autoethnographic fragments, such as shamanic "journeying" with her university students and her (aforementioned) isolated experience on a Welsh mountain during an all night shamanic vigil that was clearly deeply significant for her, spiritually, and for the unfolding of this volume.

Greenwood offers an approach to magical consciousness and nature religion rather than discrete definitions, and this seems fitting given the slippery matter of magic and consciousness and the diversity of nature religions. A case for the crucial roles of participation and animism in magical consciousness is well argued, applying not only to Modern Western Pagans (e.g. Gordon the Toad), but also to non-Western indigenes (e.g. the Cree, also discussed). Such commonality across cultures supports the idea that some pagans are indeed indigenous (chapter 7) or "new/indigenes." Nonetheless, it is clear that indigenes and new/indigenes are not the same, and Greenwood's analysis of those pagans who may romanticise nature, such as Patrick "Jasper" Lee (p.77), Wiccans engaging with the "Wild Hunt" (chapter 6), and the newage core-shamanism of Leslie Kenton (p.177), is critical without being insensitive. Greenwood also questions the environmental credentials of some contemporary pagans and explores the differences between those who actively participate in their nature spirituality as road-protesters in contrast to those who view nature through rose-tinted spectacles.

Readers familiar with postmodern and more recent shifts in humanities and social sciences research might be wary of approaches which appear to apply across cultures, time and "humanity" (perhaps) at the expense of cultural diversity and nuance. Any sense of difference is interpreted as a "context-specific expression of one aspect of what it is to be human" (p.213). Context is significant, since "magical consciousness is a type of thinking that is explained and defined in different ways cross-culturally" (p.206). Yet more importantly, magical consciousness is "potentially innate to human beings" (p.206) and "the *only essential difference* is one of context" (p.209, my italics). Despite a nod to cultural specificity and context, it is the possibility that magical consciousness is potentially an innate human propensity which drives the book. Is magical consciousness a sufficiently robust concept to engage with the complexities of and differences between the deeply altered consciousness of San (Bushman) shamans when performing Eland spirit helpers or encounters with nature during children's pond-dipping? So long as cultural nuance and the spectrum of magical consciousnesses are foregrounded, perhaps the answer is "yes," and Greenwood's concept of magical consciousness sits happily alongside other generic terms such as "shamanism," "animism" and "nature religion."

A tension endures, however, not only because magical consciousness is theorised as singular, but also because it is understood as not limited to human cognition since it is "a part of nature" (p.viii). It also appears to be "potentially innate" only to human beings (p.206). Can other-than-human people partake in this magical consciousness? Is it a matter of humans needing to tune in to what other-than-humans do all of the time (i.e. magical consciousness)? Are humans then active and other-than-humans passive? A cognitive or psychological approach to nature religion may risk anthropocentrism and cognicentrism, and neglect the agency of non-humans as well as the multi-layered nuances of altered consciousness. Animism is an important component of Greenwood's concept of magical consciousness and she argues that a cognitive approach reconciles the academic/practitioner divide thanks to this component (p197-8), yet an animistic approach might accomplish this without the need for a notion of magical consciousness. It is also questionable whether broad "awareness of holistic interconnections and cosmologies" resolves the dualism between Western and non-Western cultures (p.90-1), in that this awareness does not address specific sociopolitical issues, such as disputes over the appropriation of indigenous religion; nor does a cognitive approach address the clash of worldviews of archaeologists and pagan protestors at Seahenge (p.78-85), especially since there is already greater dialogue between the groups interested in sacred sites than Greenwood allows (p.84).

The animistic component of this book is the most salient, since animism been much neglected by scholars until very recently, and it is now being incorporated into paganisms. Animism "expresses the idea that the world is inspirited" (p.ix). Increasingly, pagans are engaging with nature as local, inspirited landscapes consisting of potentially violent, sometimes reciprocal, relational agents that must be respected and negotiated. While Greenwood argues paganisms are more consistently "esoteric" (p.184) than indigenous/animistic, heathenry in Britain marks one of a number of polytheist traditions, which are becoming more indigenous and animistic as they mature (cf p.131-2, 184). Such polytheist traditions might offer more compelling case studies over Wicca (chapter 6) for discussion of animistic magical consciousness. The way in which pagan animism is rooted/constructed in landscape is a further omission.

Greenwood makes a significant contribution to the study of nature religion and paganisms in considering some interesting ethnographic examples and examining these, at times critically, within the rigours of an animistic approach. A number of theoretical considerations raised by this volume could be developed. Greenwood attempts to reconcile the universal, a singular concept of a/the magical consciousness potentially applicable to all humans, and the particular, a concept of magical consciousness that is animistic and therefore localised and multi-layered. By way of contrast, what is universal to human people and other-than-human people in animistic (indigenous nature religion) contexts, is embodied and participatory engagements with relational agents in living landscapes. Animism itself, then, might sidestep the need for a concept of a singular, universal (to humans) magical consciousness. [Robert Wallis]

References:
Greenwood, S. 1998. The Nature of the Goddess: Sexual Identities and Power in Contemporary Witchcraft. In: J. Pearson; R.H. Roberts and G. Samuel (eds)

Nature Religion Today: Paganism in the Modern World: 101-110. Edinburgh: Edinburgh University Press.

Greenwood, S. 2000. Gender and Power in Magical Practices. In: S. Sutcliffe and M. Bowman (eds) *Beyond New Age: Exploring Alternative Spirituality*: 137-154. Edinburgh: Edinburgh University Press.

John Bishop and Sabina Magliocco, directors, 2007, 'Oss Tales. Media Generation, Portland, Oregon . DVD with PDF study guide. $24.95.

The annual celebration known as 'Obby 'Oss, which occurs every year on May first in the fishing village of Padstow, in Cornwall, attracts thousands of visitors and is a major attraction, despite the ambivalence of the town toward promoting what is strongly felt to be a local event. Despite evidence which suggests a modern origin of the festival (the first documentation was in the early 18th century), both local and visiting celebrants believe that the origin of the'Obby 'Oss goes back into the mists of time to Celtic fertility rites. The legend of the antiquity of the festival provides the town of Padstow with a pedigree of tradition, giving coherence to the residents of a town frequently feeling identity conflict and economic pressure due to the settlements of outsiders. The town also becomes an annual focus for Pagan visitors who want to experience what they believe to be an authentic survival of a living Pagan holiday. Given the immense popularity of this festival and the emblematic status it enjoys, it is truly astonishing how little actual academic attention 'Obby 'Oss has received. What little there is has focused on debunking its ancient origins or examining performative aspects such as music or dance.

Sabina Magliocco and John Bishop's fine film production and compilation is, therefore, a very welcome addition to the corpus of material relating to 'Obby 'Oss. This DVD is not just one short film, but four, spanning from Padstow in the 1950s to Berkeley, California in 2004 where the Oss is reimagined by Berkeley Pagans. Together the quartet shows the impact of representation on tradition, and the ways in which those representations impact interpretation and practice. The set includes a new digital version of the classic 1953 film *'Oss 'Oss Wee 'Oss* conceived by Alan Lomax, George Pickow and Peter Kennedy. This short piece, filmed in 1951, is truly a folkloric gem, and deserves a brand-new audience, possibly more for understanding the artifice that has frequently gone into documenting folkloric performance, than for the art of the film itself, which is also quite masterful. Despite the way in which Lomax and his collaborators orchestrated and created the context for the film, there are some truly beautiful visual moments there, which capture what is genuinely an incredible Cornish tradition. Magliocco and Bishop continue with their own follow-up, *Oss Tales*, which reconsiders the role and position of this festival in 2004. *Oss Tales* not only includes clips from the Lomax production as a touchstone and point of commentary for the contemporary iteration of this festival, but the filming and interviews demonstrate the relevance and importance of this event to the people of Padstow. The filmmakers also highlight the changing nature of the festival, the additions over the years, and the ways in which Padstonians allegiances to either the Old 'Oss or the Temperance 'Oss indicate longstanding family and class divisions within the town. Despite the intriguing notion of ancient survivals which dominates much of the scholarship, the matter of allegiance is possibly one of the most interesting aspects of the festival. Given the fact that it was an aspect which emerged in the 20th century, it demonstrates how traditions and festivals adapt to accommodate particular social and cultural needs, and the ways in which they acquire new meanings and complexities over time.

In the third film, Bishop and Magliocco shift attention to Berkeley, California, where a group of Pagans have incorporated and reinterpreted aspects of the 'Oss festival into their Beltane celebrations for over 20 years. *Oss Oss Wee Oss Redux; Beltane in Berkeley* shows the creative process of Pagans in putting together ritual practice and the types of tradition, scholarship and iconography that informs that creative process and the recontexualization of tradition and lore. The Berkeley 'Oss and the Padstow 'Oss may have some structural similarities, on face value they may share some elements, but the community function and interpretation are wildly divergent. In the final segment, Magliocco and Bishop discuss the process of putting this DVD together, providing the reflexivity and commentary that ties the project together. Importantly, they interviewed Peter Kennedy and George Pickow who discuss the ways in which the 1953 'Oss film was devised and shot, which provides fascinating insight into the ideologies and agendas of folklore research and collection at the time. It should be noted that this set comes with a classroom study guide, which makes the project as a whole even more valuable. Highly recommended. [Amy Hale]

Dave Evans, 2007, *The History of British Magick After Crowley: Kenneth Grant, Amado Crowley, Chaos Magic, Satanism, Lovecraft, The Left Hand Path, Blasphemy, and Magical Morality*. Hidden Publishing, London, 435 pp, index, bibliography. ISBN 978-0-9555237-0-0, Paperback, £20.90

Since the groundbreaking work of Ronald Hutton on the history of Wicca, and latterly Druidry, in Britain, writing about the history and culture of Paganism, while certainly still challenging within the academy, is becoming more accepted to the point where it has spawned its own conferences, numerous monographs, and journals. Likewise, studies of Renaissance and early modern magic, and fraternal organizations such as Freemasonry and the Ancient Order of Druids are also acceptable topics for research because they appear to be sufficiently distant and harmless topics so as to not be tainted by any real belief on the part of the researcher. The Hermetic Order of the Golden Dawn and

Theosophy, while possibly still considered slightly odd, are condoned on account of their impact on art, culture, and politics of the nineteenth and early twentieth centuries. However, the study of modern and post-modern magics, or magicks (I shall follow with this insider spelling convention through the course of this review), is still in such a nascent phase as an academic topic that there is almost no yardstick by which to measure it. How do we start to look at such contemporary groups as the O.T.O., Chaos Magick, TOPY, Satanism or any of the various Left Hand Paths which have emerged since the 1950s? Dave Evans writes of the "Continuum of evil" within modern occult communities, where some Pagans will characterize Ceremonial Magickians as more fringe and dangerous, partially in an effort to make themselves look more moral in comparison. Dave Evans challenges this paradigm and presents us with the argument that modern magick is more than worthy of our attention.

In *The History of British Magick After Crowley*, Dave Evans provides a balance to the focus on modern Paganisms, which has emerged from recent scholarship, to focus on the influence of the legacies of Crowley, Austin Osman Spare, and HP Lovecraft, among others, on what is known as the Left Hand Path magickal communities and individuals in Britain after 1947. This is a reworking of Evans PhD Thesis, so it is academically framed, situating the researcher not only within the discipline of history, but also ethnographically as a researcher participant, thus providing the book with a sense of intimacy and honesty as well as the validity that results from insider knowledge. This is an unorthodox book in method, topic, and structure, which may make it frustrating for more traditional academics, but Evans justifies his choices well, and the nature of the topic requires a more challenging treatment. Yes, this book is academic, but it is also personal and playful, which in many ways adds to its richness and actually to its authority, almost like an experimental ethnography which conveys the values of the movement by challenging the reader with a nontraditional presentation of the material. In addition to a summary of academic perspectives on modern magicks, Evans does a very useful, and also brave, job of discussing his position as both scholar and practitioner in a movement that is fractured and frequently undocumented.

Evans begins by explaining his theoretical and methodological stance, he then provides an interesting overview of texts and individuals that seeded the magickal culture in the 20th century, including brief biographical sketches of Aleister Crowley and Austin Osman Spare, neither of whom are the focus of this study. Evans then provides a more thorough examination of some of the most important practitioners and magickal trends which emerged in Britain, providing concentrated research on the lives and work of Amado Crowley and Kenneth Grant. Evans does a particularly through job of debunking Amado's claims to any genuine association with Aleister, but nevertheless acknowledges the importance and efficacy of his work to his followers. The final portion of the book is a close look at the development and influence of Chaos Magick in late 1970s Britain. Chaos magick has received relatively little attention from scholars, and Evans' connection with the rise of punk and the social conditions of the pre-Thatcher years really help to give the reader a clear understanding of the resistive nature of this movement. Similarly, this focus on the conditions that fostered Chaos Magick helps to put other, more orthodox initiatory systems of magick in Britain into their own historical context as a mirror of British society and culture. That Evans acknowledges the contributions of Jaq Hawkins and Lionel Snell (aka Ramsey Dukes) to modern magickal theory is edifying.

This book certainly provides historical information that will be of use to any researcher in the field, but it will also be of immense interest to practitioners who are not only interested in the history of their magickal communities, but also of the social and cultural conditions that drove their development. Evans draws on his own experiences with British magickal culture for his sources as well as texts in print and the wealth of discussion, debate and documentation that exists on the Internet. It is clear that Evans intends this work as a starting point for scholarly discussion and as the groundwork for future research in this difficult area. In this quest he has succeeded admirably. [Amy Hale]

Robert Conner, *Jesus the Sorcerer: Exorcist & Prophet of the Apocalypse*, Oxford, Mandrake, 2006. Paperback. 320pp, index, appendices, bibliography. £UK 12.99 $US 25

Early on in this book Robert Conner sets out his intentions: "this book entirely dispenses with the pleasant pretext that the life of Jesus is or ever was truly relevant to much of anything... (but)... Jesus-in-the-mind-of-believers is another matter entirely" (page 11 onwards).

Although there have been several "Jesus was a magician" exposé-type books in the past of varying luridity and lucidity, few have employed the depth and quality of reasoning exhibited herein. Robert Conner has produced a relatively brief, if dense, overview of the evidence that the historical Jesus was far more of a sorcerer than modern (and early modern) Church authorities would ever prefer to be made public. This is not ever an easy read since there is of necessity much analysis of various Biblical languages, and a grasp of Biblical history in the reader is assumed. Unlike some of the other books in this vein it is certainly not a piece of lightweight fluff or disposable conspiracy-theory material for airline reading and suchlike since it demands the attention of the reader and rewards that effort with manifold gems of information and new ideas.

Jesus the Sorcerer is not a deliberately anti-Christian book; however, by its very nature, it has to be critical of Church manipulation and suppression of text over centuries, the nature and practice of literal belief and, as Conner acidly describes it, "some of what passes for New Testament scholarship" (the inherent biases within which receive a deserved roasting in these pages). As a necessary side-effect (but not intentionally) the book also does great philosophical damage to fundamentalist literalist reasoning, thus it will not win many plaudits from less flexible reviewers. It is to Conner's credit that he does not divert his efforts into the simple polemic that the material he covers here could easily have catalysed, since his findings expose several very easy targets for attack.

This worthy book examines and supports the notions that Jesus was an exorcist, a magical healer, a sorcerer, and a seer and had knowledge of curses and much more, which will be of the most interest to the JSM readership, and which forms the framework of the book. It also gives coherent support to the notion that Jesus might have been at least bisexual if not homosexual, and was probably illiterate, all of which will also not win Conner any medals in some quarters; however, his reasoning and use of evidence is quite superb, on the magical front especially. Although this book will appeal to scholars of the period and the subject, and is perhaps essential reading for the scholar beginning to investigate the area, it has far broader appeal. The first 45 pages or so, discussing the general method of history and how to assess the veracity of sources would be of use as a series of *caveats* and methodological prompts to virtually any researcher. The analysis of how un-authentic any aspect of the current Bible is should also be required reading for any scholar of the subject. The tyranny of print is so often submitted to, but as Conner most ably demonstrates, nothing in the current Bible is even third-hand information, and we are continually at the mercy of repeated linguistic mangling, translation accidents, church manipulations, and simple copying errors in everything, which we presume from that most problematic text. The alert reader might spot that Conner is, in this book, using those very same sources to propose certain interpretations, which is a thorny problem, since might he also be falling foul of those same source errors. He extricates himself from this tar-baby conundrum capably by demonstrating rigorous reasoning and use of supporting sources.

Each chapter closes with lengthy and detailed endnotes, which provide extensive additional material. The useful index and extensive bibliography ranges from learned journals and premier-league University Presses to more populist freelance works, to give a broad overview of research into the topic, and this section alone would provide a very useful compendium for a postgraduate paper literature review.

That Conner manages to tackle a profoundly problematic subject with good grace, and, in places, a delicious, crackling dry wit, is to his credit. The only small criticisms are that this is obviously abstracted from a much larger and broader work that has been cherry-picked for maximum impact in the given page count (since fewer readers might perhaps take on a 700, or 1000-page version, with the necessary extra expense of production). While this slightly detracts from the flow on occasions, it was most likely a necessity in order to have the work more physically publishable. I hope that this challenging but fascinating book will gain the audience it deserves, which should be broader than the scholars at whom it is initially aimed, and that not many copies end up on fundamentalist pyres.

It is perhaps a measure of a book for review as to whether the reader ever wishes to read more material by the same author. I do. Recommended. [Dave Evans]

Review of Wilby, Emma. 2005. *Cunning Folk and Familiar Spirits: Shamanic Visionary Traditions in Early Modern British Witchcraft and Magic.* Brighton: Sussex Academic Press.

Emma Wilby opens her book with 'a cunning woman's tale': Scotswoman Bessie Dunlop was tried for witchcraft in 1576 and the summary of the trial's lengthy proceedings (nine pages of Wilby's Preface) informs us that Bessie had an intimate and long-standing relationship with a 'ghost' named Tom Reid. Wilby argues that such accounts of human engagements with spirit familiars – 'encounter-narratives' – are consistent in witch-trials and confessions in the sixteenth and seventeenth centuries to the extent that this feature must be considered seriously as evidence for actual belief. This leads Wilby to argue that a veneer – albeit an all-pervading, official one – of Christianity overlay enduring traditions of pre-Christian 'shamanic' practice in Britain.

At first glance, such an argument is problematic: scholars post- Margaret Murray and Montague Summers have deconstructed witch-trial and confession evidence to establish that much data is unreliable, extracted under conditions of torture and riddled with witch-hunt propaganda discourse, derived from the 'learned' or 'elite' medieval theologians. The notion of an unbroken 'old religion' of witchcraft appears to be a fabrication, with apparent vestiges of folk-belief insufficient as evidence in themselves. Wilby's re-visiting of the evidence is certainly 'courageous' (as Hutton's rear-cover plaudit puts it). Her book is also refreshing in moving beyond metanarratives: she does not support the notion of an 'old religion' nor an enduring singular 'tradition', and she does not read the trial and confession sources uncritically. Rather, she approaches the sources with the interpretative framework of 'shamanism'.

This, of course, has its own problems: shamans are paradoxical to the extent that every definition offered can be challenged, and 'shamanism' as another '-ism' suggests something orderly which everyone would recognize, yet the diversity of shamans resists such generalisation (see Harvey & Wallis 2006). We continue, nonetheless, to call shamans 'shamans' and shamans continue to do what shamans do. So Wilby's approach to shamanism as a constructed term appropriate for assessing early modern accounts of cunning folk and witches, is intriguing – particularly with her contextualisation of shamanism within 'animism'.

Although animism is clearly important to Wilby's discussion (there are nineteen entries in the index and animism is first mentioned on p14) there is no explicit definition of the term until half way through the book (p128). I was also disappointed to find no sustained engagement with how animism (particularly in shamanistic contexts) is constituted, particularly in light of recent theorising. Revising Tylor's 'old animism' notion that animists mistakenly perceive inanimate objects as alive in some way and containing 'spirit(s)', recent scholarship engages with 'new animism' as a relational ontology wherein humans are understood as one 'people' amongst a diversity of 'other-than-human people' including tree people, cat people and stone people. Humans are not privileged in this worldview; indeed they depend on harmonious relations with non-humans. Shamans are often the agents who negotiate harmonious relations if a seal-person or other 'prey' has been offended. Ambivalence is crucial to understanding a pragmatic animist worldview where humans must of necessity do violence to other 'people', whether plant or pig, and other-than-human people do violence to us – to a panther or virus, human people are prey of sorts. By altering consciousness (or deploying adjusted styles of communication), shamans are able to engage with other-than-human people: shamans 'do' animism by brokering good relations between humans and non-humans.

Wilby's approach stands between old and new animism, her interest being the shamanic doing of animism by early modern witches and cunning folk in their engagements with helping spirits and/or demons. Wilby attends to the moral ambivalence raised by an animist ontology (if it existed) in early modern Britain (p224): there were cunning folk who tended to help (healing sickness, finding lost property) using familiar spirits, and there were witches who did harm (blighting crops, causing sickness) aided by demons. But there was much crossover: in pragmatic circumstances there was not a simple 'good/bad', 'black/white' distinction (p154-6), but a precarious greyness. It is somewhat confusing when Wilby distinguishes between maleficent witch and benevolent cunning person and their respective animal familiars and demon familiars (p58), marks ambiguity and permeability (e.g. p123), and then uses these terms interchangeably throughout. But this is a useful reminder that early modern ontology resists our modern wish to compartmentalise. While Davies (2003) suggests, then, that descriptions of fairy encounters are more corporeal than spiritual (Wilby note 28, p174), from the perspective of a morally ambivalent animist relational ontology such encounter-narratives disrupt the sacred-profane dichotomy per se.

Wilby persuasively argues for early modern animism in Britain. While it was the official religion, a veneer of Christian belief overlay enduring pre-industrial folkways, with Catholicism itself having many 'pagan' aspects and Protestantism being the main harbinger of change. Wilby is persistent in reminding us that early modern life was starkly different from our own, not only in terms of hardship and daily toil, but in relationships – between humans, animals and otherworldly creatures, with spirits often living nearby, in a stone, tree, crystal or bottle (p77). She offers evocative descriptions of intimate engagements with animals, hinting at why it is that frogs, snails, rabbits, cats and hares might be perceived as 'visionary familiars' (p228-31). Previous literature has neglected these familiars and Wilby's attention to detail leads to a more nuanced consideration of how these familiars were constituted as 'envisional spirit-guides' (p242). Scholars have also focussed on elite conjurations of spirits to the neglect of examples of conjuring among cunning folk and witches (p81), and concentrated on the witch's journey to the Sabbath (as did the persecutors of witches) because these accounts are so bizarre and titillating, at the expense of the rich resource of encounter-narratives (p174). Rather than highlight hysterical elite narratives (balancing Davies' [2003] focus on elite discourse and neglect of encounter-narratives [p51]), Wilby's attention to encounter-narratives situates everyday magic in community relations. Those that are able to intercede in the 'supernatural' may be able to help but they also have the resources to cause harm, and cunning folk and their spirit familiars were demonised as witches and demons by neighbours. This situating of everyday magic vis-à-vis witchcraft accusations is reminiscent of indigenous contexts (e.g. Evans-Pritchard [1937] on Azande witchcraft and in Amazonian shamanism/sorcery [e.g. Fausto 2004]).

Scholars have also supported a 'downward filtration' (p112) of witchcraft belief, originating with elite theologians. Wilby revises this trend, arguing that the reality was more complex, involving an upward process (p164): while the learned discourse on witchcraft and demonology indeed filtered down, the already extant, enduring and widespread beliefs in fairies and other folklore likely also influenced the elite. The established assumption that the cunning person/witch did not believe what they were saying/confessing is, Wilby argues, overstated (chapter 6, especially p96), indicating how fairy and other indigenous beliefs fed into elite narratives. Many witches who initially denied involvement in witchcraft and subsequently confessed under torture, explained their denial as a silence/secrecy pact made with the devil. It is compelling that relationships with fairies often involved similar silence/secrecy taboos (and tellingly, this reluctance to talk may be one reason why we know so little [p90-1]). The witch's pact with the devil may derive as much from encounter-narratives including specific demands from fairies in return for help, as from elite Christian sources (p163). In some cases, cunning folk saw no incongruity over their Christian beliefs and engagements with elves and fairies: 'Joan Tyrry (1555) claimed "the power of God taught to her by the ... fairies be both godly and good" ' (p97). Yet, 'the devil told Suffolk witch Mary Skipper (1645) to go to church "and make a great show, but if she attended diligently he would nip her" ' (p98). While demons might demand that the Christian faith be renounced, so too did fairies. And both witches and cunning folk might be required to bargain with their soul, engage in marriage and/or sexual relations, and make sacrifices/ offerings of blood and milk, to their spirits/demons. Again, Wilby argues this is evidence that such negotiations were as much a part of indigenous belief as of elite narratives of witch-pacts (e.g. p101).

Wilby offers sustained discussion of witches/cunning folk as early modern shamans. In her reading of the sources, spirits were used for healing, finding lost goods, identifying criminals, divining the future and talking to / mediating the dead – indeed many familiars were 'ghosts' themselves (p68-9). When healing, cunning folk used blowing and sucking techniques and these are strongly reminiscent of shamanic practices (p137). They also endured dismemberment, had their souls stolen and undertook hazardous journeys and magical flight to the otherworld (p151). When entering the fairy realm (for the cunning person) or travelling to the Sabbath (for the witch), the spirit/soul left the body, perhaps constituting evidence for trance practices (p102). She identifies trance as a defining feature of shamanism and instead of assuming encounter-narratives are fictional, she addresses these experiences, sensitively, as a 'reality' (p164, 168).

Less convincing is the focus on the visual nature of the trance-encounter-narrative which might tell us more about ourselves as specularist moderns than about early modern (or indigenous) ontologies. Scholars of shamanism have tended to over-emphasise the visuality of altered consciousness and the discrete nature of 'trance'. Rather, altered consciousness is fluid, aural and somatic experiences may be as crucial as vision, and the senses may be entirely disrupted (synaesthesia). With the notable exception of Rasmussen's ethnography of arctic shamanism, Wilby's sources on shamans are consistently secondary (which seems out of character for a historian), and framed by transpersonal psychology (e.g. Kalweit) and neo-shamanic discourse (e.g. Drury, Harner). The onus is on cunning folk and witches as mystics and monists, revealing a bias to her reading of the sources in the latter part of the book (p219-20). Wilby sees shamanic marriage / sexual relations as 'a metaphor for mystical union' reflecting 'a universal symbol of mankind' (p238) and suggests that 'to some degree the visionary capacities of medieval saints and mystics can be seen as expressions of the perennial "shamanistic tendencies" of the psyche' (p223). This interpretation is at the expense of shamans as agentic animists pragmatically negotiating with other-than-human people, as the new animism approach to shamanism suggests. The way in which the book covers such a range of sources might give the misleading impression that the disparate sources across Britain and through two centuries are coherent and related. And while Wilby briefly mentions contemporary witchcraft and neo-shamanism, I think it is incumbent on scholars to engage with these contemporary manifestations more rigorously, particularly given the influence academic works have on contemporary practice.

I have argued elsewhere (e.g. Wallis 2002, 2003, 2004; also Blain & Wallis 2006) that altered consciousness (if not trance) is useful when approaching many shamanisms; yet for purists, 'shamanism' in the *locus classicus* of Siberia is incongruous with 'trance' (e.g. Hamayon 1993). Certainly, application of the terms 'shaman' and 'trance' both within and outside Siberia requires caution. Hamayon (1996) proposes that the 'spirit marriage' is more relevant than 'trance' when approaching Siberian shamanisms – and Wilby herself offers numerous examples of this practice among cunning people and witches. So, not only does the term 'shaman' work consistently in what might appear to be an incongruous setting, but it also re-configures our understanding of witches and cunning folk. They were not practicing an enduring shamanic old religion, nor were they an elite-formulated fabrication. Approaching them as animist shamans embedded in local community relations constitutes a considerably nuanced analysis. [Robert J. Wallis]

References:

Blain, Jenny and Robert J. Wallis. 2006. Ritual reflections, practitioner meanings: disputing the terminology of neo-shamanic 'performance. *Journal of Ritual Studies* 20(1): 21-36.

Evans-Pritchard, Edward E. 1937. *Witchcraft, Oracles and Magic Among the Azande*. Oxford: Oxford University Press.

Fausto, Carlos. 2004. A Blend of Blood and Tobacco: Shamans and Jaguars among the Parakanã of Eastern Amazonia. In: Neil L. Whitehead and Robin Wright (eds) *In Darkness and Secrecy*. Durham, North Car.: Duke University Press.

Hamayon, Roberte N. 1993. Are 'Trance', 'Ecstasy' and Similar Concepts Appropriate in the Study of Shamanism? *Shaman* 1(2): 3-25.

___. 1996. Shamanism in Siberia: From Partnership in Supernature to Counter-power in Society. In: Nicholas Thomas and Caroline Humphrey (eds) *Shamanism, History and the State*. Ann Arbor: University of Michigan Press.

Harvey, Graham and Robert J. Wallis. 2006. *Historical Dictionary of Shamanism*. Lanham, Maryland: Scarecrow Press.

Wallis, Robert J. 2002. The *Bwili* or 'Flying Tricksters' of Malakula: a critical discussion of recent debates on rock art, ethnography and shamanisms. *Journal of The Royal Anthropological Institute* 8(4): 735-60.

___. 2003. *Shamans / neo-Shamans: Ecstasy, Alternative Archaeology and Contemporary Pagans*. London: Routledge.

___. 2004. Shamanism and Art. In: Mariko N. Walter and Eva N. Fridman (eds) *Shamanism: An Encyclopedia of World Beliefs, Practices, and Culture, Volume I*. Santa Barbara, Cal: ABC-CLIO.

Obituaries

Malcolm Lyall-Watson, scientist, author, explorer 1939-2008

Polymath is a word that is perhaps too often thrown around casually; however, Malcolm Lyall-Watson may have been such a creature. A precocious young scholar, he studied at South Africa's University of the Witwatersrand from the age of fifteen and within five years had passed degrees in botany and zoology. He continued to study, gaining qualifications in geology, anthropology, chemistry, ecology and marine biology before taking a doctorate in animal behavior under Dr. Desmond Morris (author of *The Naked Ape*), the curator of mammals at London Zoo. Watson joined BBC Television as a producer-reporter, designed zoos (he was Director of Johannesburg Zoo at the age of only 23), ran a safari company, and founded a marine national park in the Seychelles. He traveled the world, exploring and writing, including spending twelve years living on a boat in the Amazon while performing research, was a passionate speaker at the International Whaling Commission, and introduced both the showman-psychic Uri Geller and the arcane intricacies of Sumo Wrestling to a British television audience. It is for his challenging popular science and paranormal books that Watson will best be known to JSM readers, since many of them contained accounts of inspiring and unexplained events Watson had witnessed on his travels. Titles such as *Supernature* and *The Romeo Error* were compendia of investigative travelogue and amazing, leading-edge ideas garnered from around the world, covering a breathtakingly broad and diverse area of study including psychic surgery, tribal rituals, the natural history of the wind and pheromone communication between plants. Having little regard for scientific propriety and usually refusing to accept the accepted wisdom on any topic, Watson was very much a man for investigating what might be happening, not for "pooh-poohing" the remarkable or controversial. His findings have been the catalyst and inspiration for many more recent scientists' work.

John Symonds, writer, playwright, biographer and publisher, March 12th 1915-October 21st 2006

John Symonds, who has died, aged 92, was one of the few remaining witnesses to have known the highly influential British magician Aleister Crowley (1875-1947) when they were themselves adults. Symonds, an editor of various London magazines, playwright, and author, met Crowley a year before the old man died, and for reasons which are still somewhat unclear and disputed, Crowley appointed Symonds one of his literary executors. This claim was regularly disputed in legal battles in later years with the OTO in America; however, prior to this in the 1960s and 70s Symonds and Kenneth Grant (another executor) worked together in producing wonderful examples of Crowley's works, either as reprints or first publications.

Symonds wrote considerably on other subjects, including plays, children's stories, four biographical-cum-analytical books about Crowley, and a very creditable biography of H.P. Blavatsky. His work on Crowley was not always well-received, the late Israel Regardie (a former secretary of Crowley's) calling Symonds "that most hostile biographer." Regardless of his reception, it is no exagerration to state that without the publication efforts of Symonds (and Grant) Crowley could easily have been a forgotten figure by the 1970s.

Albert Hoffman, Chemist and Philosopher 1906-2008

The Swiss chemist, Albert Hoffman, who died in April 2008, aged 102, is best know as the chemist who invented LSD, but his scientific work was considerably more broad, leading to over 100 published papers and many books. A leading researcher and lifelong supporter of research in consciousness and related fields, he also served on the Nobel Prize Committee, was an environmental lobbyist, and a Fellow of the World Academy of Sciences. The Multidisciplinary Association for Psychedelic Studies (www.maps.org) is one of many research fora online which continue to discuss his work and influence, and they were instrumental in organizing an academic conference in 2006 to mark Professor Hoffman's 100th birthday, at which the delighted and still sprightly professor was in attendance.

Taken as a figurehead by the alternative consciousness and counterculture movement, it is no surprise that his name will be familiar to many in the neopagan field, since alternative states of consciousness (be that chemically-assisted or otherwise) are a regular topic of discussion. The reader is referred to the review of Andrew Letcher's *Shroom* in a previous JSM for further discussion of the role of entheogenic substances in magical fields.

Ernest Gary Gygax, writer and mythologiser 1938-2008

Gary Gygax was not an academic in any sense of the word, but his work has affected many academic fields. He took a few classes in anthropology at the University of Chicago, but his life was largely based in commercial sales until he hit upon the idea of a fantasy role-playing game (and some later novels), which he developed and which evolved into *Dungeons and Dragons,* and this became a multi-million seller in the days before computer gaming. There has been considerable debate in the popular and academic press as to accusations that Gygax's creation (much imitated by other writers) actually encouraged participation in non-Christian religions, or, as seems more likely, it simply tapped into the time (and wallets) of a ready market of pagans, sci-fi "geeks" and others who wanted an entertaining diversion, an adventure and a social forum in which to be creative, and do battle with goblins and elves, without leaving their kitchen tables.

In the same way that it has been argued that the Indiana Jones films encouraged some children to grow up wanting to be archaeologists and that Carlos Castaneda's dubious claims led to a growth in anthropology class sizes, it is possible that without Gygax and his development of numerous creative and entertaining mythological-mental landscapes some very large areas of pagan imagery and ritual design (and thus their academic study) would not have arisen *at all*.

There is a general saying about such board-table activities like this that "it is only a game," however, Gygax endured several serious death threats from extreme religious groups who objected to his invention and the assumption that it was leading all of the world's Christian youth into a dangerous pact with Satan, but it was prolonged ill health rather than religious zealot assassins that intervened and led to his death at the age of 69 in 2008.

Alan Miller, Thelemic scholar, occult philanthropist and psychologist 1943-2008

Alan Miller, who has died at the age of 65, will be best known to occultists and academics under his pseudonym of "Dr Christopher

Hyatt," a pupil of Crowley's pupil Israel Regardie, a double PhD, a controversial psychology writer, the financial backing and motivating force behind Falcon Press in the USA, and a staunch Thelemite. Besides his own writing work, he was instrumental in encouraging and supporting (in some cases by actually employing) the noted magical authors Lon Milo DuQuette and James Wassermann early in their careers, and for publishing numerous titles by the important magical author Robert Anton Wilson and other occult luminaries. On a physical level he donated considerable sums to the *Ordo Templi Orientis*, including being a major donor for their restoration project of the original very large paintings for Aleister Crowley's *Thoth* tarot deck, plus other worthy causes.

His own voluminous writings were often controversial, in the "rascal guru" style, such as his *Undoing Yourself* and *Black Books* series, which were intended to shock the complacent and force the torpid to think for themselves. Since his death, Falcon Press appears to have sadly split into rival litigious factions, and only time will tell what effect that conflict has on the volume, spread, and quality of new Thelemic publishing in the USA and beyond.

The Journal for the Academic Study of Magic (JSM)

Back numbers

JSM 1: ISBN 978-1869928 674, £13.99, Airmail $25, 200pp
Beyond Attribution: The Importance of Barrett's Magus/ Alison Butler * Shadow over Philistia: A review of the Cult of Dagon/John C. Day * A History of Otherness:Tarot and Playing Cards from Early Modern Europe/Joyce Goggin * Opposites Attract: Magical Identity and Social Uncertainty/Dave Green * 'Memories of a Sorcerer': notes on Gilles Deleuze-Felix Guattari, Austin Osman Spare and Anomalous Sorceries./Matt Lee * Le Streghe Son Tornate: The Reappearance of Streghe in Italian American Queer Writings/Ilaria Serra * Controlling Chance, Creating Chance: Magical Thinking in Religious Pilgrimage/Deana Weibel

JSM 2, ISBN 978-1869928 728, £19.99, 420pp
Alien Selves: Modernity and the Social Diagnostics of the Demonic in 'Lovecraftian Magick': Woodman/Wishful Thinking Notes towards a Psychoanalytic Sociology of Pagan Magick: Green/A Shell with my Name on it: The Reliance on the Supernatural During the First World War. Chambers/The Metaphysical Relationship between Magick and Miracles: Morgan Luck/Demonic Possession, and Spiritual Healing in Nineteenth-Century Devon: Semmens/ Human Body in Southern Slavic Folk Sorcery: Filipovic & Rader/Four Glasses Of Water: Snell/The Land Near the Dark Cornish Sea:. Hale/Kenneth Grant and the Magickal revival: Evans/Magic through the Linguistic Lenses of Greek mágos, Indo-European *mag(h)-, Sanskrit màyà and Pharaonic Egyptian ¡eka: Cheak/The symbolism of the pierced heart: Froome/ Nicholas Roerich: McCannon/Book Review, etc.

JSM 3, ISBN 798-1869928-964, 300pp,£19.99 (post free)
Buffy and Beyond: Language and Resistance in Contemporary Teenage Witchcraft: Sanders/Witchery as a New Language of Female Identity: Lee/Creative Revolution: Bergsonisms and Modern Magic: Green/Discovering the Witch's Teat: Magical Practices, Medical Superstitions in The Witch of Edmonton: Hayes/The Re-Enchantment of the Medical: An examination of magical elements in healing: Lowery/ Apparitions, Ghosts, Fairies, Demons and Wild Events: Virtuality in Early Modern Britain: Marshall/Living the Mystery: Sacred Drama Today: Laity/ Is there esoteric symbolism in H.P.Lovecraft's The Dream-Quest of Unknown Kadath?: Geall / Becoming a Sorcerer: Jean-Pierre Bekolo's Quartier Mozart and the Magic of Deleuzian and Guattarian Becoming: Gorman / Book Reviews

JSM 4, ISBN 798-1869928-391, 390pp, £19.99 (post free)

The Practitioner, The Priest, and The Professor: Perspectives on Self-Initiation in the American Neopagan Community: Marty Laubach, Louis Martinie' and Roselinda Clemons/The Trinity of the Hebrew Goddess: A Guided Presentation Of Goddess Narratives and Submerged Beliefs: Jayne Marie DeMente/The Topography of Magic in the Modern Western and Ancient Egyptian Minds: Steven M. Stannish/The science of magic: A parapsychological model of psychic ability in the context of magical will: David Luke/Is Magic Possible Within A Quantum Mechanical Framework?: Steve Ash /Angels with Nanotech Wings: Magic, Medicine and Technology in The Neuromancer and Brain Plague: Catherine M. Lord/Rowling's Devil: Ancient Archetype or Modern Manifestation?: Lauren Berman/"Delivered From Enchantment": Cotton Mather, W. B. O. Peabody, and the Struggle against Magic: Carl Sederholm/In a Mirror, Darkly : A comparison between the Lovecraftian Mythos and African-Atlantic mystery religions: David Geall/The Journey of The Lion King and the Collective Unconscious: Melinda Marsh/"The Third Time's the Charm": Mythic Operative Magic in the Merseburger Zaubersprüche: Michael Moynihan/The Old Irish Impotence Spell: The Dam Díli, Fergus, Fertility, and the Mythic Backround of an Irish Incantation: Phillip A. Bernhardt-House/Reading the Turkish Coffee Cup and Beyond: The Case of North Cyprus: Gulnara Karimova/Reviews

**111 Magdalen Rd
Oxford OX4 1RQ
Tel 01865 245301
Fax 01865 245521**

Thousands of titles
(new, secondhand & bargains)
search & orderable on our website

mail@innerbookshop.com
Open 10-5.45 - **Mon-Sat**

Books for mind, body and spirit

www.innerbookshop.com

*From Alchemy & Chaos Magick
to Wicca & Zoroastrianism*

Visit us (and the Magic Café next door) and see our **Noticeboards** for Oxford and National events or use our **Mail-Order Service** via telephone or fax as well

PAN'S DAUGHTER
The Magical World of ROSALEEN NORTON
By NEVILL DRURY

ISBN 978-1869928-318,
168pp / 48 illus / £9.99/$14.95

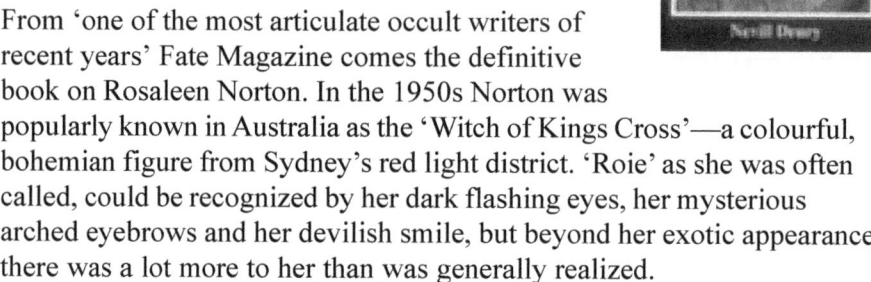

From 'one of the most articulate occult writers of recent years' Fate Magazine comes the definitive book on Rosaleen Norton. In the 1950s Norton was popularly known in Australia as the 'Witch of Kings Cross'—a colourful, bohemian figure from Sydney's red light district. 'Roie' as she was often called, could be recognized by her dark flashing eyes, her mysterious arched eyebrows and her devilish smile, but beyond her exotic appearance there was a lot more to her than was generally realized.

A natural trance artist, she experimented with self-hypnosis and as a result of her visionary explorations portrayed a wide range of supernatural beings in her paintings and drawings. However her 'pagan' art plunged her into continuous controversy. Widely criticized for allegedly bizarre sexual practices with her lover, Gavin Greenlees, she was regarded very much as a renegade from mainstream society.

This biography—the first account of her life as a whole—provides a detailed evaluation of both her magical beliefs and her art and includes a fascinating selection of previously unpublished material.

Praise for the Australian edition:
'. . . a fascinating study. Drury's understanding of the occult and spiritual realms makes Norton's art and life comprehensible. . . '
- Sydney Morning Herald

Mandrake publishes a wide range of challenging, leftfield titles. To see more visit
www.mandrake.uk.net and/or download a catalogue

Lightning Source UK Ltd.
Milton Keynes UK
UKHW011433031222
413284UK00002B/70